Conversations
with
Gaia
The Soul
of the Earth
Volume 1

Tom T. Moore
with
Layne Kopas

Flint Hills Publishing

Conversations with Gaia – The Soul of the Earth Volume 1
© 2025 Tom T. Moore

Cover Design by Amy Albright

Flint Hills Publishing
Topeka, Kansas
Tucson, Arizona
www.flinthillspublishing.com

Printed in the U.S.A.

Paperback ISBN: 978-1-966323-14-3
Ebook ISBN: 978-1-966323-15-0

Dedication

These books are dedicated to the thousands of people all over the world who have sent me questions to ask since 2005. I would have thought to ask these questions. Thank you!

Thank you, Carissa Liberatore, who began the compilations, but the coming birth of her baby girl took precedence.

And to Layne Kopas who spent thousands of hours compiling, arranging, and then "fine editing" the books. I could never have done this without Layne's assistance.

And naturally to my family, who accepts me the way I am, and my soul path.

A Note to the Reader

This two-volume series contains profound information Tom T. Moore channeled from "Gaia"—the energy that is often described as "the soul of the Earth."

Search your intuition to learn how to best use this volume. Perhaps you'll dive into it, reading from cover to cover. Maybe you'll scan the Table of Contents for topics that jump out. Or you can flip through the book, asking your guides to direct you to a particular page.

However you use this book, the magic lies in the fact that these messages, channeled through Tom, are from a powerful, wise, nurturing entity charged with the monumentous job of maintaining our beautiful planet.

Tom has dedicated himself to asking Gaia probing questions while also creating Benevolent Prayers to manifest highest and best outcomes. As Tom explains, you too can open this line of communication. And a practice of saying Benevolent Prayers **out loud** will bring wonderful things to your life, our world, the Universe.

Let this book be a positive resource as well as inspiration for your journey.

TABLE OF CONTENTS

Preface
from Tom T. Moore

I was inspired to develop The Gentle Way philosophy in the 1990s after reading a channeled article by Robert Shapiro in the *Sedona Journal of Emergence*, where one sentence said you could request benevolent outcomes in your life. I took that farther, requesting Most Benevolent Outcomes **out loud**, first for mundane requests, then using them in my business. This eventually grew into *The Gentle Way* series of books, and I was voted "Best Self-Help Author" for three years in a row by the readers of a health magazine. I'm told that in the future, scientists will rediscover the power of the verbal voice, known in ancient times.

In 2005, I first discovered that I could converse telepathically with another fragment of my soul during a seminar in Sedona, Arizona, conducted by Dick Sutphen, who coined the term "vortexes," denoting the high energy spots around this area. On the second day of the workshop, Richard put us into a light, altered state with the goal for us to try automatic writing. Instead, I decided to try and contact an American Indian Shaman living in the 1600s in the western part of North America, named in English, "Reveals the Mysteries." He had been channeled for me before by Mr. Shapiro. I said, "Reveals the Mysteries, are you there?" He responded, *Yes I am, Tom!* I thought, *Wow, this is great!*

He went on to tell me that I was to "reintroduce people to The Gentle Way." He gave me the title of my first book the first time we communicated. He went on to tell me I would write books. I protested, because I'm just a business guy in international film and TV program distribution and thought that's what I would be doing until I retired. He said, "No, BOOKS!" So, I said okay and wrote my first book in about 100 days. If you look at my website, www.thegentlewaybook.com, you will notice that it says "book" and not "books" as I could not imagine being able to write more than one book. Years later I would learn that the statement that I would "reintroduce people" referred to a life I had 12,700 years ago on the island of Poseidia, during Atlantean times. I was told that I had been inspired to create The Gentle Way and had one million followers. I have asked Gaia if my impression that the term "Gentle Way" is being used more frequently these days is correct and she responded: "...you are correct here. It is like the 100th Monkey Theory where the population starts picking up on the use of certain words and spreads it far and wide. It will continue to spread even further in the coming years."

I have since learned that **anyone** can communicate with any being in the Universe because we all have the pineal gland in the back of our heads that works as an antenna for all types of telepathic information. Scientists so far have only been able to prove that it secretes melatonin. Part of my soul contract in this life is to encourage everyone to begin communicating during meditative sessions.

Before long, I began to communicate with my own guardian angel whom I named Theo because he said humans do not have the vocal cords to pronounce angelic names. I learned that our guardian angels are actually known as "golden light beings," old souls that through millions of years have raised their vibrational levels to the point that they glow a golden light. There are a little more than one million of these old souls taking care of hundreds of thousands of people during all our lives on Earth. These lives are all taking place at the same time, because we are in a special "space-time continuum," created by the Creator of our Universe for what is called "the Earth Experiment." Creator knew we needed a lot of assistance during these lives where we agreed to be veiled from knowing about the thousands of lives we had lived on other planets. Creator believes that we will come up with solutions to problems that no other race of beings in our Universe was able to solve. My guardian angel Theo humorously told me that Creator had put out a job description that said, "Only golden light beings can apply."

Creator wanted to see if the four negative energies could be worked with, while the rest of our Universe and the **trillions** of other universes were all created in the ten positive energies. The ten positive energies seem to have their limits, since most of our Universe was stuck around 5.3-to-5.4-dimensional focus. When the "Explorer Race," as we are called, begins to travel to the stars around 3250, we will take small bits of this negative energy with us, assisting first the 20,000 planets that are part of the Federation of Planets to absorb the energy, and then they will spread it to millions and then trillions of other planets in our Universe. Eventually, I'm told that this will spread to all the other trillions of universes.

When Creator first created several hundred galaxies—each different from the others—this is where the story of Gaia begins. Over millions of years, Gaia has attained a level called "quantum mastery." Gaia tells me that she (I prefer to use the feminine form here) is able to handle all the 12 parallel Earths that Creator created as part of that special space-time continuum. When I asked if her soul was larger than others, she said, "No." But she said I could compare her to the "conductor of an orchestra." That's an understatement, since there are four million souls assisting her on all 12 parallel Earths. Using the Edgar Cayce books as a starting point, and since I knew I had had at least one life during Atlantean times, I began asking dozens of questions about Atlantis and then Lemuria which went much further than the questions Cayce was able to ask in his time period. It resulted in a whole book about these two lost continents.

This book contains information I channeled from "Gaia"—the name I and many others use for the entity that is the soul of our Earth. For specific details about my communication process, see Appendix I near the end of the book. I will emphasize two important points about this process: there is a "set of rules" whereby Gaia cannot give me the information sought until I think of the question. I have asked her who put these rules in place, and she responded: "That is an excellent question, Tom. You set these rules in place—you, meaning all of the souls who are taking part in this great experiment. You decided that it is you that must discover these events and things, not I. Therefore, I can only answer what you ask of me under this set of rules you have established for yourselves."

The second important point I want to share is that anyone who takes the time and sets their mind to it can communicate with Gaia. Again, consult Appendix I for more information about how you too can establish this wonderful connection. This is a rich resource I encourage you to use. As Gaia herself has said, "I am a great resource, but you have to ask for my assistance, just as you do for your guardian angels and guides. I can provide great riches for those who wish, simply by manifesting them. I can give you knowledge about the cosmos and your origins, but you must ask. The general population does not think that they can carry on a conversation with me as you and some others do around the world. They just have to open themselves to the possibility of doing so and then practice as you are doing. I am there always for you and wish you all to succeed in your lives."

Nearly all of all the questions you will read in the following chapters were sent to me from the readers worldwide of my free weekly newsletter. I don't charge for these newsletters, as they are my gift to the world. If you wish to subscribe too, just go to my website's first page, at **www.thegentlewaybook.com**, where there is a sign-up box. And because I am only human, I do want to emphasize that although I try my best to receive messages accurately, I do not get it right 10 to 20 percent of the time. And if there is information in this book that you find difficult to hear, I encourage you to say a Benevolent Prayer for an outcome that is for our highest and best.

Finally, I want to express my appreciation and gratitude to Layne Kopas who carefully combined through years of questions I had for Gaia, assembling them into subjects and taking great care with proof editing.

Now for the story of Gaia's journey to Earth.

Chapter 1
Introduction to Gaia

Voyage of Gaia

Gaia, is the long asteroid that passed through the solar system just a rock? And was it ensouled? What was its origin? How was it created?
Yes, it is just a long oblong rock, we can call it, and, yes, it was ensouled, but no, it was not inhabited. The soul that inhabits it is on a journey to study stars and planets as I once did for millions of years of your time. Its speed allows it to cover distances between solar systems quite fast.

Was it created by a solar system blowing up, sending shards out all over the galaxy?
Yes, there was a time when it was part of a planet that was torn apart during the Star Wars, or Reptilian War as you now term it. That gave this asteroid the speed it travels at now. There will be more like this in the future, but not before you learn how to protect Earth from a collision that would wipe out much life on Earth. You will learn how to move the trajectories away from Earth and into deep space.

Gaia, **how fast did the asteroid you ensouled travel?**
In Earth terms, over 100,000 miles per hour.

So, not 200,000 or more? I want to get this correctly.
No, stick with that figure. It was just a little above.

Gaia, is the asteroid you ensouled still in this solar system and if not where?
No, it is no longer in this solar system but is still in this galaxy. It is now ensouled by a younger soul that is exploring this galaxy and having conversations as I once did with the suns, planets, and moons along the

way. And yes, it is using those energetic pathways to portal hop. It will take several million more years first to explore this galaxy, and then it can choose other galaxies, even though they are not as compact as they were when I began my voyage that led me to Earth. I wished the soul well.

How long in Earth years did it take to cross each galaxy?
Depending upon the galaxy, it could take over a million Earth years, Tom.

Gaia, did you ensoul an asteroid or a comet during your sojourn through the galaxies?
Good question, Tom, but no, I was not a comet. I was able to steer it, as I mentioned before, but not because it was a comet. I had the ability to steer it in any direction I wished.

And I assume you could control the speed?
Quite so. Each galaxy took quite a bit of time, even though they were compacted at the beginning.

Can I assume that this was almost at the speed of light?
Even faster, as I used those portals that existed between galaxies and within the galaxies to hop from sun to sun and planet to planet where I could instantly ask questions. Even then, it took millions of Earth years, and as I mentioned before, I was constantly in touch with Creator asking questions that would be far beyond your understanding at this time.

Why would a soul be attracted to ensouling a sun, planet, or moon in let's say the Sombrero Galaxy as compared to the Milky Way Galaxy? And why would a soul ensoul a moon instead of a sun or planet?
Notice how different these galaxies are from each other. You can say the same for all the trillions of other galaxies in Creator's Universe. Each soul again has a different interest. To you, it would seem that there is not much going on in the average moon, but that is not correct. You could look at them as small planets, each with their own dynamics. Those souls that ensoul suns have a completely different interest than do those souls ensouling planets and moons. You have experienced just a little bit of the difference when you have had conversations with Sun Soul. You described it to your readers as trying to have a discussion with a physicist. The souls

that ensoul the Milky Way like having a huge sun they orbit around, while those in the Sombrero Galaxy enjoy their plane of existence. We could go on and on with differences in these two galaxies. Each galaxy has its own unique energy, which is something for your scientists to research in the future.

What were you studying and learning? And did you converse with the souls of the suns and planets or was it mostly conversations with Creator?

All three, Tom. I had many conversations with Creator learning why and for what purpose he created these galaxies that are all different from each other. And I also had many conversations with the souls that made up each galaxy as to why they were attracted to those particular galaxies. This is getting a little beyond your understanding at this point, but the Explorer Race will see great differences in each galaxy when you begin to travel to the stars around 3250. Each soul has a different interest, as we have touched on before.

Gaia, when did you form the goal of learning about the whole Universe? Was it when you were born? I know that might not be the term to use.

Yes, when I was created, Tom, I had my soul interest in learning everything I could about the Universe, with the further goal of wanting to care for a living planet. Creator recognized my dedication. We had many discussions along the way, as I asked questions. Yes, it would seem at times as if I were the kid that would not shut up asking questions, but Creator always had time to answer my questions, just as Creator will happily answer any of your readers' questions should they desire. Creator can be in a trillion places all at the same time.

Always remember that Creator can create anything from scratch.

Are there any other quantum master souls ensouling planets in this Universe, and what about suns?

You would think there would be a number in the trillions of galaxies, but you could count the number of souls that have achieved quantum master level of learning on one hand. We all communicate with each other on occasion.

How many galaxies were in existence when you began your journey?
Hundreds, but not thousands or millions as you were thinking. You might say it looked daunting, but Creator said that needed to be my path to much more understanding.

You mentioned that there are very few quantum masters in our Universe. Are all of them ensouling planets, suns, or a mixture?
Good question, Tom. A mixture. Each of us has our soul interest and these interests vary widely.

Are any of them in this galaxy?
No, quite far away in distance.

Gaia, when you ensouled an asteroid, how large was it and was it in this Milky Way Galaxy?
It was not in this galaxy, Tom, but one quite far away. Keep in mind, there are no distances for us, and the asteroid I was chosen to ensoul was chosen because it would encounter a large number of solar systems, asteroids, and individual suns and planets. Plus, to answer your first question, it was large by your standards—almost a planetoid—although not in that class for your more scientific readers, Tom.

What were you able to learn from that experience, Gaia?
There were so many things, Tom, some beyond your knowledge at the present time, but, as you can imagine, the variety of the places I visited gave me insight into a wide variety of planets, suns, and special energies.

Were you able to control the direction and speed?
Just to a slight degree, Tom, as there was no need to with this asteroid. It went where I needed to go.

What were you able to learn?
Certainly, as I mentioned, I was exposed to a wide variety of planets and suns, and the different types of energy they would emit.

Gaia, first, did you arrive to take over running the show here before Earth was moved or after, and how many Earth years ago was that?

Did the four million other souls arrive at the same time, or when?
Yes, Tom, let's see if you can receive this, this morning—I think you can.
No, I did not arrive before Earth arrived, but shortly thereafter. You might
say in an instant, Tom, as we don't waste time on this side as there is no
time. So, how many years ago, you ask?

Yes, over two million I would assume?
Yes, quite a bit more than that in order to properly prepare Earth to receive
your souls.

So, 60 million?
Yes, that's getting closer, but actually even earlier—over 100 million
Earth years ago. I know from your perspective, Tom, it is a lot of time, but
we did not sit on our hands, you could say. We had plenty of work to do
along with the four million other volunteers. This is a very complex planet
that needed to go through certain stages of evolution itself in order to arrive
at a time when it could host humans. Keep in mind before you arrived we
had to populate the planet with most of the animal, plant, bird, and insect
life. That was a huge undertaking, and, naturally, as the Earth changed
over those time periods so would all that life change and adapt too.

So, yes, I've been here a long time, Tom, and will be here long after the
Earth Experiment is finished as we will host people from all over the
Universe who wish to come and visit such a varied world. As you have
been told before, it will become a gigantic park for people to come and
experience a little bit of everything.

**Was the space-time continuum already in place when you arrived, or
was it not set up until shortly before humans and all the other
experiments were introduced?**
Good question, Tom. No, it was not long before humans arrived, but long
enough for us to monitor how the different Earth frequencies operated, as
keep in mind each timeline was a different frequency, so, let's say,
Timeline 11 would not have the severity of weather that Timeline 1 has.
So, frequencies do make a difference, but were not introduced at the
beginning, but later.

Would that have been, let's say, 2 million years ago or earlier?
Again, earlier, Tom, as humans and humanoids were already on Earth at that time. It would be more than 10 million years.

Gaia, did you have any experience before you were assigned to this planet that prepared you to work with the heavy negativity we have and are working with on earth?
Another interesting question, Tom. Certainly, I had, using Earth terms, many millions of years' experience traveling through many different energy grids, we shall call them for your readers, Tom. This was when I inhabited a small planetoid.

Was this a comet?
Yes, Tom. Exactly. Before, we have just described it as an asteroid, but in order to experience these various energy grids, I did have a long trajectory, we will call it. It was not just in this quadrant of the galaxy, you see. So, I performed a service while I was also learning about various star systems along the way, and, as you guessed, in multiple focuses.

This may all seem complex to you and your readers now, Tom, but the creator of this Universe recognized my soul interest when it invited me to do that work first, which certainly over a long period of time raised my own vibrational level—something obviously needed as you are now aware as you transfer from the Third Focus to the Fifth. Therefore, I have much experience in working with many energies, but nothing really prepares a soul to work with as much negativity as is present here. Still, I was able to acclimate slowly to the increased negativity needed for the Earth experiment.

Gaia's Origin Story

Gaia—I have a general question about your work. Please tell me about your studies and how you work with humans.
Good question about how I work, Tom. I do find time to study as I have recently worked on becoming a quantum master, and certainly the duties of keeping up with all the needs of this planet are quite challenging because it includes the Explorer Race that will someday go to the stars and

planets and educate and change them forever. There will be movement across the universe as what your Explorer Race does will have a rippling effect across the universe; this is already happening, although you won't be able to see or learn about that for several hundreds of years. It will seem you are progressing slower than you actually are.

There are many challenges and obstacles and hurdles for the Explorer Race to overcome before you will be allowed to actually reach the stars. There will be a long period of exploration of the other planets in your solar system, which will aid you down the way or in the future to understand the makeup of other similar planets in the universe. There are so many things for you as a race of people to learn that it cannot be done in a few generations. This will happen over hundreds of years and also with the assistance of beings that are more technically advanced than you are.

Note: For more information on the explorer race read Robert Shapiro's The Explorer Race *series of books.*

I know I read you have attained either material mastery or something like that. Am I correct?
Yes. That has been one of my best accomplishments since I ensouled this planet.

So, you have achieved quantum mastery?
It was quantum mastery I've achieved during my inhabiting of this world. It is something that is hard to explain how it is accomplished, but I did. Now I am working on other things, as you say.

Gaia, I just read a *Time* magazine article that says that James Lovelock, the environmentalist, coined your name. Isn't your name older than recent times, or is it a new name?
James coined the name, although it was in existence well before the time he first used it publicly. Is that a diplomatic answer?

It's a confusing answer to me. Did he channel the name or was it given to him as an inspiration, or did he see it in some old text?
He actually channeled the name. I gave it to him.

Gaia, is it my understanding that you were ensouled in an asteroid at one point in your existence?

Yes, that is quite true, Tom. It was my training wheels, in your vernacular. There was much to be learned, even though it would seem to be an easy assignment, if you will. It was a large asteroid, yes, that moved through the universe, and I was able to communicate with planets and suns as I passed and gained great knowledge during that experience.

So, why were you chosen for the Earth by the Creator?

All souls have certain specialties and interests, and I was unique in my interests so the Creator of this Universe felt that I was the right soul for this job as I could have the experience with the planet for several million years of your time, even before humans were ensouled here. I was ready for you by then. At least I thought I was, but having a free choice and veiled from knowing about yourselves is truly unique in this and any other universe. It has meant growth for not only your souls, but for me too.

Did another creator create you too?

Yes, yes. I was attracted to this Creator's Universe just as many, many other souls were because it is so unique among creations. It was exciting, if you wish to use that word, and we all knew great growth would be the result in taking part in this.

As a soul, do you normally reside on the earth? Do you surround it? Do you completely permeate it?

And what a good question from you this morning, Tom. I do reside, if you will, in the earth and my presence expands as needed to the surface and all through the earth. It's very difficult to explain in your third dimensional thinking, but as a soul I can be everywhere at once, just as I'm speaking to you right now. I am cognizant or aware of everything on this, and in this, planet.

Months later I would ask a similar question, receiving more information:

Do you remain, more or less, in the center of the planet, or do you expand yourself to cover the whole planet, or do you move around?

An excellent question, Tom. Let's see if you can receive this. I tend to move around in my body. I am not like the fragment of your soul that remains basically in place during your waking hours. I have the ability to move around the planet in milliseconds of course, plus I can send out parts of myself to keep tabs, so to speak, on developments on or within my physical body. Naturally, I have the ability to be in thousands of places all at the same time. I am not limited. As your Theo says, we're multi-taskers.

Gaia, how many people around the world are communicating with you at the same time as me?
There are several thousand, but not as many as you might think, considering the world's population. It is something I am easily able to handle, should there be thousands more that wish to communicate with me.

Are most of them in India, or are they really scattered around the world?
A majority of people are in India, but there is good representation in Europe, and even a few souls in the United States and a few more in Canada. It all adds up when you add all the people in and on all the continents of the world, keeping in mind the time differences as many will meditate to talk to me either in the evening or morning time as you do.

Are you, Gaia, a combination of souls or energies, or was there some misinterpretation since you have many souls that you allow to live on and within you?
I am basically a complete soul, but of course that means I am part of a larger mass of energy of all that is. I welcome all the many souls and fragments of souls that choose to reside here.

Your awareness is not constricted by our time, is it?
No, I am aware of the Earth from conception to the end of its days.

It could be sad I suppose to know of one's ending, but then are you aware of what you will do next after you have finished here?
Somewhat, but that is a little veiled for me as I have much to do and accomplish myself before I take the next step.

I'm still trying to nail down the inconsistencies between what I receive and what actually happens, so here are more questions I asked Gaia:

Certainly, my inability to receive you correctly has to enter into the equation, but when you say something using a phrase that I would not use, then that leads me to assume I received the message clearly.
Yes, but not always, Tom. Still, be patient and you'll see at least one of these events soon.

Perhaps patience enters into the equation too Gaia.
Certainly, it does too, you see.

Gaia, I have always imagined you as a ball of energy, but can you be further defined as an "electromagnet intelligence?"
That's correct, Tom. Therein lies our ability to create and work with the physical world. Your scientists can put their heads together to figure out how we exist in the quantum world, but it will take literally thousands of years for them to understand.

So, I guess someone could call you "Electro Lady" or some such name.
They can call me anything they wish, Tom. I am always available to any human being who wishes to communicate.

Gaia, do Theo's (Tom's guardian angel) answers and yours reflect the collective conscious, my truths, or what is real about a subject?
You are always dealing with a collective conscious when you communicate on a soul level. We are always connected to each other, and that includes all on this dimensional level. That does not mean we are not individual souls with our chosen areas of expertise, but that we do have the advantage of this beautiful connectivity. Yes, you could use the phrase "one for all and all for one," which has a layered meaning.

When you ask these questions, we are able to pull in the information from thousands, if not millions, and, yes, billions of souls. You were told long ago, Tom, that these answers are filtered by your education, spiritual beliefs, and so on. That is for every human that asks us questions. You and a few others do your very best to stay as neutral as possible, so your answers will be closer to the truth as we can give you, based on all these factors. As we have also told you in the past, the information you receive will be studied for a very long time, and even the answers you receive incorrectly will cause people to think and discuss and ponder. This material will act as a steppingstone for many to come in future times.

Gaia, I'm asked how you can read the thoughts of humans—whether it be compassion or violence or do you not need that as you look at the overall vibrational levels as we very slowly raise them?
Yes, I don't have to read them per se, although I certainly can. I am in second-to-second communication with all those GAs (*guardian angels*), as you call them, involved in the Earth Experiment, but keep in mind I also have the capability to see far into your future and I know that your path is now set to, as you put it, slowly raise your vibrational levels over time.

I am also in second-to-second contact with your souls as they write their new history and constantly look to balance all your lives on Earth. Keep in mind that description given to you before of a giant energy soup. Obviously, that is a 3D description for you now, and over the years you will come to understand this, and there will be those that come along who will seek better descriptions as your vibrational levels increase. There always has to be something new to learn and there will be more revelations not only through you, Tom, but through and from others as well. Still, using this description, this energy soup, allows us to be in second-to-second contact for not only the present, but the past and future as well.

Gaia, I'm asked how specific is the data you can and do know regarding human thoughts, such as those of compassion or violence, even in a single day?
Tom, I can tap into this information second by second should I desire, but in a way, there is no need as I know all of your futures and all of your pasts. Of course the future and even the past, changes according to your actions in the present moment, but the future looks brighter every day, I will say. There are more thoughts of compassion and fewer of violence although it might not seem that way to you now. You are unable to view your vibrational levels rising, but I can. I encourage every one of your readers, Tom, to send light to the planet each day. Send light and love and

even say a prayer for those less fortunate and your future will be glorious. Rise above your personal concerns and say Benevolent Prayers for others. That will raise your vibrational levels each time you do so.

So, to summarize, yes, I have the ability—should I desire—to monitor any individual person, but I do it more on a total world basis, and in constant communication with all of the souls participating in the Earth Experiment. We all set a path as we go along that will be the greatest learning for each soul fragment.

Chapter 2
Earth Movement

A note from Tom:

Longtime readers of my newsletters know that Gaia had told me to check in every six months about the percentage probabilities for giant earthquakes on the West Coast and for the Yellowstone Volcano to erupt. This has been ongoing for several years.

She did say that in-between the six-month checks, if I saw a large migration out of California and a fairly large migration in, that meant that she had been given the go-ahead to proceed with the earthquakes and Yellowstone eruption. Never did I dream it would be a catastrophic fire that would burn half of the Los Angeles area, but that's what happened. So, on January 18, 2025, for my six-month update, here are my questions:

Recent Discussions of Massive Earth Movements

Does the LA fire event tie in with previous prediction of mass earthquakes along the West Coast?
Yes, Tom. I have been given the go-ahead by your souls.

What will be the timing of the earthquakes—2025, 2026, 2027, or later since it will take a few months for those in the Los Angeles area to come to the realization that they must move?
It will not be until 2026, Tom. You're right, people are clinging to the hope for a quick rebuild, which will not occur.

Will the quakes start in Southern California and where, and how far up the coast?
Yes, right along the San Andreas fault line and all the way up past

Vancouver over a period of a few days.

How far inland in California, Oregon, Washington State, and Canada?
Even past the mountains, Tom, as there are fault lines that have not been discovered as of yet. Going over the mountains will not be sufficient protection.

What about Yellowstone and the percentage, which was at 73% as I recall?
It is now close to 93%. People must move away from that area when they experience rumblings increasingly severe.

And I assume the volcanic cloud will extend all the way to Chicago as you previously told me?
Exactly, Tom.

So, this time you are not including the Mississippi Valley?
Correct, Tom. It will remain fairly stable.

Any precursors for the West Coast quakes and Yellowstone?
The earthquakes—smaller ones on the West Coast will become more numerous and as I mentioned, Yellowstone will awaken.

I assume there will be a number of mudslides with the next rain event in the LA area?
More reasons to move away from that area. It will be very unstable.

You mentioned several years ago that the oceans of the world would rise three feet. Is that still your plan, or will there not be sufficient land to drop into the ocean for the rise in ocean levels?
That will occur, Tom. Glad you remembered that (with a little help from Theo). There will be sections of the coast that will tumble into the ocean along the West Coast. Not the same as when the Atlantean Islands sank and the oceans rose 45 feet, but still there will be displacement.

Gaia, will the Arial Seamouunt volcano, located 300 miles off the coast of Oregon, erupt in 2025?
Yes, Tom. One of the precursors of more to come.

The following questions were asked January 25, 2025:

Gaia, what is the probability of the large earthquakes in 2026, and how large will they be?
Let's see if you can receive this this morning Tom. Needless to say, the percentage of probability is quite high—over 95%—yes that is correct. The largest of the earthquakes, keeping in mind that there will be several thousand, will be over 8.0–8.3 to 8.4. As I said before, these will be the largest in recorded history.

So, I must ask, since they are not 100% for the quakes or for Yellowstone erupting, how would we go about landing on the smaller percentage, if that is a possibility?
It would seem so, but as we draw closer to 2026 the percentage of possibility will continue to rise. Since all your lives are taking place at the same time, you are all experiencing these events in your future.

Will the quakes extend all the way to Alaska, and if so into the interior or to the Aleutian Islands?
All the way to and slightly past the Aleutian Islands, Tom.

Will any tsunamis be created either by the movement under the ocean, or by land dropping into the ocean?
Yes, large tsunamis—multiple ones—will be created by these earthquakes.

How large?
Over 30 feet—quite destructive.

I assume Hawaii and Japan, and perhaps even the Asian mainland and Australia will be affected?
Yes, even Europe to a lesser extent. Those who live in Hawaii and Japan will have to quickly move far inland to not be affected by the tsunamis.

What about Mt. Rainier?
The shaking will cause it to lose its mantle, wiping out the valley below.

Will Mt. Vesuvius and Campi Flegrei erupt in Italy?
Not at this time.

Why did you and our souls decide not to include the New Madrid fault in the Mississippi Valley?
We all agreed that releasing the pressure on the West Coast was sufficient at this time, plus the souls living in the middle of North America needed the experience of helping the survivors of the events on the West Coast and Yellowstone.

What size will be the precursor earthquakes?
Several in the 6.0 to 6.5 range.

How soon after those will come the large movements?
A matter of weeks, as there will be many smaller earthquakes in between those.

At what depth will these quakes occur? 6.7 miles or 9 kilometers?
Exactly. Even shallower at times.

Will more of the lower West Coast land be lost than the upper?
Slightly more.

Will the slippage of the North American Plate over the Pacific Plate be 28 to 30 feet?
Yes, that is a large slippage that I need, since there has been none for eons of time.

What will be the length of time of the major quakes—the number of months?
They will continue for several months at above 7.0.

Will the earthquakes begin near Tijuana and work up to the North, or will they begin more toward San Diego or even Los Angeles?

The origination will be closer to Tijuana, Mexico.

Will these be the largest earthquakes in recorded history?
Yes, plus the number will exceed those recorded before.

During what part of 2026 will be the large earthquakes and the eruption of Yellowstone?
More towards the middle of the year. The smaller earthquakes will begin in the first three months of the year.

Will part of the destruction include taking down the mountains in Southern California, allowing the Pacific weather systems to flow across the Southwest and then eastward through Texas and the Southern states?
Yes. Arizona, Nevada, and New Mexico, plus the far western part of Texas will see annual rainfall of 30 inches to 35 inches and then Central and Eastern Texas and the Southern states will see 60 inches or more of rain, drawing on the Gulf of Mexico, turning them sub-tropical. These rain events will cross the Atlantic Ocean bringing rain to the deserts of Africa, bringing them back to life.

What reasons did you have for delaying these events in the past?
There was a great amount of learning and growth during this past time period, but now a large percentage of the population needs to experience earthquakes and volcanic eruptions. Some will heed the warnings and leave, having experienced this in the past, but there are those that will refuse to leave, ignoring the warnings, just as their guardian angels are instructed to keep them there.

How will the Trump Administration handle the disasters?
Poorly, as you can imagine, since this is beyond what has ever happened to your country in the past. Assistance will have to come from those who risk their lives to save others. There will have to be fuel dumps for people to refill their cars, since many will have to leave California without filling up their gas tanks. Las Vegas will see a large influx of refugees who will fill the hotels there, and will become a hub for assistance, since the city has many flights per day in and out of the city.

In the same session, I decided to ask my own Guardian Angel Theo to verify the answers I had received from Gaia:

Theo, did I correctly receive from Gaia about the earthquakes and eruptions?
Close to perfect, Tom. We know how hard this is for even you to accept, but it has always been on your soul contract to warn people of the coming catastrophic events.

The following questions were asked Feb 2025:

Gaia, will Santorini have a major eruption and will the precursor quakes on the West Coast just be a few at the 6.0 to 6.5 level or thousands like Santorini?
At this time, I am not planning a major eruption, but certainly more adjustments in that area. These earthquakes will subside in the next few weeks. The precursor earthquakes in 2026 will be similar in nature—hundreds of smaller earthquakes, but larger ones mixed in. This will let the population know larger ones are on the way. It will be their last chance to move out of those areas.

Gaia, what will be the effect on El Salvador?
There will be adjustments all along the "Ring of Fire," as it is called, just not to the extent as there will be from Northern Mexico up through Alaska.

Gaia, could you be more specific regarding Vancouver, Vancouver Island, White Rock, Langley, Burnsby, and the interior such as 100 Mike House?
That area along the coast will experience a number of seven to nine level earthquakes. There will be major destruction and loss of life for all who do not move away from that major fault zone, along with yes, tsunamis created by the movements. They must move well over the mountains into the interior of Canada.

Gaia, will food be able to be grown in the Midwest of the United States?
Not for some time, due to the ash cloud from Yellowstone that at times will blanket that area. As I stated before, much of your produce will have to come from Mexico and South America.

How long will the ash cloud last? Will this cause the world temperature to drop?
Look for it to last for several years. The northern part of the country, as I have stated before, will experience a perpetual winter during that time period until the ash cloud dissipates. The world temperature will drop a degree or two.

Am I receiving all this correctly from you this morning?
Yes, Tom.

Gaia, what will be the death toll?
Several hundred thousand to over one million people, whose soul contracts are to experience this event. The West Coast is heavily populated, and many will refuse to move even with the advent of the precursor earthquakes. Yes, the death toll could be even higher, but I'm giving you what you can accept at this time.

Gaia, will there be chaos or martial law?
Just as with any large event, National Guard troops will be brought in and even Army and Marines will be posted, although their lives will be put in jeopardy too. Thieves will also be buried in the rubble of houses they attempt to burglarize as the earthquakes continue.

Gaia, will the free energy machine help?
Yes, those that construct or buy the machines this year will not have to rely on electricity provided by companies when their electrical lines collapse. They will also be small enough to be take with the families as they evacuate the West Coast.

Any effect on upper New York and New England?
A huge influx of refugees who have friends and family in that area, plus centers to accept these people will be established.

Gaia, what is the probability of large earthquakes for Taiwan?
They will experience tsunamis like most of Asia, India, and Australia/New Zealand.

Gaia, any effect on the East Coast, U.S. economy? How long will it take to

recover? What about the stock market?
There will be a flood of refugees to the East Coast—thousands. It will take many years to recover. The stock market will reflect this. Some businesses will thrive if they provide services needed in this recovery.

Gaia, is there any safe place to live in California?
Certainly, nowhere along the coast deep into the interior. There will be certain mountainous areas that will shake, but not as severely as the coastal areas. There will be damage, just not as severe.

Gaia, when the earthquakes come to California, will there be great pollution and even nuclear pollution?
Yes, Tom, that will be a byproduct of the movement of the crust.

How will you handle that?
Just as I have done for centuries with other large movements. Given a little time, the pollution will sink to the bottom, Tom, and will be absorbed back into the floor of the ocean.

What about the nuclear pollution?
That will take longer, but you—meaning humans—will find ways to contain this pollution.

Gaia, you said one million casualties was all I could accept last time, so what will the worldwide total be—10, 20, 50, 100 million or more? And what will be the percentage for the West Coast, Hawaii, Japan, etc.?
Let's see if you can receive this, Tom. There will actually be over 100 million casualties from the earthquakes, the eruption, and tsunamis caused by the earthquakes. It will be closer to 200 million than the 100 million figure. Yes, you are receiving me correctly. You can see why your souls resisted and dragged their feet, shall we say, but these adjustments in my mantle must be made, and I have put this off as long as possible. But don't forget that these soul fragments need this experience.

So, I am not just giving a figure?
No, you are very close to the actual number of worldwide casualties, as you term them.

What percentage of the total is the West Coast?
30%.

Hawaii?
1%.

Japan?
7%.

Don't forget that there will be tsunamis for Asia and even Australia, but even other locations, along with the three-foot rise in the oceans with the displacements. Those percentages seem high for Hawaii and Japan, as they will have warnings. But there will be multiple events.

Gaia, what is the greater perspective and purpose of 2026—to bring people together?
If it was just that simple. I have warned people for several years to leave the coasts, not only for me to give them a rest, but also I knew I would be given permission eventually to make these earth changes. As you have been told numerous times, Earth is a living thing. I am the soul that ensouls Earth. These events will reduce the population on Earth. It had reached its peak and was slowly starting to reduce, but this will quickly reduce the population even more. There will be millions of people that will assist in the recovery in some way, and then there will be those that will try and take advantage, all the way from thievery to making money on those directly affected.

Gaia, how will Bangladesh be affected, and are there any places in the world where land will rise?
The majority of Bangladesh will go under water either from the tsunamis or the rise in sea level. There will be a great loss of life there. The major rise in land will be around the Yellowstone Super Volcano.

Gaia, how will Port Charlotte, Florida fare?
Like all of Florida, the rise in the oceans of three feet will cause flooding.

Gaia, what about Silicon Valley, plus the nuclear power plant near the coast?

All heavily damaged by the 7 to 9 earthquakes. There are safeguards at the plant in case of earthquakes which will keep the spread of nuclear waste down. Silicon Valley will cease to exist as a place to work, since the earthquakes will continue for months.

Gaia, what will be the height of the tsunamis on Hawaii, Japan, the Philippines, Australia, New Zealand, and India?
They will be several that will be over 100 feet high in Hawaii, Japan, and the Philippines, but even Australia and New Zealand may see 30-foot tsunamis, although they are thousands of miles away, and there will be a dissipation, but not completely. India's coast will experience large tsunamis.

Questions asked March 2025:

How will Boise, Idaho be affected?
Heavy ash clouds at times, with numerous earthquakes, caused by the eruption.

How much worse will be Yellowstone than Mt. Saint Helens?
Yellowstone is in all sense of the word a Super Volcano. Multiply the immediate affected area by at least 10 times.

Will the ground be covered in ash in Minnesota?
Large portions of this area will be covered by the continuing eruption.

How much change in the weather?
As I have stated before, the thick ash clouds will not allow the snow to melt in the summer, thereby keeping temperatures low year-round.

How much less land will there be in California, Oregon, and Washington?
Use a general figure of 10%—still enough to raise the ocean levels around the world by three feet. And the same all the way up through Alaska.

Will there be any growing areas left on the West Coast?
It will be extremely difficult to farm, due to the continuing earth movements. This area will take years to rebuild.

What effect will there be on the Philippines, Sydney, Melbourne, Auckland, Christchurch, and Auckland New Zealand?
All of these locations will experience tsunamis. Not just one, but multiple. Those whose soul contracts are to survive, must move quickly to higher ground and be prepared to stay for weeks.

What about St. Louis?
Heavy ash clouds at times, but liveable.

Gaia, what will be the damage by the earthquakes to Phoenix?
Minor damage from the earthquakes as they will be felt hundreds of miles away.

Gaia, which mountain range or ranges should people move past to be safe—Cascades, Sierras, Rocky Mountains?
Well past the first two you mentioned, but to be completely safe, past the Rocky Mountains.

Keep in mind that people should request MBOs to move to the safest place for them. They will then be guided. May we remind everyone that these are prayers and will be answered.

Gaia, will Mumbai be submerged in 2026, and what about the India islands of Lakshaweep, Andaman, Nicober? (Asked March 2025)
Mumbai and the islands will experience several large tsunamis. People will need to leave the coastal area and abandon the islands if they wish to survive.

Gaia, how will Bangladesh be affected, and are there any places in the world where land will rise?
The majority of Bangladesh will go under water either from the tsunamis or the rise in sea level. There will be a great loss of life there. The major rise in land will be around the Yellowstone Super Volcano.

Gaia, how will Port Charlotte Florida fare?
Like all of Florida, the rise in the oceans of three feet will cause flooding.

Gaia, what about Silicon Valley, plus the nuclear power plant near the coast?
All heavily damaged by the 7 to 9 earthquakes. There are safeguards at the

plant in case of earthquakes which will keep the spread of nuclear waste down. Silicon Valley will cease to exist as a place to work, since the earthquakes will continue for months.

Edgar Cayce had a prediction regarding the South Pacific. Were these quakes what he predicted?
Yes, in a way, Tom, but keep in mind his predictions were based on the timeline you were on at that point when he was given the predictions, and now you are on a more benevolent timeline; although when the movements I have previously described occur, many people will think the end is near. That's not correct. I simply must release the pressure built up from these plate movements, or to use the old saying "you ain't seen nothing yet" would apply, as they would be so cataclysmic as to fit within his predictions. That WILL NOT HAPPEN—yes, emphasize that for me, Tom. I know you do not wish to touch on this too much, Tom, but the question was asked by your reader, so we must answer.

Gaia, how will the flow of wind and rain after the earthquakes of 2026 affect hurricane season?
Dramatically, Tom. It will be hard for them to form due to the flow of wind across the southern part of the United States. Up until now, the storms have formed off the African coast and traveled westward, breaking apart or gathering strength. After next year, that flow will be reversed and storms that form in North America will travel across the Atlantic and will bring copious amounts of rain to the African desert. Good question.

Gaia, are there timelines where the earthquakes and volcanic eruption will not occur?
An emphatic no, Tom. I need these adjustments on all timelines. What will be different will be many more people will heed the warnings and not need to experience the earthquakes, or they will experience a lesser intensity by leaving earlier than the lower timelines. Again, for this timeline, request an MBO, as you call them, to be guided away at the right time and for a perfect place to live.

Gaia, can the cactus in the Sonoran Desert survive the ash clouds, even if they are less?

The ash clouds will not be as intense or constant in that area, so yes, they will survive.

Gaia, how can Canadians and even those here in the U.S. prepare for an influx of refugees? Stock up on food, medical supplies, wood—what else?

Neither government will even entertain the idea of massive earthquakes and a super volcanic eruption until next year. Therefore, it is up to individual families to slowly stock up on what you need to survive these events. Much assistance will come from other countries, and of course from areas not affected directly by these events. Once you feel you have sufficient supplies for your family, then look to see what you can do to gently suggest to others that it is always good to have extra supplies of food, water, etc.

Gaia, how many cubic tons of earth will be blasted from the Yellowstone volcano?

These numbers will not even be able to be calculated by your volcanologists, but easily millions of tons of ash will fall, and not just for a short time—we are talking about well over a year—even years.

What percentage of the wheat crop will be destroyed, and will farmers ever produce wheat again?

With the change in weather patterns, other parts of Canada and even the United States will be able to grow wheat. Canada will be warmer farther to the North. Much wheat will come from other countries.

How long will a bread shortage last and should people buy extra flour and store it?

The shortage of bread will not happen overnight, depending upon the source of your bread, but it will occur. Stocking up on extra flour would be a good plan.

Gaia, do you have any plans to activate any of the 95 volcanoes discovered underneath the ice sheet of western Antarctica?

No, Tom, this whole area will remain dormant for many years to come. There will be great melting of Antarctica in the coming years, but this is due to the warming world temperatures we have discussed before.

The following questions were asked in April of 2025:

Gaia, what effect will Yellowstone have on Saskatchewan Canada and specifically Melfort?
Lower Saskatchewan will experience ash clouds that blow east from Yellowstone. Melfort is far to the north and will see an increase in their population from people forced to move. Don't forget that Canada will be warmer to the north with the changing climate.

Gaia, what effect will the earthquakes and Yellowstone eruption have on the internet, banking, and large retail stores?
As we have mentioned before, people on the west coast, and yes, even those closer to Yellowstone will have to rely on the Starlink satellites for internet service. The Federal Reserve will have to step in to assist those refugees whose banks will be destroyed. Records will be lost, and it will be imperative for those who become refugees to prove what their banks had in their accounts, unless there are records stored elsewhere.

Large retail stores such as the Walmarts and other retailers will suffer loses and their chains of supply will be interrupted, forcing them to find other sources. There will be shortages of certain products—a long list, which is why we suggest stocking up on essentials.

Gaia, what about Ohio in 2026?
Ash clouds at times in the northern part of the state, but livable.

Gaia, what about Visakhapatnam on the East Coast of India?
Large tsunamis. Move or be inundated multiple times.

Will the Yellowstone eruption effect the formation of hurricanes?
No. Just the weather in the upper part of the United States and the lower part of Canada.

Which mountains on the West Coast will be taken down—just the ones surrounding Los Angeles, or more up the coast?
Primarily those in the lower part of California. Still there will be great destruction all up the West Coast. Many avalanches in the mountains.

Will the highways out of Los Angeles become impassable?
A definite yes. Many will become trapped trying to leave. They will have to walk out.

Will Lake Okeechobee be affected?
It is far enough inland to only be affected by the storms.

Gaia, how will Long Island and Lower Manhattan fair?
With the rise in the oceans three feet, places that have flooded in the past will experience this full time. Barriers will be built, but this will take time.

Gaia, where will the level 9 quakes occur on the West Coast?
Up and down the whole coast, and if some place does not have a level 9, 8s and 7s continuously will occur. These will not be one-time events, but continuously over months—again, this has never been seen in modern times.

What about the migration of birds, due to the ash clouds?
Yes, they will be prevented from their natural migrations. They will have to adapt.

Will air travel be suspended around the world?
No, only in the areas affected by the earthquakes and ash clouds. Airplanes will have to be rerouted to airports where they can land and take off safely. This will be a big adjustment.This adjustment will last for many years.

Will both America and Canada experience a depression?
Yes, both economies will suffer, with other countries contributing to assist those who are able to leave the West Coast and from under the ash cloud.

What about Apple and Amazon?
They will have to shift their operations to the East. The operations on the West Coast will be destroyed.

Gaia, how will Iowa, including Fairfield, do regarding the ash cloud from Yellowstone.
Not as well as you think. It will all depend upon the direction of the wind.

It will be livable, and Fairfield a little more so.

What about Redding, California?
Quite unlivable. The earthquakes—and there will be thousands, will take out all the electrical and water supplies, and many buildings will be destroyed.

Africa and Earth Movements

Will Africa experience any tsunamis or volcanic eruptions in the next five years, and should they move away from the coasts too? (Asked July 2021)
Moving away from the coasts is not just for the North American coast, but worldwide. As the climate warms, so will the rise in the seas of the world. For Africa, it will be more storms—some will be beneficial for parched areas, and some will be destructive. Africa has less of a problem with volcanoes, so nothing in the short run.

Asia and Earth Movements

Gaia, is there any probability of a volcanic eruption in the next two years of the Akahoya volcano located south of Japan? (Asked March 2018)
No, Tom. There has been a buildup of magma there, but there will not be a volcanic eruption there anytime soon.

Geologists say the last time it erupted was 7,300 years ago. Is that correct?
Within a century or two, Tom.

Did it erupt at the same time, or shortly after Mu sank into the sea after the hydrogen-type bombs ripped it to shreds?
It occurred very close to that time, Tom. As you might guess, the sinking of the continent threw everything out of order.

So, should I adjust the time period when Mu sank from 7,500 years ago to 7,300 years?

No, keep that figure for now, Tom, as it took time for the buildup to occur.

Gaia, what is the highest probability during the next 10 years for tsunamis, earthquakes, and flooding for Hong Kong and SE Asia? (Asked March 2017)
As we have repeatedly pointed out, any city existing on the coast will have great flooding issues because of the rise in ocean levels. Not only that, but with the warmer temperatures not only in the atmosphere, but also in the ocean, comes greater storms—typhoons as they are called in that part of the world. So, there will be a migration of people from the coast into the interior as will happen around the world. I did give you warning five years ago. These storms in general will be larger and more numerous than in the past. That you can take to the bank, Tom.

California and Earth Movements

Gaia, when the quakes come to California, how will Mt. Shasta fare?
Yes, it will be affected to a certain extent, as even though it is away from the coast there will be great shaking which will be felt for hundreds, if not thousands of miles in some cases, Tom. Mt. Shasta will absorb most of this, but still the residents will definitely feel the effects.

Gaia, what is the probability of Mt. Shasta or Lassen being active in the next 40 years?
Less at this time, Tom, but don't forget your souls have a big decision coming up soon as to whether they wish to have a major eruption of the Yellowstone volcano, or a smaller, but still dynamic one. What they decide there will affect the other volcanos in that region. As you saw with the La Palma volcano, its eruption has been steady, not explosive, but still destructive to those whose homes were in the path of the flow of lava.
If Mt. Shasta did come back to life, how would it affect the people of Telos who live in a little higher frequency?
It would affect them too, so that is another consideration. They do great unseen work with their dream schools. My preference and of most of your souls would be to leave this region quiet.

How will the political landscape change in California when there are

fewer people there?

Yes, an interesting question, Tom. They will certainly remain a blue state, as they are called, since they will see all the resources the federal and state governments provide the citizens, many of whom will have lost all their earthly possessions. If anything, they may be more liberal. Then, for those who must leave California altogether, you will find they will affect other less liberal states, in some cases providing the tipping point to change a state from a red state to a purple or blue state.

Carbon Monoxide a Predictor?

Gaia, does the sudden release of carbon monoxide on the West Coast from California up to the north signal a major earthquake on the way?

This is an interesting development on the scientific side in finding new ways to predict earthquakes, but at the same time, the release of carbon monoxide does not automatically mean a severe earth movement. This needs to be studied much more to see what other factors enter into knowing that a significant earth movement is, but days away. Those additional factors were not in play, so therefore there will be no major earthquake along the North American coast. Yes, there was a slight movement there, thereby releasing the gas.

Caribbean Islands and Earth Movements

Gaia, do you have any plans to awaken the dormant volcano in Jamaica?

No, Tom, their greatest worry will be the rising ocean levels.

What percentage of Jamaica will be affected?

Obviously, the whole island will be affected in some way, but the bays and inlets will be most affected by the rising ocean levels. Any low-lying area will be inundated, and where the land and beaches are not completely covered any storms, not even hurricanes, will cause water to come farther inland and flood those homes and businesses near the waterfront.

China Earthquakes

Gaia, what is the probability of one or more earthquakes of 6.0 or higher for Southern China in the next five years? (Asked June 2020)
Quite high, Tom. Remember that there is constant movement of the continental plates, and pressure must be released.

Continents and Destruction

Gaia, is a similar situation happening today as it did in Atlantis? Force of one versus the force of many?
As we have stated before, Tom, there will never be another conflict that will result in the destruction of whole continents, as it did for Atlantis and Lemuria. As we have stated many times, you passed that marker back in 1987 at the Harmonic Convergence.

Controlling Volcanic Eruptions

Will there come a time when we learn to control volcanic eruptions?
Yes, but this will be fairly far in your future, Tom. Several hundred years. You will long before then learn how to utilize the heat generated by the volcano, and thereby partially control it, but if I wish to bring large amounts of magma there for an eruption, all they will be able to do is move out of the danger zone.

Dormant Volcanoes

Gaia, with dormant volcanoes erupting and the strength of earthquakes increasing, does this signify that an even larger event is coming that will change the face of the Earth? (Asked February 2020)
Interesting question, Tom. As I just recently said, the Earth is a living thing. That is quite hard for the average person to accept. When it breathes, the land moves—sometimes in mysterious ways to humans at this point in your development, since you have a long way to go to understand the true geology of the Earth. It is like looking through a keyhole. You can only see so much. What I'm saying is that what you are seeing is my normal movements of this living being. You can look at your records and see this is no different from any other period of time. That does not discount that in the future, your souls may say that they want a major movement and

activity that we have discussed before, or it may be a series of smaller movements. That has just not yet been decided for that time period between 2022 and 2027. Again, it is up to your souls.

El Salvador

Gaia, what is the highest probability for continuing quakes in El Salvador?
Almost 100%, Tom. This area is quite quake prone and will continue to have small, medium, and large quakes in the future. The people who live there chose, before birth, to live in a quake prone area of Earth in order to experience these during their lifetime. There will be those who will learn to build better quake-resistant structures to lessen the effects of earthquakes.

Fault Lines

Gaia, do the fault lines emit RF (radio frequency) transmissions just before an earthquake, or do they emit these RF transmissions all the time?
Good question, Tom. Yes, they do emit some RF transmissions constantly at normally a very low level, but certainly before a major earthquake movement these transmissions do increase. The "trick," if you wish to call it that, is to discover which transmissions are the precursors to an earthquake and which ones are from normal movements of the fault line.

I must ask, aren't geologists already monitoring these fault lines?
They are monitoring the fault lines more for movements rather than RF transmissions, Tom. They need to expand their monitoring to include more or different types of data.

So, if you know a geologist out there, perhaps you could GENTLY suggest that they set up RF transmissions monitors at the same time as the seismic monitors.

Gaia, does helium leaking from a fault line signify a coming earthquake?
Yes, it does at times, but not others, Tom. This is not one of those absolute

precursors we have spoken about before an earthquake occurs, but, yes, it can be one of many. In the instance asked about, it is simply my letting off steam, shall we say. It is relieving pressure in an area where if I did not do this there would be a buildup to the point where the Earth would move. So, to summarize, other factors must be weighed before saying that just helium being released to the atmosphere is the key ingredient to an impending large earthquake.

Gaia, will the torrential rains on the West Coast act as a lubricant to the fault lines, or will it just run off into the ocean?
Yes, an interesting question, Tom. On the surface, to use a little pun, it would seem that the rains, as the ground seemingly has reached its capacity to absorb, simply run off into the rivers, lakes, and ocean. Yet there are places where the water does not run off, but slowly and, in some cases at a rapid rate, goes into lower caverns, cisterns, and, yes, the fault lines all along the coast.

And to answer your question, yes, it does act as a lubricant, and is one of the many factors which will allow me to move the fault lines all along the coast. Obviously, there is a reason the San Francisco area is being inundated at the present time, as I have said in the past that area would be the first to move. Water will move anything if enough of it is used. You could compare it in a way to the fracking done in the middle of the country. Notice how there are earthquakes in areas that had seen little or none before.

Flooding
Gaia, are there any areas in the United States and Europe that will remain relatively safe from flooding and natural disasters?
Here we get into soul contracts, Tom. I will remind your readers that I wish people to move away from the coasts. They still have not formally recognized the rise in sea levels, but you can see the results of that rise in how far inland the flooding reaches. This is not limited to just the East Coast of North America, but the Gulf Coast and West Coast will experience severe flooding too.

But you have been given a tool to keep you safe. You can request a Most

Benevolent Outcome, as you call them, for the PERFECT place for you to live to be able to weather any natural event. Listen to those whispers in your head and circumstances will suddenly open doors so that it might send you to live in another section of your city, or perhaps far away. There will be many parts of the world that will not be touched by any natural disaster—you just have to request to be in one of those places.

Iceland and Earth Movements

Gaia, will the volcano in Iceland release pressure on Yellowstone and the same question if Mt. Taupo erupts in New Zealand? (Asked July 2021)

I applaud the person who asked this question as volcanologists certainly need to study the connection between volcanoes on this planet. That being said, it does have some effect, as I can release pressure in Yellowstone by having a fairly safe eruption in Iceland. It does not have as much of an effect if the volcano in New Zealand erupts. The Yellowstone volcano has a huge caldron underneath the surface that volcanologists are aware of. This is a dynamic environment that is constantly changing. As we have spoken before, I have not been given the go ahead to have a major eruption there by your souls, so therefore I use a volcano such as Iceland to in the short run relieve pressure, but that time could end in the next couple of years, and it all depends upon the intensity. Don't forget that this is a living planet, and volcanoes are simply part and parcel of this changing world.

Italy and Earth Movements

Gaia, you said there was a low probability of Mt. Vesuvius erupting in the next five years. What about Campi Flegrei, and is it connected to Mt. Vesuvius? (Asked January 2017)

Yes, it is connected to Mt. Vesuvius, Tom, which is a given. And, yes, I am adding to the caldron there at the present time, which is causing the seismographs to be jumping, but again, the probability of this volcano erupting in the next five years, along with Mt. Vesuvius is low, but as we have covered the probabilities for Vesuvius for 10 years, so, yes, you can add in Campi Flegrei. Both will be highly destructive. I am giving fair warning time that this area will be beset by lava flows again.

This will accomplish a number of things for me, but also for the souls who inhabit that area and need that for their list of Earth experiences. So, to summarize, yes, there will be continued rumblings in that area telling the residents that those volcanoes are awakening again, but nothing major will happen in the next five years.

Gaia, is the activity of Mt. Etna about the same or is it rising in intensity?
No, just about the same, but steady, shall we say. It is definitely not decreasing, Tom, but it does have its ebbs and flows where it may appear to increase or decrease. This is a good place for me to release pressure, as the land is not so inhabited, and everyone stays well away.

Gaia, does Mt. Etna have cycles or are they just irregular eruptions?
The cycles, as you can imagine, are under my control, Tom. So, yes, they are cyclic, but so far, your volcanologists have not been able to determine those cycles as their information is incomplete regarding the history of eruptions. And that can be said for all my volcanoes.

Is there an interdependence between Mt Etna and Mt. Stromboli? Together do they lower the probability of a Mt. Vesuvius eruption?
You have been told before that all of these volcanoes are connected, but again this has yet to be proven by your volcanologists, just as your geologists have yet to prove there is an absolute connection on the Ring of Fire so that when there is an eruption on one part of the Ring there can be an equal reaction clear across the Pacific Ocean on another part.

Regarding lowering the probability of a Mt. Vesuvius eruption, those two do keep the pressure from building too much at Mt. Vesuvius, but there will come a time when the probability is high for the caldrons to fill there and erupt. That is quite a few years in the future at this time.

Does Mt. Etna have greater eruptions at the same time as Mt. Stromboli or separately?
Separately, but there can be exceptions to this if I build up enough pressure by moving large amounts of lava into both.

Where does the plate margin run in Italy?
Just connect the dots, Tom. That will be close to the plate margin.

Gaia, is Mt. Etna in danger of slipping into the sea as some scientists suggest?
Quite so. I know you thought I would say no, or that it would be far in the future—and it is in the future—just not as far as you and other scientists might think. Should I decide to activate Mt. Vesuvius and the other volcanoes in that area in the coming years, Mt. Etna could very well slip. Obviously, this would cause a catastrophe for the Mediterranean basin, but I have warned you previously that these volcanoes around the world are connected, Tom, and Mt. Etna is part of that network, we will call it.

Gaia, why did you choose this time period to have the earthquakes in Italy that destroyed centuries-old buildings?
A simple answer, Tom, as we have discussed before. I must relieve the buildup of stress in that fracture just as I have other earthquakes around the world for the same reason. A more complicated reason has to do with those who need the experience of an earthquake. Yet, that does not in itself go far enough. When people build on top of my fault lines there will always come a time, whether it is in 10 years or a thousand, when I must relieve the stress between two plates, we will call them, and shift. Those that live close to other fault lines, such as the major or even minor ones in California, know subconsciously that they are living on borrowed time. Yet, they are drawn to live in these areas like a moth to fire. Yes, you can use the term "Year of Living Dangerously," but make "Year" plural.

Lights from Earthquakes

Gaia, please comment on the various theories of earthquake lights—those lights generated, it seems, by earthquakes.
Yes, there have been some good studies on this, Tom, so I will not spoil the fun of their studies in this area, except to say they are on the right track and soon they will be able to simulate the creation of these lights in a laboratory. These are electrical charges, Tom. The scientists just have to determine how they are generated and on what light spectrum.

Long Term Predictions: Next 100 Years: Earthquakes and Volcanoes

Gaia, will you continue to have earthquakes and volcanic eruptions over the next few hundred years?
Yes, of course, Tom. The Earth is a living entity. What will change will be the human species' ability to predict these events and not be caught up in them as you are in this time period. Houses in earthquake-prone areas will be much more structurally sound, or there will be laws in place that houses cannot be built in these areas. Houses that are occupied in earthquake-prone areas will have devices to warn the occupants that an earthquake is imminent and will evacuate in time so that there is little or no loss of life. For volcanoes, it will be a similar situation. No buildings will be allowed to be built near the volcanoes, and those that are occupied will be given sufficient warning to evacuate prior to the eruption.

So, the earthquakes and volcanic eruptions will stay at the same intensity as they are now and will not decrease?
Quite correct, Tom. All of this is set up, you could say, as teaching purposes so that those in these occupations as volcanologists and geologists will always have something to study and learn. This will carry over as you explore other worlds and see the similarities and differences between your planet and others.

Magma Flow

Gaia, scientists are speculating that the moving flow of magma under Earth's surface will either cause a pole shift or will possibly stop and change direction due to Earth's magnetic field. Comments?
Yes, a heady topic you might say, Tom, so I will give you a basic answer to your questions. You have been told many times in the past that I do move my magma from one place to another. That is a given. Regarding a shift in the poles, that will not happen. Again, I have repeatedly said that the shift in magnetic north will continue on its slow path. There will be no dramatic shift in, let's say, the near or foreseeable future. Do I use Earth's gravitational field to assist me in moving the magma? Certainly. I also use the gravitational pull of the other planets and the Moon to assist me, and, yes, the Sun will send magnetic waves upon my request.

Keep in mind these are all symbiotic relationships I have with all of them as I also assist those other planets in ways your scientists will not discover for hundreds of years. Your scientists are just scratching the surface in studying my inner workings, and they know this. They will have many more speculations in the future—some not so accurate like these are, and eventually quite accurate ones as instruments are invented that can peer into my inner workings. That is part of their learning process and must be learned prior to you traveling to other solar systems in what to you seems far off.

So, to summarize, no shifts in my poles, but, yes, I do use Earth's gravitational and magnetic fields to assist me in changing the direction of magma under the surface.

Gaia, I must return to the pole shift one more time, trying to make sure I'm correct. Did the poles shift twice, including 50,000 years ago, or just once?
The pole shift that occurred during what was called the First Destruction is correct, Tom. The First Destruction was not man-made in any form. Was there a previous pole shift? Perhaps, but it did not affect the Explorer Race in any way. Whether the poles shifted once or twice or several times—yes, several—during millions of years is unimportant. The fact is the race that lived in Antarctica perished when they refused to move. So, go with just the one pole shift as it affected millions of people living on the shores of the continents and, in those places where it turned much colder, those who lived in the interior had to adjust, leave, or freeze.

Gaia, why are deep holes suddenly appearing in the Mt. Baldy Sand Dunes on Lake Michigan?
Yes, the area under the sand dunes is eroding, Tom, and the holes that are appearing are the least resistant to erosion. There are caverns underneath the sand dunes and there are gaps where the sand is falling into the caverns. This will continue, Tom, so you should warn the person who wrote to you, along with any others, that these sand dunes are becoming dangerous.

May I remind everyone living in a northern climate that you can request a Most Benevolent Outcome for one day of sunshine per week. I suggested

Saturday as that's when most people are out shopping, attending sporting events, and running errands.

*And before anyone decides to pick up and move, whether it's to the next town or halfway across the world, request a Most Benevolent Outcome for the **perfect** place to live.*

Moving Earth – Is It Required?

Gaia, will there ever come a time when you will cease to need to move the Earth?
Tom, it will be hundreds if not thousands of years before I cease to move the Earth. You have to bear in mind that the Earth is a living entity on its own. Moving the Earth is part of that process. It's as if the Earth wanted to yawn, to stretch itself. I am the keeper, you might say, of this process. You understand I will be here long after you humans have left after finishing the Earth Experiment and returned to your lives on your home planets. That's the way it should be, although for many of your readers to even consider such things is baffling because you're veiled—I recall having discussed this many times, but to answer your reader's question, as long as humans live on the surface of this planet, you will experience earthquakes.

Will they always be as violent as some are during this time period?
Yes, but you forget one thing—humans will be better able to adapt to these movements with better structures, or even better, choose to not live in these "hot zones" as they'll be called. Certainly, there will always be people who put up with, shall we call it, these movements, but they will know the right places to live to have homes and businesses that will not be in the worst part of the zone. So, you see, there will continue to be choices—to live in an earthquake prone area, where I am moving the earth, and if they do the most gentle part of the zone, and to build so that, yes, even the streets and buildings are built in such a way as to be able to live there.

All of these are choices; always remember the Earth is a living thing and cannot and will not stay in the same position.

New Madrid Fault

Gaia, what is the highest probability of the New Madrid fault staying quiet in the next 10 years? (Asked February 2020)
Quite high, Tom. At present, I have no plans for the fault line to become active. I only would have activated this fault line had you not had the Harmonic Convergence.

But what about all the information you gave me at one time about this fault line?
You could say that was another probable future. At the present time, it is much more about the West Coast.

Northwest Coast of America

Gaia, what will happen to the islands in the South Puget Sound including Anderson Island, when you finally move the fault lines?
These islands will move along with the North American coastline, you see. The quakes will be felt quite severely all throughout this area, and, yes, there is the danger of tidal waves or tsunamis, although the height will not be the height of, say, the ones in Japan. Still, the residents there should have supplies on hand as the major thrust of rescues and salvaging operations will be in the more densely populated areas such as Seattle. So now is the time to stock up on supplies.

Gaia, is it true you have a new volcano off the coast of Central Oregon, and if so, what are your plans for it?
Yes, there is, Tom. I have many other volcanic vents throughout what is termed "the Ring of Fire." Scientists have already been studying underwater life around these vents or volcanoes and the life there can be quite unique. It is no different with this small volcano. It is also another way for me to heat up the water temperature for not only the ocean, but to help me warm the atmosphere. So, the small volcano does multiple tasks for me, along with releasing pressure. If I did not have ways to release pressure at this time, there would be a major earthquake to release the built-up pressure. That is not desired by your souls at this moment in time.

Gaia, when and if you move the fault lines near Seattle, will you move just the fault line under the city, or will you move the fault known as the Strait of Juan de Fuca, or will you move both and how far to the east will it cause damage?

Yes, to both questions, Tom. Both fault lines will move significantly. That whole area is subject to large movements and so that will occur; although, Tom, as I mentioned, not until the area around San Francisco moves quite violently first. As you have noticed, there is somewhat of a progression, as pressure is released at one part of the Ring of Fire it causes another to erupt within days or weeks. So, I encourage everyone to heed my warning.

Gaia, how far east in Washington State will be affected by the probable upcoming quakes in several years? (Asked November 2017)

All the way to the Cascades, Tom. They have fault lines in this area and there will be great movement and flooding. At the very least, move over the mountains and away from Mt. Rainier.

Oklahoma Earthquakes

Gaia, is it just fracking causing the earthquakes in Oklahoma or are they movements you are making for some reason?

The fracking coincides with small adjustments I'm making in the crust or mantle of the Earth. There is no real cause for alarm by the residents there. There will be no massive earthquake in their future, just many small ones, but certainly no large ones in the near future, Tom. The land in Oklahoma has some minor fault systems, which have yet to be discovered by your geologists. They are more sensitive to fracking than, say, other oil fields where this method of extraction is used.

Gaia, will your earth movements in Oklahoma stop if and when they cease fracking operations and injecting waste water back into the "Arbuckle," or will it continue?

Good question, Tom. It will cease eventually, but it will be like the proverbial bowl of Jello. The movements will continue for a while, but will slowly lessen until they reach the level prior to the beginning of fracking and wastewater injections.

Will you be able to repair yourself after all the drilling and fracking?
Yes, I could do this tomorrow, but for the Earth Experiment. This is part of your learning—to repair the holes you drill and cavities you have made. I could do it, but you will do it as part of your learning.

Gaia, there have been a number of earthquakes in Oklahoma, including the largest one in their recorded history. Why are you moving the crust there?
Yes, Tom, I realize that the residents in this part of North America have not felt earthquakes before, but part of all those factors the Sun mentioned was present in order to assist me in moving my crust there. You could say, and be pretty accurate, that these moves are needed to bring about the movement of the whole New Madrid fault line, as keep in mind all these pressures must build for that to happen. There are fault lines there your scientists did not expect to find.

Gaia, is there a geographical reason why storms veer away from Enid, Oklahoma?
Yes, it is interesting that your reader noticed this. There are certain, shall we call them, magnetic abnormalities underneath the surface there. I know you thought perhaps someone was doing a little creating or co-creating with me, but that is not the case here. The magnetic deposits, we will call them, cause the storms to veer away. Someday they may investigate, but for anyone wishing to live in a pretty safe place in Oklahoma, this town would be a good choice.

Pacific Islands

Will the eruption of Kilauea have any effect on any volcanoes around the world, especially on what is called the "Ring of Fire?"
Yes, Tom, you will see more activity, just not any major eruptions. If you look at a map, this volcano sits in the middle of the Pacific and so technically you could say it is not on the Ring of Fire, but it is connected to my veins of lava, so your scientists will get an inkling of how it connects. It will cause debates—is it connected or is it just a "coincidence" that there will be some other activity somewhere else in the world?

Philippines and Earth Movements

Gaia, what is the probability of the Mayon Volcano violently erupting in the Philippines in the next five years? (Asked Marach 2018)
Yes, Tom, the probability is low at this time. There is much movement of magma in that area and will continue to be, but in the short time period of five years the probability is low. Extend this on out and, yes, the probability rises dramatically.

Will there be plenty of warning so that people can move out of the way?
People will look at something happening on the other side of the world and will think that it does not affect them, Tom, but they are dead wrong. The Earth is a living thing, and I must manage this, yet within the confines of what your souls desire and must experience as part of the Earth Experiment. I have continued to warn you to pass along to people to move away from the coasts.

Yes, but a very few people, as part of the whole, is a very small percentage.
This will grow, Tom, over the next few years—you will see. Remember, you were told that a lot of what you are receiving today is for people in the future. You assumed it would be after your death, and, yes, that's true too, but it is also for people in what I consider the near future too.

Predictions of Earthquakes by Scientists

What is the probability of scientists or geologists learning to predict earthquakes in the next ten years?
Better devices for measuring are on the way, but they will not be fully developed by then. Progress is being made, but slowly. Each new device will contribute one after another.

Puerto Rico

Gaia, what is the probability of a strong earthquake for Puerto Rico in the next five years? (Asked March 2022)

It is the same as for the West Coast—approximately a 65% probability. Though it does not seem so, one will cause the other to move.

Ring of Fire

Gaia, why is the Ring of Fire so important for you to move the plates versus another part of the world?
This is all part of the evolution of this planet, Tom. Had all of you had memories of earlier times you would have seen plates moving at every period of history. That's just the nature of landmasses. So, in this time period, the Ring of Fire is active because the plates continue to move as they have for millions of years. Earth is a vibrant planet, Tom, and as humans this is part of your education to learn about the dynamics of plate movement as part of your studies to prepare you for travel to other planetary systems.

What is the symbolism, if any, between what is called the Ring of Fire around the Sun and your Ring of Fire?
They just happen to be called the same thing, although the symbolism would naturally be a person's idea that the Earth's Ring of Fire is hot like the Sun's.

What about the area around Aijic, Mexico, near Guadalajara?
Not a good place to live as they are much too close to the Ring of Fire tentacles of faults, we shall call them.

Why do some have ash clouds and some do not?
You can gain that information—at least most of it—by reading reports and studies of volcanoes. It certainly partially has to do with the lava lake sinking down to the water table. This is at different levels according to the region the volcano is in.

Sensitivity to Earthquakes

Gaia, why would a person feel discomfort, irritation, or even become incoherent for a few minutes when an earthquake happens in the world?

Yes, these individuals are what we would term sensitives to the vibrations the Earth makes, Tom. You could say they are "hard wired" to have these experiences. This is fairly rare, but there are thousands of people who have a range of feeling when I move the Earth. Studies will be done one day to see what part of the brain reacts to these subtle energies.

Would it be considered another telepathic reception?
Exactly, Tom, but it affects the part of the brain that produces this irritation or, in severe cases, incoherence. I'm afraid I cannot go farther in an explanation as we get into the parts of the brain for which you have not been educated. As you can imagine, there is a long list of feelings that have not been yet tied to certain parts of the brain. It is a little difficult to pinpoint the location when you don't know when an earthquake will occur.

Gaia, do sensitive people experience dizziness weeks before an earthquake?
Absolutely, Tom. There are a number of people that have these feelings of dizziness and even nausea before a large earthquake, even if it is hundreds or even thousands of miles away. Your bodies are built for early warning, but many people dismiss these feelings as being caused by some imbalance in their bodies at that moment, instead of asking themselves, "Why do I feel this way?" So, you should allow your antenna, shall we call it, to rise and search for the origin of the discomfort. This will be especially true for anyone living in a high probability earthquake zone. LISTEN to your bodies and act accordingly.

Super Moon and Earthquakes

Gaia, as there were no significant quakes in the world during the "Super Moon," why didn't you take advantage of that assistance from the Moon, and what else do you need in the mix to assist you when that seemed so perfect for your needs?
Good question to start the day, Tom. Yes, the Super Moon, as it is called, has already assisted me, although you may not be able to see it in those lists of earthquakes in the world. The Moon has assisted me in moving the interior of the planet the magma, you see—so that further movements and earthquakes can occur. So, the Moon was quite useful, although you have

as yet not seen the results. Now, there will be other planets, plus the Sun, to assist me with the movements to come and still along with the Moon's help too.

Weather and Earthquake Connection

Gaia, can hurricanes cause earthquakes?
Sometimes, Tom, they can, but normally earthquakes, as you know, are caused by internal movements. What hurricanes do is provide copious amounts of rainwater, which can act as a lubricant to a place where I wish to have a movement. Normally they are quite minor. Rarely are they what you would term a major earthquake. So, yes, they can, but normally hand-in-hand with interior movements to create a movement, up, down, or side-to-side.

Gaia, are the weather and economy connected, and, if so, are they affected by astrological aspects or human emotional energy?
Yes, to all the questions, Tom. The weather and economy are not just affected by one thing, but by many factors. The weather can affect the economy by having too much rain and flooding, or two little and a drought. This can negatively affect the economy, you see. Then the weather can be caused by certain astrological aspects, which assist me in many ways, including earth movements, fires, and so on, but then comes a factor your scientists have not been able to measure yet—human emotions. If the emotions are angry, it can affect both the land by loading it with high negativity, and I have to release this through storms, hurricanes, and tornadoes, which again affect the economy both negatively and positively, as there has to be rebuilding or repairs done to structures. So, yes, all are connected and the sooner your scientists figure this out the sooner they will understand the symbiotic relationship between humans and the Earth.

Gaia, is it humans who cause you to have storms and earthquakes to clear the negativity?
That can certainly contribute, since in the past I've told you that storms are needed to clear the negativity in certain areas. Earthquakes are more of a natural process, since Earth, may I remind your readers, Tom, is a living planet. I, and all those souls that assist me, are constantly moving

lava, that you can compare to blood vessels in the human body. Your geologists will learn in the future that the Earth is much more complex than even they can imagine now. This will give you a basis to study the differences in planet Earth and even the other planets in your solar system, before venturing out to the millions of other planets in the Universe. Still, Creator has a pattern, a blueprint if you will, so you will see the similarities as the Explorer Race explores this Universe.

Water Table

Gaia, can you explain to us how the water table is affected thousands of miles away from an earthquake?
No, I have already given you hints. It is on more than one soul contract to learn how all this connects. The mere fact that they do is revolutionary knowledge to some geologists.

West Coast Fault Lines

Gaia, does Hidden Valley, California, have fault lines that are not on geology maps?
Yes, an easy one to answer, Tom. The area certainly has fingers of fault lines running throughout this area all along the coast. People see one fault line running along the coast and think that is the only fault line, but that fault line has many fingers running off it; many so small your equipment cannot detect yet. So, yes, there are fault lines running all through the area. Name a town nearby and the answer will be the same.

Yellowstone and Other Volcanoes

Gaia, why did you have Mount Tambora erupt in 1815 and is that an indication of what will occur if Yellowstone erupts?
Again, we go back to these bucket list experiences, Tom, and those people worldwide were able to check that experience off their list as they had to live through times when the ash cloud prevented crops from growing and being harvested, resulting in food shortages. And I needed to release pressure from my interior. So, there were multiple reasons—there never is just one. All these events are approved by your souls long, long in advance.

As we have spoken about before, Yellowstone, if it erupts, will cause a mini-ice age, but will be limited to the area to the east we have discussed before. Still again, it will affect millions of people that inhabit that region of North America.

Gaia, if Yellowstone erupts and causes Mt. Vesuvius and one or two other Italian volcanoes to erupt, will they have the same effect of causing an ongoing winter, or are they too far to the south?
You are correct, Tom, their location will not cause a mini-ice age as would Yellowstone's eruption. However, the ash cloud produced by these volcanos will spread for over 1,000 miles in more of a southeasterly direction. Of course, there will be times when the weather systems switch the direction of the ash clouds from south to north and vice versa.

And I assume that the probability of that happening is still around 73%, with no change?
That is correct, Tom. It may remain there for many months, or climb higher, or perhaps reduce, but that probability is fairly low at this time. As you have seen from other volcanic activity on La Palma and Hawaii, this is a time where I must release volcanic pressure.
So, this isn't just a message for a certain group of people?
No, Tom, you are receiving this well.

Gaia, if the Yellowstone Super Volcano erupts sometime during the period of 2022-2027, will it cause the Long Valley Super Volcano to also erupt? (Asked October 2021)
The probability of that happening, Tom, is quite high—let's say over 50%. As you thought, they are connected.

It would seem that the ash from that volcano would also travel to the east.
Yes, but not as far due to the prevailing winds. Good question, Tom. And, yes, the Yellowstone eruption would draw from the Long Valley Caldera too.

A note from Tom about preparing for the possibility of a super volcano eruption:

I realize how concerning the information I've recently received from Gaia about possible events in 2026 is. But I've been told many times that it is my job to share the information I receive. How you react to it is up to you.

I see five options for people living on the West Coast and near Yellowstone:

1. Do nothing. Just sit back and wait to see if the precursor quakes begin in the first three months of 2026. But be aware that if these predictions are correct, things may become very difficult.

2. Everyone on the West Coast should put together an Earthquake Emergency Kit. Have you? I have a page on my website that outlines a suggested packing list: www.thegentlewaybook.com/quakes.htm#list

3. If you have investment capital, invest in a condominium or house somewhere to the east of California and the coastal states. Housing prices will start to spike as people move away from LA. If nothing happens, in two years you can sell and probably actually make a profit on your investment assuming you have only put down the minimum deposit and made payments. If things do go south, you have a place to live.

4. You can invest in a motor home or travel trailer. Travel trailers are much less expensive. I have recently seen prices in my area, Dallas, starting at under $20,000 with payments of $120 to $250 a month. Fly into DFW, rent a car, find the right one for you and then store it—do not take it back home! When you decide to leave the West Coast, you do not want to have to pull a trailer along, especially if driving conditions deteriorate. If you need to evacuate, you can rent a U-Haul trailer, which needs less gas than pulling a motor home or trailer, and it could be abandoned if only four-wheel vehicles can make it to the East. In considering a storage facility for a trailer, make sure you determine if the facility has security, electricity, and an overhead

cover. A concrete pad is preferable, but there should at least be gravel. I suggest you buy the largest motor home or trailer you can afford, as you might wind up living in it for two or three years.

5. You can decide to move now. There are many advantages to this option: lower home prices; a better selection of an area to live in, more available employment, and more peace of mind.

Chapter 3
Climate Change & Pollution

Climate Change General Review

Gaia, would you please summarize climate change, or global warming, for my readers, starting with: is this something you wish to occur?
Yes, for your readers, Tom, global warming is just that—the overall warming of the planet. And, yes, this is my plan, although certainly greenhouse gases spewed by your coal plants and such do assist me. I am warming the planet to melt the poles to a certain extent, which will raise the ocean levels. This will in turn force the populations of the world to move away from the beaches and allow them to rest. It will also alter the very topography of the Earth. During the next few years, the temperatures will continue to rise so that I can achieve these goals.

Gaia, has a similar climate change like we are experiencing happened in the past?
There is nothing new under the sun and that includes every climate you can think of over the past millions and, yes, billions of years. There are many reasons for the change in climate for Earth. Yes, poor decisions by humans in general do contribute to climate change faster than it would have, but nothing happens on Earth without agreement of your souls and my input. All of this is teaching humans about your world and what can happen if you just let society run amuck. You're slowly learning to become good stewards for not only this planet, but also many others you will assist in the future.

Your recent efforts to do away with your dependence on fossil fuels augers good news as your scientists and, yes, even those who tinker in their garages will now try and find ways to create energy without fossil fuels.

Even five years ago getting the largest governments in the world to agree on this would have been impossible. The days of depending upon oil are numbered.

Gaia, what is the future for climate activists? And how did the Portal of Light action speed things up?
The Portal of Light was a success from their desire to have a worldwide meditation. A lot of energy, and we will term it benevolent energy, was created to speed things along. It may seem there were no changes, but benevolent energy will assist in benevolent outcomes for those involved in climate activism, among others. It is not like turning on a switch. Benevolent energy clears a path.

Gaia, do you clean yourself of any of the pollution left by humans or do you wait for us to clean up the environment and leave it only to us?
Good question actually, Tom. Yes, there are some things I do to lighten the severity of what the human population does to me. These steps that I take are not known to you yet—and I am speaking of your geologists and scientists. If the human population were to suddenly abandon Earth one day never to return, certainly I would correct all the pollution and other things such as mining and drilling within a few years—some very fast and others over several hundred to several thousand years, but I know you are making progress and are throwing into the trash heap much less than you used to. One day your governments will even make it a crime, although not a severe one, to not recycle. Everyone will be doing this—not just the small percentage that are now.

So, to summarize, yes, I do take some steps to lessen the damage done by humans, but in the end, being able to see thousands of years in the future, may I remind your readers humanity will leave me in almost pristine condition when you move on to other planets and star systems in the Universe. At that time only visitors will be allowed to experience this world as sort of a vacation spot to enjoy the wide variety of plants and animals, as you call them.

Affected Animal Populations

Gaia, do the hurricanes and cyclones sweep an area of the mosquito population, or does it just increase the number with all the standing water left?
Certainly, the existing population is wiped away if they do not find shelter in houses and buildings untouched by the storm, but they are a resilient insect, Tom, and larva untouched by the storm begins their population anew and the standing water quickly swells their population again. You might call it wishful thinking on the part of humans to think that the mosquitoes will be swept away never to be seen again.

They, like all of creation, have a purpose, or the Creator would not have allowed their presence on Earth. As we have said before, but I remind you, Creator loves every single insect, human, animal, bird, and so on in this creation. The mosquitoes have their purpose on Earth and one of them is to be a carrier of diseases so that you humans will learn how to cure them, which will aid you many years from now as you encounter these same diseases on other worlds. It is all in the master plan, you can say. That is another reason why you must take it slow in reaching the stars, as you cannot have your explorers wiped out on a planet where these diseases exist.

Gaia, why have so many insects disappeared, and will they return?
The use of DDT was disastrous for many insects, killing literally billions, Tom, and is still in use in some countries. The populations will slowly rebound, as they are needed for food for your bird populations and others. There are even better ways to control the insects who feast on farm products coming in the not-too-distant future. This is all part of the explosion of ideas coming in this century.

Gaia, why so many dead dolphins on the Gulf Coast? Reports say three times the normal number.
Pollution of the waters. Dolphins are highly sensitive to this pollution as your scientists will discover in the not-too-distant future.

Gaia, are dolphins dying near the Peruvian Coast from toxins, sonar blasts, or what?
Yes, Tom. They are dying and, yes, it is a combination of factors, but not

sonar blasts I can assure you. Dolphins can take on viruses—not the same as humans, but viruses in the sea. Most of the time they have no effect on them, but in this case, they were due to a combination of factors. And, yes, to answer a question forming in your mind, they did have a little prior knowledge of this but were willing to take on the virus in order to leave the planet.

It is difficult to understand, but from their point of view it was time to move on, and the fastest way was to allow a virus into their bodies. There is also room for scientists to discover why they are dying—another lesson for the Explorer Race, as you can imagine. If they learn how to treat this disease, they will be able to treat other diseases they find elsewhere that seemingly, on the surface, would not apply to the dolphin disease, but does, Tom. So, this was a little hint to your scientists once they find the cure for the dolphins near Peru—look farther afield to see other applications.

You can always say Benevolent Prayers for anything happening in the world. That helps raise your vibrational level by showing compassion. Here we can say, "I ask any and all beings to comfort and aid the dolphins and send all our love to them at this time, thank you!"

Gaia, why do dolphins have white lung disease?
Another disease brought about by pollution in the ocean, Tom. Scientists will discover its origin, but I will tell you know it is pollution—toxic chemicals.

Gaia, is red tide killing dolphins in Southwest Florida, or something else?
No, not something else, Tom. The red tide snuffs all the oxygen out and many fish will die until your scientists find a way to destabilize the tide to break up its structure. That will not come this year or next, but a breakthrough in the study should come within the next few years. It will be a eureka moment for the person who discovers how to erase it.

*Let's say a Benevolent Prayer **out loud**: "I ask any and all beings to assist in breaking up the red tide even faster than we can hope for or expect, and* *to assist the person researching to find the answer even sooner than we can imagine, thank you!"*

Gaia, why are so many manatees dying in Florida?
Partly from the poisoning of the water flowing into the rivers they inhabit, Tom, and partly because they wish to decrease their presence on Earth. They know that most people love them, but each species on Earth has their own mission, shall we say. Each soul group was asked by Creator's emissaries to take part, and naturally as you have heard before, they could reject the request, but no one does.

How would you describe these emissaries, Gaia? Are they whole souls or are they large elements of the Creator?
Yes, they are pieces of the Creator, Tom, and do this work along with much more.

Are there toxic levels of radiation in tuna, Gaia?
Certainly, it depends upon where the tuna are caught and where they have been. There can be, but this is a small percentage, Tom. Scientists can monitor the catches and will, so I would not be too concerned with this. The tuna are there to assist in feeding you. Your body easily absorbs small amounts of radiation. I would not eat the tuna, let's say, near the Fukushima reactor, although even those fish don't really have high levels. Still, the Japanese eat so much fish that a steady diet of these contaminated fish will cause problems in the long run. Again, elsewhere in the world, I would not be concerned as long as you don't eat these fish every day.

Gaia, what is causing millions of fish to die all over the world?
Yes, again we get into not only pollutants in the water, but again my cycles. When their oxygen is cut off for a myriad of reasons, Tom, the fish perish. Your scientists will study and eventually understand why this happens and will be able to prevent it. Until that time, more millions of fish will die. You are on the verge of becoming a less-polluting society of people. You are slowly learning about the ecosystems and how delicate they are. You will someday stabilize them—which will be a great accomplishment on your part. My recommendation is to spend more time understanding why these fish died. I gave you plenty of hints and it's up to your scientists to

first identify and then suggest corrections. That is a number of years in the future, but you will accomplish this, I assure you.

Will caribou go extinct?
No, there will still be places where they can roam in smaller numbers. Then in the future they will once again thrive as the human population shrinks.

Gaia, what are your plans for polar bears?
Yes, I love these beautiful animals too, but there will come a time when they will withdraw from the earth, only to perhaps return one day in the far future. There have been and are many different forms of life that have been on Earth and are no longer here due to climate change. Obviously, one of the best known would be dinosaurs, but then you could name many others such as the mammoth, saber tooth tiger, and many, many others. This is a natural cycle, and honor their service to man as, don't forget, they have been a source of food for those who live near the poles. But, to summarize, they will withdraw in the coming years.

Gaia, why do you allow polar bears to starve to death?
Many other animals on Earth do the same, Tom, but these beautiful creatures are easy to see and their beauty, coupled with their size, makes them an easy target for photographers. This is just the natural order of things on this planet. These starvations also teach you, the Explorer Race, that allowing Earth emissions to escalate and the climate to continue to warm due to the emissions, there are consequences, and the starvation of these polar bears are just one of the results. The rise in ocean levels is not all caused by humans, but you certainly contribute. These polar bears are on their way out but will return in the future when there are a lot less humans.

*Here is a Benevolent Prayer to say **out loud**: "I ask any and all beings to aid and comfort all the polar bears and help them find sufficient food, thank you!"*

Gaia, are the saiga antelope dying off because they want to leave Earth or to teach scientists about climate change?

An easy answer, Tom—both. They will leave for a time, but like several—yes, several—other species of what you term animals will be leaving but will return one day when Earth's population of humans greatly diminishes. You—meaning humans—have done a nice job of conserving them, but the climate is not suitable for them at the present time. You are not yet at a stage where you can control your environment. That will come one day in the future.

Gaia, did humans, including Cro-Magnons, Neanderthals, and Adam models kill off the woolly mammoths, giant armadillos, and saber tooth tigers?
Yes, but climate change also contributed to their demise.

Gaia, please comment on the deformed fish showing up on the shores of the Pacific Northwest?
Yes, Tom. If your scientists study these fish, they will find other factors that caused the deformity—not radiation. Some of the ocean off the coast is highly polluted with all sorts of toxins. These deformed fish are the result of exposure to these toxins, and not radiation, as some people will jump to that conclusion.

You must clean up your oceans, Tom. As you've seen in photos and videos, this appears to be an almost impossible task now, but there will be developments, in the not-too-distant future, which will make this task much easier than can be imagined at this time.

May I remind you that this space-time continuum you are in, Tom, allows for great progress over a very short period of time. Have your readers imagine someone looking at Earth from outside and everyone would seem to be moving at 10 times normal speed. This would be the easiest way to explain it. No other society in the Universe could keep up with that speed. You are quite unique.

Gaia, why are so many marine animals dying on the West Coast of North America?
Again, this is a cycle, Tom, coupled with pollution and some of these animals' desires to return to their home planets as they feel their work is

done here now that you have advanced to the Fifth Focus. Some species will die out and although it may be hard to believe, others will take their place when Creator's emissaries reach out and request participation by other societies in the Universe. In the meantime, your scientists will study the situation and will make some discoveries as to the cause of this seemingly epidemic occurrence. All these events are the teaching tools you need, Tom. Remember what you were told before that time is still speeding up just a little more, and these learning opportunities will present themselves at a fast pace, but we are sure you humans will respond and solve what might seem to be unsolvable problems. We have great confidence in you, Tom.

Gaia, explain how you are adjusting your ecosystem in Antarctica by allowing whales to forage for krill in the bays and shell crushing crabs to climb the cliffs and shoreline?

My ecosystem is just fine, Tom, and yes, it is adjusting to the melting ice sheet covering Antarctica. This is just a natural transition, which has happened countless times before on other continents, including North America. The krill will not be decreased until the point that they do not survive. No, the whales are quite intelligent, Tom, and will not destroy the ecosystem built for their survival. Therefore, they will forage for only enough to sustain their bodies and will move to other locations to allow the bays to replenish themselves with krill. Although your scientists are concerned, there really is no need to be as the ecosystem will survive and flourish as the ice melts releasing organisms for the krill to feed upon.

Regarding the shell-crushing crabs, yes, they will have a feast for a while, but again there are many more of these soft-shelled creatures than they can kill, and they will only kill to eat, mind you. Therefore, don't be too concerned as the threats to the ecosystem will prove groundless. Take my word on this, Tom.

Cape Town, South Africa Water

Gaia, Cape Town, South Africa is close to running out of water. Will they receive any and if so, when? How does this work in your cycles and for their soul contracts?

Yes, it will be some time before they receive sufficient rain for their needs. They will have to solve this problem in the short term by trucking in loads of water, even ship containers. Naturally, the long-term solution is to have a desalination plant to convert sea water to potable water. There are smaller devices that people can use to make the water drinkable. As for soul contracts, again, I would much prefer that they move away from the coast. Yes, this may be a beautiful location, but events may occur where their lives will be in danger from the possible coming events. They are not the only coastal community having problems. I need people to move away from the coasts and I am slowly putting pressure on them to do so.

So, to summarize, no short-term relief, except for what the city can generate themselves. The rains will return, but not before they run out of water. That is the highest probability at this time.

Let's all say a Benevolent Prayer for all the residents of Cape Town out loud: "I ask any and all beings to assist the government of Cape Town and South Africa to provide sufficient water for the residents of Cape Town and for the rains to come earlier than we can hope for or expect, thank you!"

CO2 Levels

Gaia, what about the Earth's CO2 particle level reaching 400, as I saw on the news. Will it go higher and is that the major cause of weather?
Yes, to your first question, Tom. The particle level will continue to increase as, yes, it is one of the factors—again we are speaking about many which contribute to the weather patterns. You will continue to see fluctuations in the weather, from very wet to very dry and everything in between.

Gaia, does the human race add more carbon dioxide than do volcanoes?
Yes, Tom, it does. The pollutants put out around the world do add more than the volcanoes that are not so many in number these days as compared to in the past. Certainly, there will be more eruptions in the future, but they will pale in comparison to what the human race is emitting now.

But do remember, Tom, I consider this a temporary condition as free energy is not too far now in your future, and when that comes these levels will slowly reduce as more and more factories and engines of all types use this energy. So certainly, humans need to do all you can to not pollute the atmosphere until that day arrives, and I know attempts are being made to reduce the pollution.

Gaia, what does the increase in the CO2 carbon dioxide level mean for climate change and our health?
It is but one of the ways I am using to warm the atmosphere and warm the climate. There are many other factors that I use to contribute to the warming of this climate, so all the others must be considered since they are not separate. And, yes, as you were thinking, the heat from the volcanoes that are active in the world are one of many. Still, humans must stop polluting my atmosphere not only for me, but for the lives of humans and all the oxygen breathers on this planet.

You have been making strides, and although there will be a backwards slip, it will be short-lived, I can assure your readers. Events are on the horizon that will change many attitudes. I understand the duality between those that believe that pollutants are bad for life on Earth and those whose desire for profits override steps they could take to lessen the pollution.

Crystal Mining

Gaia, how do you feel about people removing rocks, gems, and crystals from you?
Yes, it would be best if they were left where they reside, Tom, but I understand, and these stones and gems and crystals understand that this is part of your learning process on Earth. In the future you will discover many more uses for these gems and crystals than you are now aware of, and it will assist you in reaching the stars. That's all I will say, as you must discover how to use these stones, we will call them, yourselves. Keep in mind, Tom, that I have billions of these stones in my body, so a few million will not upset the apple cart, we will say. Those stones you do not use— sitting in a bucket somewhere as an example, could be buried in your backyard to enjoy me again. They and I will greatly appreciate that service and act of kindness. You could even conduct your own idea of a ritual to

join us together again. I will appreciate that too.

Desalinization Plants

Gaia, will the desalination plants being built in California ease the water problem, and is there a problem of location of these water plants?
Yes, and yes, Tom. They will ease the water problem when they come online, but, yes, there is a small problem in their location as I raise the ocean level two feet. I realize it may seem to some people you are crying wolf, Tom, but even you did not understand how this will be accomplished. There is a tipping point that your scientists—at least most of them—are not aware of where the warmth of the oceans, the air, and land and so on finally tips the scale and causes wide melting of the poles. You are awfully close to that mark now. This year you will see another rise in the world temperatures. Already there are some locations noting the change, but the scientists that have noticed these changes do not wish to cause undue alarm if they are wrong. I can assure them they are not wrong; this is getting quite close to the tipping point.

Ecology: Paper Bottles

Gaia, will there be paper bottles by 2030, or will there be a better container for beverages?
Yes, Tom, there actually will be a plethora of options at that time as there are other containers that are being developed. Paper is just one of them.

How about seaweed, as I saw a story about making straws from seaweed?
Yes, you can add seaweed to the list, Tom, but again, we said a plethora of options, depending upon the liquid being sold to consumers. A couple actually more than that have not been even thought of yet but will soon be. The idea of a paper container will spur others to consider biodegradable alternatives.

Fires And Floods

Gaia, are the forest fires set accidentally or on purpose by humans part of their soul contracts?

Yes, and not as you guessed, Tom. Those accidentally set normally are soul contracts to not only assist me in regenerating the forests, but if there are houses or homes destroyed, this may be to balance having had one's home destroyed in another life by those people whose homes are destroyed. There can be also balancing that must occur if someone's home is destroyed that had not done the same to the person in a past life.

Those that set fires on purpose, again, can be both—soul contracts, but also goes too far and there must be heavy balancing done in the future. There are times when a person is sick with some sort of mental disorder that causes them to be an arsonist. Your scientists will discover—although not for many years—the DNA strand that causes this problem. Where some humans go off their soul contracts is that they enjoy it so much they set fires over and over, leading to great balancing in the future.

Typically those that accidentally set the fires as part of their soul contract feel great remorse and will do their best to balance their actions in the future. As you can see, Tom, these actions have a multitude of possible reasons. One answer does don't fit all the possibilities. And, yes, we have to look at all the people affected—from the firefighters to those whose homes are lost, to those who wish to help the forests rebound; there are so many soul contracts at work here.

*Here is a Benevolent Prayer for all the animals to be said **out loud**: "I ask any and all beings to aid and protect and keep safe all humans, animals, birds, insects, and all living creatures in the path of all the forest fires going on at this time, thank you!"*

Gaia, why are there always fast-moving fires around Southern California? They moved so fast many could not get out of the way.

Again, soul contracts come into play here. I have continually warned people to leave the coasts. That part of California is overpopulated. Those that are forced to move away from the coast will thank me later, should the probability of the earthquakes ripping through California come to pass. There are hundreds of thousands of people who still have on their bucket list of Earth experiences fires, not to mention earthquakes. And I did mention before, Tom, that the fire season would be year-round for the West Coast. Before it was more in rural areas, but now I've moved the fires, with your souls' agreement, to more densely populated areas.

Gaia, why did you, and I assume our souls, decide to have enormous fires and floods affecting people all at the same time?
Yes, Tom, both did coincide. The need for fires to rid the forests of all the old growth and allow new growth could not be held off any longer. This is a cycle for me that is several years long. There is much forested land that has not seen fires yet that will in the future. As I have explained in the past, if humans are going to live in forested areas you need to build your houses so that they are not burned down when I must have these events.

Therefore, this was not the first year of these major fires, nor will it be the last. Regarding the floods, there are many younger souls that have not experienced flooding as one of their bucket list experiences, so this accomplishes not only that but also is a wakeup call to millions of people that yes, there is a climate change, and what are you going to do about it? You can't just hide in your homes, or you will be underwater. Plus, this is another incentive for scientists to learn how to control the weather, which we have spoken about just recently. That ability to control the weather is in your future.

Gaia, you seem to have a large number of storms with record rainfalls around the world. Is this normal or do you have a reason for this?
Certainly, I do have my reasons, Tom. Some you can immediately understand regarding soul contracts we have spoken about many times before. Those souls in those situations of typhoons, hurricanes, major low-pressure systems in general need these to mark it off their "bucket list" as humans term it, and I do like that term. So, as I work closely—not apart—with your souls, Tom, they understand the probabilities of all these events literally millions of years in advance. I have spoken about this in the past, but I must continually remind everyone these events are known by your souls and they try and take advantage of them to fulfill the desire to experience everything the Earth can provide regarding experiences for their soul growth.

Therefore, besides helping your souls to cross off the experience of being in a large storm and major flooding, again, as I have spoken before, it enables me to wash away a great deal of negativity built up over time by masses of humans living in very densely populated areas. Anyone can notice even after a brief, gentle rain how clear it feels around you. This is a very important function of mine—these rains.

Gaia, are terrorists starting forest and grass fires, or are they mostly set by just arsonists and the occasional dumb campers?
An interesting question, Tom. Yes, there are a few fires we can attribute to terrorists, but the majority of fires in forests and grasslands do fall under the category of your plain old garden-variety arsonists. One benefit, resulting from the idea of terrorists wishing to set these fires, is people will be more aware of their surroundings and will report any suspicious behavior to authorities.

Gaia, why so much torrential rain worldwide?
It is all part of your climate change, Tom. That is the fairly obvious reason, but behind that are the soul contracts where people need to experience flooding as one of their bucket list items they must experience in one or more lives. You must not forget that there are many young souls alive in this time period, and whether it is raging fires in the western part of North America, or raging floods in all parts of the world, I am creating these with your souls' agreement.

Will this continue for more years?
Quite so. You could say this is just the first of several years where you will see this flooding. Eventually, your meteorologists will learn to control your weather, as you were recently told. They will not only learn how to create rain, but also how to control the amount that it rains. This will come in this century.

Of course, we have not touched on things like the refilling of reservoirs for your drinking water and other uses. If I did not have large storms at times, there would be insufficient water for your population, which has grown too large. So, the storms serve multiple purposes, and to answer your question, yes, this year does seem above average in rainfall, storms, etc., but if you look at your records you will see a pattern—a cycle. The cycle is up at this time with storms—significant ones—all across the world. And one last thing, Tom, your news reporting services also enters the equation by reporting on these storms. Only a few years ago they would have been on page four or five of your newspapers. Now they are brought to your attention in much greater detail, thanks to your instant reporting from these flooded areas.

Gaia, how do heat and fire fit into your cycles for Australia, where they are seeing almost Sahara desert-type heat, along with mammoth bush fires?

Yes, again this is a cycle where I need to renew the forest or bush land, as it is termed there, Tom. This cycle will continue on for just a few weeks more and then cooler temperatures along with rain will reappear.

Will any of this heat cycle down toward the Antarctic? (Asked January 2013)

Quite so, Tom. I'm glad you see the connection. Heat rises and is cycled out far and wide, increasing the average temperatures to the south and to the east. It will help speed the melting of the Antarctic ice cap. You'll start to see those reports in just a few months' time.

Please keep in mind, Tom, that the people experiencing the massive fires all have it in their soul contracts for this experience as part of their overall soul experiences on Earth, which, we have discussed before, are needed in one or more Earth lives.

Gaia, are any of the California wildfires geoengineered?

No, they are not that sophisticated. These fires, they will discover, began in a variety of ways, including some man-made. Still, keep in mind that even an arsonist has a soul contract to perform. They were also born with that behavior pattern in their DNA.

Gaia, I assume the wildfires in California will continue?

Quite so. As was noted on your news, this is the beginning of fire season for them. There will be more and even larger fires as I replenish the land and clear the old growths to make way for new ones. And may I add, Tom, that this is but another method of encouraging people to move away from the coasts. Earth is changing and there will come a time in the near future where the casualties from these fires and hurricanes will seem minor to what is on the horizon for the North American West Coast.

*We can at least say this Benevolent Prayer **out loud**: "I ask any and all beings to aid, comfort, and assist all those beings in the path of the wildfires to be kept safe in the most benevolent way possible, thank you!"*

Gaia, what is the most probable future for Paradise, California, that was burned a few years ago?

Yes, Tom, it will slowly rebuild as the residents that are left resist moving away from the area, but it will take many years, and if they do not build houses that are fire resistant, they very well will see this happen again in the future.

Gaia, Southern California is experiencing mudslides where there were previously wildfires. How does that assist you in your cycles, as you lose topsoil for the regrowth of trees and other plants?

Yes, but much soil is left, Tom, so don't forget this soil was from the decomposition over many, if not hundreds of years, so there is sufficient topsoil for my purposes, and more will be generated in the coming years. All one has to do is to go to a burned-out forest and see the beginnings of life there to understand this is part of the cycle of life. And, yes, this includes all those affected by the mudslides. This could be someone who simply gets caught in a mudslide and is prevented from their planned movements all the way to those who lose their lives in a mudslide where their cars were swept away or even their houses were swept away. Naturally, these occurrences are all soul contract related. Their own guardian angels make sure they are at the right place at the right time, may I remind your readers.

Gaia, are fires in the Amazon your way of renewing? Or is this another problem to solve?

Certainly, this is a problem that cannot be swept under the rug. Great pressure is being brought by countries to stop the burning of the forest. Eventually, even more assistance from other nations will be used to stop these fires. Still, that will not be enough if the farmers keep setting the fires. They will have to be forcefully stopped by laws being added and enforced. This is a problem that your governments will put pressure on the leaders of Brazil to implement. It is not too late. Eventually reforestation will take place, using these same local farmers and paying them to help reforest the Amazon rain forest. Obviously, this will not happen overnight, but eventually.

Gaia, I'm told there are many fires all over the world. Are any set by direct energy weapons, and are any related to Agenda 2030, whatever that is?

None are set by these so-called direct energy machines, which in truth are simply lasers that governments are working on as weapons, Tom. We have discussed this before, so this is not new information. Agenda 2030 is yet another conspiracy theory without any substance, other than that given by the people who made it up to again spread fear and concern in your population.

Will it be safe to return?

Marginally, yes. It all depends upon where they live and how they will rebuild.

Will this area be affected by quakes, volcanic eruptions, and more fires?

Yes, yes, and yes, Tom, depending upon what your souls as a whole wish to experience. Fires eventually are a certainty. Earthquakes? Yes, but the size has not been voted on, shall I use your vernacular? Volcanic eruptions fall under that same heading. I have told you, and through you the people who read your writings, to move away from the coasts. There are a variety of reasons, the rising ocean levels, earthquakes, possible tsunamis, and, yes, even fires and volcanoes.

Gaia, I understand the reasons for your need to cleanse the land with forest fires, but the deaths of up to 500 million animals? Please explain why you can't give the group souls sufficient warning to leave.

I cannot, Tom. This is part and parcel of you humans' learning process to take care of the Earth. In the future, you will learn how to have short periods of fires so that you can achieve what I must do on a large basis. Believe it or not, this is all part of your learning process. You will not allow your forests to get to the stage where I must have forest fires. You will do controlled fires. Yes, this will take years to achieve this, but this is in your future, but back to all the animals. Their group souls also understand that this is part of your training and experiences as part of the Earth Experiment. Their souls are removed just prior to their deaths.

Gaia, will Arizona continue to have as many wildfires over the next 25 years?
Yes, Tom, the highest probability is for those arid conditions to remain during that time period. There will be a slow change, but we will also remind your readers that if your souls decide to have Yellowstone erupt and the quakes on the West Coast to occur, there will be great changes, as more rain and storms will pass directly over Arizona.

Gaia, what is the probability people without water in 2050?
We have discussed this in the recent past, Tom. Great strides are being made to convert ocean water to potable drinking water, plus the population has peaked in the world and will slowly recede. There will be pockets of people who will have little water, but overall, there will be a sufficient supply.

Famine

Gaia, what is the probability of global-wide famine?
There will be some parts of the world that will continue to experience famine, but then there are countries that will adapt and grow hardy varieties of foods. With a warming climate, crops that could not be grown farther north will now be grown there. Farmers will adapt, along with more foods being grown in massive greenhouses, where a crop can be grown two and three times a year, where in the past there could be only one crop. Man is very resilient, Tom. You have learned to adapt over tens of thousands of years.

So, we won't be forced to consume "Soylent Green" as in the old 1973 science fiction movie, I presume?

Quite so. Cannibalism is far in your past history.

Flooding and Sea Levels

Gaia, when will the general public notice and be aware of the rising levels of the ocean?
There are already people who not only notice but have been already affected by the rising levels. This is especially true on low lying islands and ocean frontage where storms bring in surges farther inland than ever before. Again, we harken back to what you were told before. Those with access to this information are keeping it from public view as long as possible as they working to have the governments of various countries pay for barriers to protect their investments, or they quietly put these properties up for sale and let the next poor schmuck take the loss—and for the large properties it will be groups of investors that are so pleased to own oceanfront property, until they see the waters cover the coastline.

I would assume shocked would be the term to be used next year if the oceans do rise eight inches as you told me before.
Oh, yes, panic will set in, and the nations will regather to discuss the abrupt rise in ocean level. There will be a tightening of the timeline for fossil fuel emissions to be reduced.

Gaia, how will the Texas coastline, and you can add in the Gulf coastline, fare in the coming years?
There will be more storms of various sizes, Tom, that will eat away the coastline. As I have said many times, I want you all to move away from the coastlines to, at the very least, give them a rest. Many houses built on the coast will suffer damage or outright destruction

Gaia, will you melt the ice in Antarctica in the next few years to reveal ancient ruins? (Asked November 2016)
Yes, that time is coming, but not for some time, shall we say. The ruins are buried deep within the ice, or they would have already been discovered with the melting that has been going on. That said, it will be several years before the ice melts to give a glimpse of several of the ruins left over from thousands of years ago—yes, over a million, Tom, in some cases.

Would the probability of this happening in, say, the next ten years be high or low?

Low, Tom. Keep in mind that the ice is hundreds of feet thick in some of the places where there are ruins. It will be more than 25 years, is the highest probability.

Gaia, if and when the large sheath of ice breaks off in Antarctica, will that expose ruins of an early civilization, or does this ice sheath consist of only water so that when a part of it breaks off there is only more ice?

There you have it, Tom. The ice sheath is just that, ice sitting on top of water and not land. This calving or breaking away from the main ice sheath only raises the ocean levels a tiny bit with the melting, as the water displacement by the ice means no change with the ocean levels of the world.

Speaking of ocean levels, why haven't we seen anyone mention the exact rise in ocean levels, when everyone is talking about them going up? (Asked February 2017)

Yes, as was explained previously, oceanographers have been blocked from releasing this information. They are allowed to say the oceans are rising, but not how much as it would cause panic in some coastal communities. They have been hoping it was just a onetime blip and not that the water level has speeded up its rise. This year will be the time when they are forced to admit the rise.

Was I seemingly blocked from bringing this to the attention of the public?

Just a little bit as we want the timing to be just a little later.

Gaia, any particular reason for changing coastal topography?

I have repeatedly told you for several years, Tom, that I wish to give these areas a rest from overuse and pollution. I have asked that people move away from the coasts as I knew this climate change was coming. There will be many more storms in the future and even if the winds are not as great due to the action by your group saying Benevolent Prayers, there will still be flooding as I wash the surface, and there will be many structures lost to flooding every year. This should tell everyone that they need to move to areas on higher ground.

Gaia, what will become of the devastated properties on the Florida coast?

Some will never be rebuilt upon, Tom. Many people did not have flood insurance and cannot rebuild. Some of the people drowned or were killed in some way, so their families will simply try and sell the land. If you recall, I have suggested that people move away from the coasts. There are more destructive storms to come. You cannot rely on old models that said a destructive storm would only occur every one hundred years or so. Throw that model out the window. These storms will become more numerous with the change in climate. Now, the same location, or nearby, might experience a hurricane every three or four years. You have been warned.

Gaia, I'm asked how will rising ocean levels affect Central Florida?

Yes, we have touched on this before. The hurricanes will not only have storm surges on the coasts but will bring widespread flooding to the central part of that peninsula. It will not go completely under water, but they will experience more flooding in the future.

Gaia, how much of Florida will disappear in 20-50 years?

We have covered this somewhat in the past. As sea levels rise, more of Florida will experience flooding when there are storms, especially hurricanes where the water is forced farther and farther inland and will remain for longer periods of time. Anywhere close to the coasts will not be safe, and with the flooding will come vermin. I have said time and time again to move away from the coasts, especially where the land is comparatively flat. Florida will not disappear in the time period you referred to but will no longer be the idyllic place to retire.

You do not want to get to a tipping point of no return, and you will not, but it's good to have more of a consensus. People will remember these days for many years, and I want them to.

Gaia, I'm asked if New York City and its suburbs and outlying areas

such as New Jersey will have to be abandoned in what would be our fairly-near future? (Asked December 2012)

Certainly, there will be great resistance to this, Tom. Great barriers will be constructed to hold out the water, but it will be a losing battle, especially as they see storm after storm flood the streets and subway tunnels, but the abandonment of the city will come in stages, as people become tired of having to deal with flooding first in their homes and then businesses, as there are many businesses in New York City and the suburbs which need customers for their restaurants, dry cleaners, grocery stores, and so on, but certainly within 50 years it will be abandoned, along with the low-lying suburbs. As I mentioned before, the rise of the ocean levels two feet is just the beginning. Another foot will come within a few years after that. So, I'm trying to warn people through people such as yourself to move to higher ground, or you'll wish you had.

Gaia, I have a question from a reader who lives in a beautiful valley on a river with the town name Bella Coola, BC, Canada. Will your earth movements affect this little town when you begin them, or are they relatively safe nestled in between two mountain ranges it seems?

Yes, I would love to tell her she is safe, Tom, but they are only 10 feet above sea level as she noted, and a large tsunami would affect this area. They will have time to reach higher ground, but it could affect them. She can request a Most Benevolent Outcome to either be out of the area, or to be able to move safely to higher ground. The soil on which the town is built is too unstable. Enough on this subject.

Will the Dubai UAE survive your rising of the ocean levels?

Much of the city will be inundated, Tom, just as all other sea level cities in the world will have this problem.

Gaia, would I be correct in stating that you would prefer everyone in the San Francisco Bay area move away from the coast?

Yes, you're absolutely correct, Tom. It is as if you have one foot in the water already and you're saying, "Do you think it's time to leave now, or should I wait until both feet are in the water?" No matter how you express it or how you say it, there is a rise coming in ocean levels, Tom.

As you see our future, what percentage of people will make their decision to leave voluntarily as compared to being forced to?
Alas, it will be a small percentage in North America—less than two percent. In the more low-lying areas of the world, the percentage will be higher.

Gaia, I was told last year that the Gordon Michael Scallion map is a low probability. Does that still hold true? (Asked October 2017)
Yes, Tom, the flooding and loss of land on the North American West Coast will not be that severe.

I did look at a rising ocean level map and it showed part of California's Central Valley being flooded.
Yes, that will occur.

So, one more time, 62 feet is too low?
Yes, but not by too much. Stick with the 75 feet.

What is the probability of only a 10-to-12-foot rise in ocean levels, which would still flood all the coastal towns and cities, and would still cause people to move to the interior? (Asked November 2017)
Yes, that probability is quite low—less than 10%, Tom. It is a nice idea but would not achieve all of what I need, and your souls also need, but it is a probability. Again, as I have said before, the probability of the loss of coastal land is 59% at the present time and there are several years ahead.

Gaia, how far away from the coasts should people move?
That's an easy question to answer, Tom. Far enough away so that you do not tax the coastlands as you've been doing for thousands of years. Yes, there still have to be ports for shipping, I understand, but the vast majority of people do not have to live on or near a coast. Move back to the hills and valleys away from the coast. This is for your protection, safety, and for your livelihoods as you are seeing not only here in North America, but all over the world that the storms and storm surge have increased in intensity; and as was demonstrated recently, large earthquakes can occur just offshore from my tectonic plates moving and the earthquakes spawn tsunamis.

Hundreds of thousands of people are displaced by all these events and would not have suffered financial loss had they been farther away from the coastlines of the world. As you have explained to your readers before, Tom, have them request benevolent outcomes to choose the perfect, safe place for them to live.

Gaia, what are the highest probabilities for New York City, the California Bay Area, Hawaii, Guam, and Tokyo?
All the areas you mentioned, Tom, are located next to the oceans of the world. As I have said numerous times, the oceans will continue to rise, at times slowly and at other times abruptly, should there be land that drops into the sea. I have encouraged everyone for several years to move away from the coasts as they will one day face the same loss of homes as the people on the big island of Hawaii who are in the path of the lava flows from Kilauea. They all thought they were far enough away but are not. It is the same for those who live on the coasts of the world. Move away from the coasts, and that can mean just a few miles, or in some cases over fifty to one hundred miles. Take that to the bank, Tom.

Gaia, how high above sea level should one live in Santo Domingo in the Dominican Republic, and for that matter, all of the Caribbean?
Sea levels will continue to rise over, let's say, the next 50 years more than one foot. That may not sound like a lot, Tom, but any storms will push waves much farther inland. To be safe, one should live higher and farther away from the coast and the surging seas.

So, it will not be, let's say, 18 inches?
No, just a tad more than one foot. Again, may I remind your readers that I have been saying to move away from the coasts for a number of years now?

How long will it be before it is necessary for the residents of the Shenzhen province of China to move away from the coast?
They, like those who live on the coasts of Florida and the East Coast of the USA, will move after they find that these storms, or typhoons as they are called there, will repeatedly wipe out their homes and businesses. As this part of the world is so over-populated, many will transition—die—as part

of their soul contracts to experience storms and flooding.

I assume it will be the same for Shanghai and Beijing?
Worse for them, Tom, as they are packed to the gills, shall I say, with people. I have given warnings for years and now we are in a period of time where the coasts will be left to recover. Take that to the bank, Tom. There will be mass migrations away from the coastlines.

It will seem seasonal most of the time, but again with some severe storms that will be greater in intensity due to the warmer waters. Blizzards will more intense, then recovery. The warmer waters that travel up the East Coast of North America and then across the Atlantic will mean more intense storms. They should prepare and have more fuel and food and water on hand. This will become the norm for the foreseeable future.

Gaia, with summers as hot as they are, shouldn't the oceans rise faster than predicted? (Asked August 2018)
Yes, they are rising faster than the scientists predicted, Tom, but not as fast as that time period you already passed. I slowed it down, but it is still warming in the Arctic and Antarctic. Because of the warmer waters, you will also see an active hurricane season as you move into August and September, and, yes, all the way to November on your calendar. And please mention to all your readers that you have the power, through Benevolent Prayers, to reduce the size of these storms.

But again, look for a rise of a couple of inches this year. As more attention is brought about the warming of the climate, the fact that the oceans are rising will force those who are covering up the rise in ocean levels for political and business reasons to begin to admit there is a problem that will affect millions of people living on the coasts of the world.

Foliating Deserts

Will you or are you still planning to make the deserts verdant again as that was originally one of your big goals that the California quakes would assist you in doing?
Yes, that is still a goal for me, Tom, one that I plan to implement sooner as

compared to later. I want not only the desert areas of the southwest USA to be verdant again, but also the Sahara in Africa.

Global Dimming

Gaia, is "global dimming" a significant contributor to global warming?
Yes, it does contribute to global warming, Tom, and for all the reasons they have found and more. If the Sun cannot shine through the haze of pollution, then there is warming of the atmosphere. The atmosphere will only clear up with the drop in usage of fossil fuels, contrails, and other usage detrimental to my atmosphere. I am not so concerned, Tom, as I know this will pass as these energy sources are found to be no longer necessary.

Heat Extremes

Gaia, will the heat in the Middle East increase to the point where it will become uninhabitable?
No, Tom. There will remain places in the world that are desert areas for several thousand more years, but at the same time I do plan for some desert areas to begin receiving more rain. Yes, that scene of millions of flowers blooming in the desert is not just a one-time occurrence. There will be more rain in several of these desert areas in the future. Of course, there will continue to be extremes in weather occurrences whether it will be too much rain or droughts such as the one that affected the plain states and California—again, all part of my cycles that humans have no records of.

Gaia, will the average temperature of the world increase by another degree or two?
Yes, Tom. I'm continuing to raise the temperature and it will be slightly above one degree. It is coming closer to the temperature I need to raise the ocean levels.

Gaia, will Finland continue to warm up?
Quite so, Tom. They are on a warming cycle that will continue for years to come. It is all part of the global warming. So average temperatures there

will continue to rise. This will take an adjustment by the people living there, as well as having to relocate people who live too close to the ocean, which will rise two feet.

Speaking of the oceans rising, how much warmer must it be for severe melting to cause the oceans to rise?
We're almost at that point, Tom. As you were told recently, the world temperature will rise slightly over 1 degree and next year will be the same or slightly more. That will cause major melting, especially in the northern latitudes.

Gaia, is one of the ways you are warming the atmosphere by releasing kilometer-wide plumes of methane gas? If so, what does that do?
Yes, that is one of the number of ways I am warming the atmosphere, Tom. In releasing this methane gas it also warms the ocean surrounding the release, but once in the atmosphere it does help create a hole where the Sun can also assist me in warming the planet and thereby raise the ocean levels the two feet I said would occur. I have tried to give advance warning, Tom, not only to you, but using other methods for other people. I realize it is difficult picking up and moving away from a beautiful coastline, but that coastline will be in many people's backyards in a couple of years. Then, as I said before, it will be too late to save their house or to have sold it to those people whose soul contracts call for them to have a flooding issue.

So, you're creating or adding to the ozone hole, is it called?
Close enough, Tom. The release of methane gas does not seem to be connected to what humans are doing in polluting the atmosphere. It contributes, Tom, but I would have still released the plumes of methane gas as I do wish to raise the ocean levels and am using all the tools at my disposal to do just that. It is just that humans are noticing all these events taking place just now, so they are scrambling to try and understand it. You might say they are two steps behind what is happening on a planetary basis.

Gaia, will coral reefs survive during the coming years, or will they die due to the warming of the oceans?
No, they will not all die, but, yes, in some locations they will continue to

die as they are on a certain temperature range that must not be too warm. However, there are even millions of locations where they will continue to thrive. This is a cycle of mine and the waters will cool back down in the future, although it will be some time. I do not wish to destroy the homes of the billions of sea creatures inhabiting the reefs of the world because there is a symbiotic relationship with all sea life.

Gaia, many reefs are dying all over the world. Will they survive?
Yes, Tom. They may retreat for a time, due to pollution and water temperatures, but they will rebound as the human footprint reduces and the animals that build these reefs can again flourish in the seas. The reefs may appear dormant at certain times, but, again, there will be adapting, and reef life will return in all its beauty, of that I can assure all your readers now and in the future.

Gaia, how many degrees, if any, will the world temperature rise in the next five years? (Asked December 2018)
Yes, Tom, the world temperature will continue to rise as the climate continues to change. That is a given.

Are we talking about one, two, or three degrees?
It will rise a little faster than they estimate at the present time. More in the order of 1.7 degrees Fahrenheit.

Did I receive that correctly, Gaia?
Yes, you are very close, Tom. Use that figure.

Will the Southeast part of the U.S. see a more significant rise in average temperature than the Central South?
It will be about the same for both sections of your country, Tom. The warming of the climate will mean hotter summers at times, but then the conditions for storms to increase not only in size, but also frequency. Again, I am still urging people to move away from the coasts for a number of reasons. I will continue to raise the level of the oceans, just not as dramatically as the past few years. The warming of the waters will also increase the intensity of the storms that are created out in the Atlantic and the Gulf of Mexico. Take that to the bank, Tom. There will be more coastal

flooding associated with these storms.

Gaia, when will this world heat wave end?
As we have spoken about before, this is all part of the cycle. You have had hot years, cold years, and those in between. This one is a longer cycle as the Earth is warming from the poles outward. Another teaching time for Earth humans. This is more a cycle of heat, then cool, then heat again. I have said before that the Earth was warming, and that the oceans would rise. That has happened. So, adapt. If you live in a northern latitude, perhaps you should consider buying an air conditioner and learn how to adapt to warmer summers, along with more violent weather.

Gaia, you previously said the California drought would last several more years. Has this changed and if so, why?
I did change the flow of precipitation at the request of your souls. As has been pointed out in your news reports, it would require about four years of precipitation to end the drought. They are not out of the woods, shall I say, by any means. This simply gives them more time to introduce ways of conservation, too long to go into detail here. The melting snow will cause other problems that must be solved, such as flooding. As I have repeatedly said in the past, people should be moving away from the coasts for a variety of reasons, including the melting of glaciers raising the sea levels. These levels will rise faster than your climatologists currently estimate.

Gaia, will Greenland completely melt one day, and if so, when?
Not completely, Tom, but let's use the figure that over half of Greenland will melt into the sea. This will occur within the next one hundred years, so it will be a slow melting process, and your thinking is correct that it has to do with the movement—the very slow moving—of the magnetic north, in combination with climate change. And, yes, for any doubters out there, the climate of Earth is changing.

Why wouldn't Greenland be affected by Yellowstone as you said winters in the northern part of the USA, and I assume lower Canada, will have harsher winters?
It will have some effect, Tom, but the majority of the colder winds will be to the south.

Insect Population

Gaia, has there been a huge drop in the insect population in the world, and if so, what is the reason?
There are a number of factors that have reduced the insect population, Tom. Homo sapiens, naturally, are at the top of the list as you require more and more space and take away the habitats of insects. And, yes, on that list of causes is herbicides. Several of these you will see reduced or completely outlawed in the future. Then there will be a very slow return of several of the insect populations. There is a reason for the insect population to exist, Tom. They are not just an annoyance, as they all have a purpose. Humanity's job is to figure out their benefits, and not just the detrimental aspects. They can be food, as an example, as many are high in protein. Your scientists need to think outside the box, I believe, is the common saying. Much study needs to be done. Provide more grasslands and woodlands for them and those that use them for food, such as birds. And on humanity's side, stop having so many children, as you are at a level I do not wish to go much above.

*Let's say this Benevolent Prayer **out loud**: "I ask any and all beings to protect the insect population of the planet, and to rid ourselves of harmful pesticides, and may the insect population stabilize in the most benevolent way for Earth, thank you!"*

Invasive Species

How do we handle invasive species in our lakes, forests, and in and around our houses?
This is all part of the Explorer Race's learning process. You have far to go—you just cannot see it yet. You think you've made good progress, and you have, but you have far to go in learning to control your environment in a benevolent way. You will not always make the best decisions regarding invasive species, but they are there to teach you lessons, and you will learn much in the next 100 years. Take that to the bank, shall we say?

Kermode Bears

Gaia, why are there only 400 white Kermode bears left in the wild?
A victim of humans, Tom, reducing the area they can roam free. They will return once the humans start lowering in numbers in a century or two.

There are 4,000 tigers left in the wild. How long will they survive in the future?
Again, the population is forcing them into smaller and smaller areas. When they eat people to survive, their days are limited as hunters come after them. Again, they will return in a few centuries.

Landmark Changes

Gaia, will any recognizable landmarks such as the Alps, Amazon rainforest, Venice, the Arctic, or Antarctica disappear in the next 25 years due to climate change? Also on the list would be Florida, California, and New York City.
There will continue to be a warming climate change, Tom, during this period of time. The Arctic will shrink, but Antarctica will continue to slowly melt, with the ice edges continuing to shrink, giving people a view of the landmass they have never seen before. The same with Greenland, where large portions of the island will lose its ice sheet. Those are givens. What is not given is California, Florida, and New York City. There are probabilities for those locations where they will dramatically change, or like the rest of the world slowly change due to the warming climate. Your souls have yet to choose their course, as there are many factors to consider—not the least of which is what learning can come from experiencing dramatic change. This will not be decided in 2019, but the choices will continue to narrow as we approach that time period of 2022 to 2027.

Gaia, will frozen bodies of the people who inhabited Antarctica when the poles shifted ever be discovered?
Yes, they will, Tom, but it will not be for many years—yes, over 50 that you were thinking, and even more. Antarctica will continue to slowly melt, and eventually ruins will be found of a city, and an archeological study will need to be organized and funded to go there during their summer period to start excavation. That's when the first frozen bodies will be

discovered. So, a long time, relatively speaking, in mankind's future. And, yes, you can ask Antura to show these people, should you desire. There are records.

Gaia, what percentage of climate change is due to humans, and what percentage is due to natural cycles, which you have mentioned before? Good question. Only a little less than twenty five percent of climate change can be attributed to humans, Tom. As I have told you before, Earth is a living thing and has cycles spanning over thousands of years. Your records just do not go back far enough to see or have recorded them. Still, that 25% is a large enough amount that it can speed up or worsen the climate change. You are making good progress, although it may not seem that way, in curbing your pollution of not only the atmosphere, but the land itself. Keep stepping up your efforts, and great progress will be made in the next 50 years. That may seem like a long time to you, with your shorter lives on Earth, but in my way of viewing things it is quite short.

Everyone on Earth is becoming much more knowledgeable about pollution, as you can see from news reports and documentaries. Plastic will be replaced by biodegradable containers. There will be a development in breaking down plastic, so that it can be recycled and returned to the Earth. You'll see.

Gaia, will we make significant progress in the next five years to reverse climate change, or what do you want and are planning? (Asked May 2021) Your first goal is to stabilize your environment. That should come in a little more than five years. Then after that you can begin to reverse the major detrimental effects. The conversion to electric cars and trucks will be but one of many actions we see happening in the next five to ten years.

Therefore, the stabilization, would you say, will be in seven or even ten years? The number would be closer to seven, assuming everyone gets on board with these plans. There will be some resistance in such countries as China, but that will slowly end with the introduction of the free energy machines. Coal, gas, and oil will have limited use in the future. You will all breathe easier—literally.

Gaia, is having multiple snowstorms and extremely cold weather a notice to everyone of climate change, or is it just that many people needed this experience?
Yes, Tom, everyone needed this experience, but it is also a note to all those who doubt climate change that they should get on the train to fight climate change, which can be done in so many multiple ways.

Plastic Waste

How will we eliminate micro plastic from our bodies?
That will come with using the biodegradable containers.

When will plastic packaging be removed in stores?
That goes hand in hand with the development of the new containers. AI will help here.

Is there a technical institute for dealing with plastic?
Again, we return to our earlier response that there are scientists working on new containers. Larger corporations that spend millions of dollars on plastic containers are researching the use of other materials. Breakthroughs will come fairly soon, with a slow roll out.

Pollution

Gaia, what is the highest probability for using the HUC enzyme to produce clean energy?
This is truly a historic discovery, Tom. Much work still has to be done in the coming years, but again it is but another discovery that will be widely used. It is truly clean energy.

Gaia, when will we figure out how to get rid of the garbage island in the Pacific?
This will take some time, Tom, but eventually a sort of scoop will be used, and massive tons of the garbage will be taken to a location and recycled or destroyed in furnaces.

Gaia, is the idea or invention by the young man about cleaning the oceans using the ocean currents viable, and if so, will it be implemented or will some better way be discovered?

It does have some viability, Tom. Funding will be a little difficult. And, yes, there are other people working on this same problem, but his may be the first to be tried.

Gaia, will this latest effort by Ocean Cleanup be successful?

To a certain extent, yes. Still, more ways to recycle this enormous amount of plastic in the ocean must be found in order to justify the expense of having several ships in the ocean rounding up this plastic. There is still much to learn and implement, but the Ocean Cleanup is a nice beginning. And as they point out, the real pollution comes from the rivers of the world, and it will be less expensive to first gather the trash at the mouths of rivers by smaller vessels, and then eventually to stop using plastic and instead use containers that are easily recyclable. Still, in the future are those containers that quickly disintegrate after use.

Gaia, what happened in Indianapolis, and several other places it seems, where there was snow with the consistency and form of plastic?

Yes, here we get into pollution, Tom, as obviously there has to be a reason why you could actually burn this snow and it will give off a pungent odor and will not melt like other pure water frozen substances do. They will need to study where this came from and what pollution causes the snow to take on this consistency and molecular structure. Scientists need to study this problem and study the molecular structure. They will then discover the origin of this pollution.

Gaia, will the floating structure created, I assume through inspiration by the teenager, be successful in removing plastic from the oceans?

Quite so, Tom. Yes, the young man was inspired, and although this will not solve the whole problem, it will remove tons and tons of plastic from the ocean once these floating devices are installed. The only delays will be for funding, but the recycling of the plastic will help alleviate or lessen the role governments must play in ridding the oceans of this trash. They will ask for more "crowd funding" once the first one proves successful.

Potable Water

Gaia, except for reducing the population, are there other solutions coming along for potable water?
Several will be used. Water from the ocean will be pumped in and the salt content removed. The pumping stations will be built quite quickly after an easier method of converting the water will be developed. People will get used to having tanks connected to their houses so that rainwater can be collected and stored. And then there will be methods of causing the clouds to generate precipitation. They will call it "cloud activation." Your meteorologists still have much to learn about controlling the weather, which you will do in the future. This will include generating the clouds, as this can be done.

Gaia, I saw a feature length documentary on water, and wondered if the river in West Virginia that is polluted could be purified, and if so, exactly how?
Yes, Tom, it certainly can be purified, and with not too much effort. So, there is more than one way to purify the water there. They can take vials of purified water—basically water where there has been prayer or intent to send love to the water and then release it into the river just above the drain of the chemical plant. That water will join with the polluted water and will be purified for drinking.

The other way—and if people wish to do both that is fine too—they can stand on the side of the river and pray or send beautiful intent and love to the water and that will also purify it too. So, you have two ways of purifying the water. Once it is purified it will stay that way—yes, even if more pollutants are discharged into the river. You humans are much more powerful than you can imagine, Tom. You just have to set your mind to it, to use an old expression.

Gaia, what is the best way to clean up the polluted mine water in Colorado?
Yes, your scientists have not discovered the way to do that yet. Therefore, I must let them, per their soul contracts, discover how to do that. It will be done by converting molecules, we will say for your purposes, into other

types of molecules somewhat through a system of osmosis. That's as far as I can go.

And, yes, your idea of having a large number of people stand at the water's edge and pray for the water will also work on a short-term basis, but if there are more pollutants added, then you must do the whole process over again. It would be nice to say a Benevolent Prayer for someone to discover how to clean the water sooner than you can hope for or expect. That will help someone focus on the problem at hand.

*Let's all say this Benevolent Prayer **out loud**: "I ask any and all beings to assist someone in discovering how to clean polluted water sooner than we can hope for or expect, thank you!"*

Recycling

Gaia, what is the highest probability for recycling now that China is cutting down on waste imports?
It is time, Tom, for all these countries to step up and recycle on their own. This will take some time, and, yes, there will be places where plastic bottles and other potential recyclable items are dumped into landfills, but this will also cause governments to encourage the use of bottles—glass—and to encourage the use of filters in the home. There are many other ways you have not explored yet to recycle or cut down on the use. Necessity is the mother of invention, is a good saying to use here, Tom.

Sea Stars Dying

Gaia, why are so many sea stars dying?
Yes, they have been poisoned by certain elements in the sea, Tom. Scientists are working on the problem to discover why this has occurred, but, yes, on a higher soul level, the group soul wishes to reduce its presence on Earth. There will still be many remaining, but the poisoning allowed the group soul to do other things.

So, the sea star population will partially recover?
Exactly, Tom, but it will take some time since its existence is threatened.

Seed Repository, Norway

Gaia, please comment on the storing of seeds in Norway.
Yes, Tom, an interesting development you might say. And, yes, Monsanto's involvement is especially intriguing. Are they worried that their chemicals could actually be poisoning the earth? The idea of storing seeds on the chance of disaster can be seen as wise for the long run. It's just the motives behind this decision leave questions. Remember, Tom, that we allow humans are to make decisions, and humans felt that storing pure strains of these seeds was best at this time. I have no fault with their decision. Whether they will be needed in the future I will not say as it might in some way affect their work.

Sequoias

Gaia, are the trees in the Sequoia National Forest over 3,000 years old, and are they stressed for some reason?
Yes, Tom, they are quite a bit older than 3,000 years. The attempts to judge their age has ranged as high as 6,000 years, which is fairly close to their actual age.

So, not older than that?
Correct, Tom. Use that figure.

Why do some people feel they are stressed?
Because they are, Tom.

For what reason?
This is a very stressful time for these magnificent trees.

Would it be because they sense changes coming for them?
Yes, Tom. There is a high probability of change coming.

Will it be fires, or something else?
That is one probable reason.

Is there any probability of the trees undergoing earth movements?

There you have it, Tom. For them there is a high probability of great movement. They are able to sense these things years in advance.

Why can't you protect these trees?
All souls that agreed to contribute to life on Earth agreed to what you would call the rules of existence. Let's leave it there, Tom, for the time being.

Gaia, what will happen to the Sequoias when California quakes and is it true they are the plant record keepers?
The last question first, Tom. Yes, those beautiful ancient trees do store and keep records of plant lives. Humans are just not able to communicate with these ancient soul fragments yet. This will come in the future. And, yes, many will be lost in the shaking. They know this and are prepared. Still, many will survive and flourish as there will be many fewer humans around to possibly damage their existence.

Snow Fibers

Gaia, please explain the snow "fibers" found along with the rust-colored dust photographed.
Yes, Tom, these are pollutants picked up in the atmosphere. They can be traced back to certain factories, not so much to airplanes, but certainly they did contribute to this toxic residue. This was not directly created but was the result of a mixture of pollutants that will be found in analyzing the residue. As I have said before, Tom, you humans must learn to clean up your atmosphere, and I know you will. It just will not be done overnight is the highest probability, but it will be a byproduct—cleaner skies—once free energy is implemented.

Gaia, why are seashells found in the Chilean mountains?
This is more the result of upheavals of the land, Tom, and not that the land was much lower at that time.

Sustainability

Gaia, what are the best constructive practices for ecosystem

sustainability?
We could spend hours on that subject, Tom. Suffice it to say that learning to respect all beings as creatures put on Earth by Creator, and understanding they are ensouled too, is a good start. Supporting recycling, and if it is not in your area, work so that it becomes a reality. Love the Earth. As I have explained before, it is a living thing. Giant progress will be made this century, if everyone pulls together. Stop having so many children. The Earth cannot be sustained for a long period of time with so many people. I will have to step in, and I can assure you, people in general will not like that path. Say benevolent prayers for the Earth each day, just as you do, Tom.

Tornadoes

Gaia, what is the source of the negative energy released by tornadoes, and is it localized or gathered from a wide area? And also, it seems to people that it causes negative energy. Please explain.
Yes, Tom, let's see if you can concentrate on this. Tornadoes do release this negative energy for me, and as you have noticed recently, some of these tornadoes are quite powerful, meaning there was a lot of negative energy being released. That you understand. This energy is gathered from not only the localized area, but even far beyond that, as this tornadic energy sucks up like a sponge all the surrounding negative energy for miles. Naturally, the reason they take the path they do has to do with individual soul contracts and who is supposed to experience these funnel clouds. As I have said countless times, Tom, but I understand that it must be said for each event or series of events, each soul fragment must experience natural disasters during one or more of your lives, so those souls experiencing those tornadoes signed up for these lives knowing full well that they would experience this at a certain time in their lives.

So, to answer the first part of the question, the energy is gathered from a wide area and dissipated and actually changed through this transfer of energy. To answer the second part of the question, it may seem as if it generates negative energy to you, but remember, there is great compassion shown to those who have these experiences and contributions are made to get the survivors back on their feet, so this compassion—even those just viewing the damage—generates a loving energy which replaces the negative energy and helps to raise the vibrational level of the whole population. So, there is a great benefit that results from any natural disaster, whether it be tornadoes, earthquakes, hurricanes, or any other natural disaster, as you call them.

Keep in mind that, yes, the Earth is a living body and, yes, it moves and changes just as your bodies do, Tom, but obviously in a different way. So, you can say that for any living body, whether it is human, animal as you call them, planets, suns, and so forth. We are all living entities. Humans will slowly learn the symbiotic nature that is present here and elsewhere in the Universe. That is part of the learning experience for the Explorer Race.

Although Gaia did not address it in her response, hate, fear, depravity, and anger are all included in what would be considered "negative energy."

Gaia, are we missing something regarding why tornadoes seem to follow certain paths over a long period of time? Or is it truly as the meteorologists say that it is all because of the location of the jet stream?
Good question, Tom. Yes, the main factor is the location of the jet stream during the spring and summer period, but, yes, there are also other elements present on and below the surface, which can attract these tornadic winds. Your scientists will have to develop better instruments in the future to see what is happening below the surface, and eventually they will notice certain elements present in these tornado prone areas.

Keep in mind there are soul contracts at play here. Theo has told me it's your guardian angel's job to have you at the right location at the right time to experience whatever event you're supposed to experience. That could be a tornado, hurricane, earthquake, or even an auto accident where you are injured or killed.

Gaia, will the tropical cyclones affecting Australia, New Zealand, and the Pacific Islands increase in intensity over the next few years?
Yes, they will, Tom. Eventually things will settle down, but not for a few

more years. This gives me the chance to blow off steam, you might call it. Everything on Earth is part of a cycle. Eventually the pendulum will swing the other way. Trust me when I say that those living on the coasts of the continent and islands need to keep aware as these storms can and will suddenly increase in intensity. They need to have supplies on hand for those times when there is no electricity and no running water and food is scarce.

Water Shortages

Gaia, what is the probability of there being a worldwide shortage of water in the future?
No probability, Tom—at least not worldwide. Certainly, there will always be certain places on Earth, the deserts I'm referring to, that see little or no rain each year, but even those will be shifting in the future.

Gaia, are we supposed to find new ways to supply water to drought-stricken communities? I know you said one way was for wells to be driven, but are we going to be forced in the short term to find other ways to produce water?
Yes, Tom. That is one of the reasons for this cycle. It is a learning cycle for humans too as you must adjust to these changes. Creating ways to recycle water and, yes, that does include recycling wastewater, are among the ways to weather a drought. Yes, even starting to put barrels under rainspouts from roofs may be needed in some areas. You just have to put your thinking caps on, you see.

Gaia, so just to continue this discussion and wind it up, have you created waves, too, that appeared to be energetic?
Yes, but with an atmosphere, Tom, they are harder to notice. There were instruments that have recorded these energies, but have, so far, gone mostly unnoticed by your scientists.

Gaia, do you see the need for constructing water pipelines in the U.S. from east to west, or perhaps installing saltwater conversion plants?
Certainly, one or more saltwater conversion plants on the coast—but far enough inland not to be affected by the rising ocean water levels—would

be good. I will also remind everyone that this is a cycle, and cycles have beginnings and ends. There will also be other changes in my crust or mantel, which will allow more weather systems across the southern part of your country. But, again, the conversion plants would initially be more costly than say a pipeline from the Mississippi River, yet, it will not affect the water level of the river as you can imagine it would have to be a giant pipe to bring water to not only Arizona, but New Mexico and, yes, West Texas. And may I remind everyone that there are vast stores of water below the surface, which have yet to be tapped. I think these are enough hints for those who might wish to ponder solutions—short term and long term.

Gaia, will Arizona have sufficient water in the future?
A calculated, yes, Tom. There will be more water resources identified. Plus, there will be better water conservation. Toilets that demand or that work with less water will be introduced.

Is there an ocean under Arizona?
Not so much an ocean as large pools of water. It will be expensive to tap those resources.

Will Arizona continue to get hotter?
In the short term, yes, but there are changes coming where I will funnel storms and such over this land, providing them with more rain.

What is the highest probability for Arizona in the next 20 to 30 years? (Asked March 2020)
This time will be a time of transitions. Keep in mind that your souls have not decided upon Yellowstone and West Coast earthquakes. Those will cause dynamic changes for Arizona if they are approved, so the jury is still out here, you could say. Yellowstone's eruption will affect the northern part of Arizona at times. Many more people will come to Arizona to live, but at the same time, the mountains will not block the rains from the West Coast.

Will Arizona be relatively safe in the next 20 years? (Asked September 2021)
Yes, in the past I have said they will have more rain, and they will have

flooding at times until they construct proper drainage. It will also be hotter at times until you have global warming under control—and that will eventually happen. Humans have so much to learn at this point in time, but you eventually will.

Gaia, will Arizona, including Prescott, be a safe place to live during the next 20 years?

For the most part, yes, Tom. It all depends upon where you live. Prescott, Phoenix, and Tucson will all be fine. Those that live in the forested areas certainly know that there will be fires as I clear the land. Sedona will be fine, but Flagstaff will have a few problems to deal with, but overall there will be no major earthquakes, just rumbles and those that they feel from other parts of the country, shall we say.

You have said previously that they would begin receiving more rain than they have in the past. Would this still be a high probability?

Quite so. That is in my plans to, again, bring growth to this desert land. As each year passes, we can update, but Arizona, for those that are able to adjust to the heat, will continue to grow.

Gaia, does drought transmute negativity, and what determines your need for extreme cycles?

Yes, Tom, drought conditions do tend to burn off, shall we say, negativity. This planet is alive and moving—more so than almost every other planet in this Universe. Extreme cycles were determined millions of years ago, although this may be hard to believe. These cycles must also be signed off on by your souls, and they do it for learning purposes so that they will understand how to run the Universe one day. This is, after all, Earth School. They can learn all the basics here.

Weather Systems

Gaia, is the Gulf Stream slowing down, and if so, how will it affect the weather?

The Gulf Steam works in cycles just as everything else on Earth, Tom. Yes, it slows down, then it may speed up. And, yes, it does assist me with weather patterns. Let's leave this for your geologists and meteorologists to study. As I have said before, we do not wish them to become bored. There are many, many, tie-ins between what is happening on the surface, and even under the surface, and their effects on Earth's weather.

Gaia, have there been improvements in weather modification that we have not heard about?
They continue to conduct tests, Tom, but they are years away from being able to control the weather. Will some of their experiments cause changes in the weather? Yes, but not consistently. That's what is frustrating to these scientists. It might cause a change one time and absolutely no change another.

How far in the future is the highest probability for being able to control the weather? (Asked September 2017)
Farther out than you might think, Tom. It will certainly be at least 25 years or more before you are able to make any headway to first knock down the intensity of huge storms. I cannot say any more as these must be discoveries for someone to have their "ah-ha" moment. Real control of the weather will be more on the order of over 50 years. It will give your scientists something to work on their whole careers.

Gaia, does a hurricane or severe storm cleanse negativity?
Yes, it does to a certain extent, Tom. Water is a great neutralizer, and it can absorb these negative energies and pass them out to the ocean where they are dissipated and then converted to benevolent energies.

Gaia, is cloud seeding safe in desert areas such as the UAE?
Yes, it is safe. Cloud seeding of different forms has been used for thousands of years.

Is the quality of the rainwater the same?
Almost, but it is still quite drinkable.

Gaia, does the low-pressure system that began in Hawaii and has grown into a series of what is known as "bomb cyclones" signal a change in climate, or is this something more of a cycle for you?
This is all part of the La Niña cycle where the upper part of North America

has these low-pressure systems, while the lower part has warmer and dryer weather. Again, this weather is something that all the younger souls need to experience—rain, flooding, blizzards, etc. On the upside is that the lakes, rivers, and streams will be replenished.

It would seem this would also act as a grease to allow earth movements?
It will, but not the large earthquakes we previously discussed. Smaller ones, yes.

Are other planet locations going through the same conditions, and what about drought?
These same weather systems circle the globe, so you will see reports of Europe experiencing abnormal conditions. Parts of Africa will receive little precipitation. There are many very young souls that need that experience of drought.

Gaia, with the warming of the oceans will there be more hurricanes as strong as Patricia (2015), or will that one stay the record?
That one will be the record for some time to come, Tom, but there will be one or two more in the future that will be as strong, if not a little stronger. The fact that people are learning to pray for these storms to weaken is a big development. I might remind your readers, Tom, in such places as the Philippines and Japan that they too can say Benevolent Prayers for the storms to weaken and I will oblige as all of you must learn that you are junior creators in training, and these storms can be controlled with a little help from your friends.

The fact that Patricia did minor damage in comparison to what it was capable of should give you an insight to what can be accomplished. I also moved the storm a little to the south so that the heavily populated Puerto Vallarta tourist area would be spared. That was all due to your Facebook friends saying the Benevolent Prayer in unison, along with countless prayers said by those in the storm's path.

Chapter 4
The Nature & Characteristics
of Planet Earth

Agartha, Inner Earth

Gaia, is there such a place in the inner Earth as Agartha, or is this perhaps a combination of the different inner worlds, or is this one of those inner societies you have spoken about before?

Yes, there is some confusion here as we mentioned before that there are over 20 societies living beneath the surface, most of them at different focuses than those of you on the surface. None of them are part of the Earth Experiment, and there have been just a few times when those on the surface have stumbled upon them. This was not by chance you understand, but to create mysteries to introduce you to the concept that there can be civilizations living beneath the surface of any planet you reach in the future. Agartha is but one of these societies and is forbidden from contacting you except during dreamtimes such as you do with the Lemurians at Mt. Shasta.

What about the depiction of the whole inner Earth being one gigantic world unto itself?

Again, over-dramatized, Tom. Certainly, there are some enormous caverns, as I have mentioned before, with its own light from crystals, but not as depicted in the artist's drawing.

Antarctica Polynya Hole

Gaia, will the large polynya hole in Antarctica remain, and what is the cause?

Yes, for the scientists involved it is certainly something that they will study for years. Therefore, I cannot give you too much information at this time. Suffice to say, it will remain a large cavity in the ice and that in turn will have an effect on the melting of ice—that is a given—even with the cold, the Sun will at times touch all the exposed surfaces. They will have to study the dynamics of this huge area opening up. I told you before I cannot give you all the answers if it infringes on soul contracts, and in this case it will.

Australia Black Mountain

I'm told that nothing grows on Australia's Black Mountain. Why is this the case?
The soil lacks the nutrients needed for anything to grow. You ask why? It has nothing to do with any ancient war as you were thinking, Tom. This is a natural event, again, for your geologists to study—another mystery for them to solve in the future.

Have there been people who disappeared there, and if so, for what reason?
Yes, but for natural reasons and not, shall we say, unnatural. This mountain has much to reveal but will take more study.

Brunhes-Matuyama Magnetic Reversal

Gaia, did the Brunhes-Matuyama magnetic reversal event occur 781,000 years ago and was it a slow or fast action? And did this cause the destruction of the society on Antarctica?
Yes, Tom. Your scientists are fairly accurate in reading the changes in the layers of Earth. And, yes, this did cause the society living on Antarctica at that time to be destroyed. A few were able to survive, but this did occur quite suddenly, and they were not prepared to handle the severe climate change. They were warned it was coming but did little to prepare or leave.

Did any of their souls join in the Earth Experiment?
No, Tom. This group wanted nothing to do with the Earth Experiment after having their lives cut short by my reversal of poles.

And what was the reason you reversed them?
It was to set up the continents in preparation for the Earth Experiment,

Tom. You could use the analogy of setting up a Monopoly board for the game. In this case, everyone taking part had different starting points.

Cascadian Subduction Slippage

Gaia, what is the probability of the Cascadian subduction slippage in the future, or is this tied to all the West Coast probabilities? (Asked August 2020)
Yes, Tom, they are all connected, which your geologists have not yet determined, although there is speculation that they are. There will be slippage. The question is, how much and in what increments shall I adjust. As I have said in the past, the probability for these adjustments, you call earthquakes, is over 60% in the next five years. You have been asking for updates every six months, so let's continue on that schedule.

Earth Growing

Gaia, is Earth still growing in size?
Yes, to a certain extent, but not as some readers would think. The Earth attracts meteorites each and every day, adding just a tiny bit of mass to the Earth. And naturally, the Earth expands in the Fifth Focus just as you do, but it is all in proportion so that it truly is not noticeable.

But again, to answer the question—yes, but by tiny amounts each and every month as Earth's gravity attracts foreign objects, we will call them, into the atmosphere.

Electromagnetic Waves

Gaia, some scientists are saying that there are electromagnetic waves given off prior to an earthquake. Is this factual, and if so, how much warning can they give?
It is factual, Tom, and they will find it an important precursor to an earthquake. In many instances it will be several days and weeks prior that the readings will increase.

Fires and Floods

Gaia, why did you, and I assume our souls, decide to have enormous fires and floods affecting people all at the same time?
Yes, Tom, both did coincide. The need for fires to rid the forests of all the old growth and allow new growth could not be held off any longer. This is a cycle for me that is several years long. There is much forested land that has not seen fires yet that will in the future. As I have explained in the past, if humans are going to live in forested areas, you need to build your houses so that they are not burned down when I must have these events.

Therefore, this was not the first year of these major fires, nor will it be the last. Regarding the floods, there are many younger souls that have not experienced flooding as one of their bucket list experiences, so this accomplishes not only that, but also is a wakeup call to millions of people that, yes, there is a climate change and what are you going to do about it? You can't just hide in your homes, or you will be under water. Plus, this is another incentive to scientists to learn how to control the weather, which we have spoken about just recently. That ability to control the weather is in your future.

Gravity And Magnetics

Gaia, is gravity based on magnetics?
In a way, Tom. Certainly, you've seen demonstrations of magnets both attracting and repelling each other, so you can say that is involved in creating gravity on the surface of this planet. To go farther would require a discussion based on science, which we cannot do with you, Tom.

Do humans develop magnetic attraction to Earth?
Again, we must keep this simple for you and your readers, Tom. You do have magnetic capabilities in your bodies, and certainly it responds to the magnetism in the Earth.

Ley Lines

Gaia, where does the energy of a ley line originate, how does it stay in a line, and do all planets have ley lines, or are we unique in having them?

First, the last part of the question. No, you are not unique as almost all have some sort of energy lines circling these planets. That should give your scientists a hint that they are quite necessary for the function of the planet. Planets without ley lines could be termed "dead planets" as they have no energy. There are few of these. They await a soul to ensoul them and allow them to come alive. So, it is myself, along with the trillions of other souls in this Universe that have a hand in creating these energy rings.

I go back here to saying that your scientists have just scratched the surface (yes, a little pun there) in their studies of these energy rings. Some day they will learn why great structures were built along these lines. Your ET aunts and uncles had a hand in pointing out the place to build these pyramids and other related structures. The people living at that time only had a little more knowledge in this area than you do today. They relied on the ETs to guide them.

Are some ley lines stronger than others or are they equal in strength?
Almost equal, but there are differences in their frequencies, and again, this is something for your scientists to study in the future as their instruments progress.

How do they flow in continuous lines?
We must allow these scientists to have their "ah ha" moments, Tom, although this will be quite a few years for them to come to accurate conclusions. So far, it is speculation.

Gaia, are there any special energies in the Dallas-Ft. Worth Metroplex that seems to attract a lot of events, from weather related to the Ebola outbreak here?
Yes, Tom, there are certain special ley lines that travel through this area and attract humans. And where there are humans, naturally, I have to at times have giant storms to release the negative energy that builds up.

And to answer your question about why you live there, we needed you to be one of the anchors energetically. There are certain people who are able to anchor energy, Tom, and you are one of them. It's not something you're even aware of, but you do act as a catalyst. Many other people are attracted subconsciously to your region either for work, love, or in actuality, the energy of this place. We know you prefer to feel the energy of the mountains, but your energy was needed here, and you agreed on a soul level, Tom.

So, there are ley lines that criss-cross this region?
Certainly. This is a subject that will be studied in the future as your scientists learn more about the energies of the Earth. Why else would ancient temples and pyramids be built in certain locations? The people of those times were given information as to where to build what you consider to be monuments, but really do serve a more important purpose. This information will be discovered again in the future.

What does it mean to anchor a grid point, and what is a grid point?
Your energy is anchoring or assisting in anchoring a part of the Earth grid. This is an unseen energetic force that is laid over the landscape. Your scientists have much to learn about these energies. Here again we get into an area where a person having studied these ley lines would ask more detailed questions. Where these lines intersect are considered grid points. That's where you come in to assist me.

Light Generation

Gaia, how do you generate light in your caverns for some of the societies to live, such as the Lemurians?
Yes, Tom, let's see if you can receive this. The light is generated as you call it by certain crystal formations. It is not the rocks, but the crystals that generate light as heat in the deep interior is translated into light for the caverns. And to answer the question you have forming in your mind, the heat is transferred to light and the caverns remain at a steady temperature.

Then there are no crystals that automatically generate light on their own?
No, Tom, there are no crystals that automatically generate light. The light has to come from somewhere and here the heat of the Earth generates light and also gives the caverns a mild steady temperature all the time. There are no fluctuations as there is on the surface.

Lightning Storms

Gaia, what is the purpose of lightning in storms, as it frightens not only animals but humans as well?
Certainly, your scientists have studied and will continue to study lightning in storms for many years to come. Lightning assists me in building up the storms so that they are able to cover a wider area. The lightning energy does just that. Of course, it accomplishes other things too—lightning strikes can injure or even kill humans and animals with the souls' permissions as part of their soul contract. Animals are able to feel this energy at a higher level than humans, so studies are needed at some point as to what animals feel that humans do not.

Magma

Gaia, news reports say that there is a buildup of magma under New England, but it will be a long time before eruption. Are they correct?
Close to accurate, Tom. It will be thousands of years, so it should not be of worry for anyone living there today, compared to the people who live near Yellowstone, and to the east. In terms of years, as I have said before, that is a high probability.

Why the magma buildup?
It is just part of my planet dynamics, Tom. It is something for your volcanologists to study in the future. It's all part of my inner dynamics that will provide thousands and thousands of hours of study as your instruments become better and better at probing not only Earth's interior, but other planets as well.

Gaia, do you have two blobs on opposite sides of the world, and if so, are these magmas or something else and what is their purpose? Is there any connection to inner Earth cultures and are these blobs needed for your stability?
Some of this I will not answer for you today, Tom, as you can imagine these are questions for your scientists to study over quite a few years before they are able to really understand my inner-Earth workings and how or what these blobs are used for. Let's say for the time being that the theory

that they are used somehow for my stability is partially true. There are other reasons for their existence. They have nothing to do with any inner Earth cultures on your plane of existence. If you recall, several years ago I said there were forms of life in my interior that are on a different dimensional level than humanity.

I will also say the magma associated with these blobs, as they were termed, does not stay in one place, but circulates. Hence, the reason why I will let those who study these things theorize.

I will add that in my meditation sessions I always send white light and love to the center of the Earth and expand it to permeate every single cell and every single atom of the interior of the Earth and all of those who live within it. Gaia says I'm one of the only ones in the world sending light to her interior, so I would suggest that everyone also do this.

Magnetic Field

Gaia, will Earth's magnetic field remain fairly stable or dramatically change?
It will not dramatically change for many, many years, Tom. I reserve that option for the future, but for now it may ebb and flow, but will remain relatively stable.

Magnetic North Pole

Gaia, has the rate of movement of the magnetic North pole sped up to 34 miles per year?
Yes, I did speed it up a tad, Tom.

Will this rate slow down, or will the speed continue?
It will continue for a while, Tom, before slowing down.

What is the purpose of the speedup?
It is part of the climate change, Tom. You will see some changes in the weather patterns, along with everyone else. In the end it will be a positive change for everyone.

Natural Disasters

Gaia, is there something you have not "spoon-fed" us yet about why we need to experience natural disasters? Why must we experience them; just because they happen on Earth?

Perhaps a little more information, today. Although it is impossible for you to see when these natural disasters—your term—occur, they occur differently on different levels of focus. You are able to experience this on a third-dimensional or even fifth-dimensional focus. On higher levels of focus they occur differently. Remember that your souls are learning how all of this works, so that when you all meld one day you will understand how everything works on all dimensional levels. This is all part of your souls' training. You could experience an earthquake, tsunami, or volcano eruption in a quantum state, but that, as you can imagine, does not give your souls the experience of having a fragment of itself experience it in the third dimension. That actually is a good question, Tom, but difficult for most of your readers to understand or accept when you must experience it in your current, past, or future lives.

Pain Felt by Earth

Gaia, when atomic tests are done, or fracking, does the Earth feel physical pain or anything?

The physical pain you refer to is a human trait, Tom. As a soul, you understand we do not feel physical pain per se. A soul accepts what is. You understand that I am putting this in words your readers can understand. Therefore, the planet does not feel physical pain. The soul that inhabits and takes care of a planet certainly has more control than you can understand or imagine at this time. The soul knows millions of years in advance where the planet is headed in the galaxy along with asteroids that it will encounter, comets that will cross its path, and even how long its sun will shine before it enters another phase of existence.

So, be good stewards of this planet you live on. This is your responsibility to take care of it just as I do as, don't forget, you are part of the Creator too. There is part of the Creator in every human alive on this planet. We know your struggles, but you are starting to reap the rewards for being veiled and not understanding you are polluting the Earth and will make it pristine again one day. We **know** this because you are in this space-time continuum and it has already occurred farther down the way, but I digress.

To summarize, the Earth does not feel physical pain as do humans. But, again, it is your responsibility to take care of it and treat it just as if the Earth is part and parcel of your family, because it is. You want to leave the Earth in better condition than you found it in this life—even if it is just a small part that you have personal control over. Make it beautiful, and honor me and my work, and the other millions of souls who work on behalf of this planet.

Poles Shifting

Gaia, I suppose my readers and I are still confused as to whether the Earth experienced a shift in poles, a pole reversal, or did the axis actually shift causing an enormous wind perhaps?
Yes, I understand it is confusing, Tom, since you are not a geologist who has studied these events. Again, we are speaking of the First Destruction. Yes, there was a shift in poles, Tom, which was dramatic as it occurred in one movement, and not like is happening now where the shift in poles is gradual. I needed that shift in poles immediately to clear off a lot of what was called the civilized world at that time. And, no, it was not a shift in the axis, but the actual movement of the poles caused frigid temperatures and winds and such to move to areas that had not experienced this. So, the Earth itself did not wobble and suddenly tilt. The axis remains pretty much where it was before the shifting of the poles.

Gaia, has the Earth changed its plane of rotation in relation to the Southern Cross and Milky Way?
There has been a slight change that your scientists—those who noticed—are a little perplexed about, Tom. It is considered a normal wobble, but is not, you see. It is just another of the many adjustments I'm making to this 5.0 density.

So, the Earth will not return to its original position?
No, certainly not for some time, Tom.

Did that include our angle to the sun, and if so, wouldn't that alter our summer and winter cycles?

Yes, there was a slight change, Tom, but not so much in relation to the Sun as to the rest of the Universe. You might say that both changed at the same time. So, to summarize for you, yes, there was a slight change, but looked upon as a normal wobble by your astronomers and scientists.

Sinkholes

Gaia, what is the reason we are seeing more sinkholes around the world? Is it true Earth is rotating slower?

Yes, the tiniest shift in rotation, Tom, can cause sink holes to develop as my Earth adjusts to new settings, you might call them. As was shown in the video, Earth elongates to a tiny setting, but that is enough to cause a slight compression of the earth's crust.

What is the reason you changed your setting?

The adjustment had to be made to bring about other Earth changes you will see in the future, Tom. This is all part of the Explorer Race's learning curve, shall we call it. When your scientists can see a difference in the rotation, this adds to their knowledge that other planets can do the same. It will aid in your knowledge and understanding of the Universe. So, yes, to summarize, Tom, I have shifted the earth's spin just the tiniest amount, but enough to cause these changes on the surface, including the sinkholes.

Will this continue for the foreseeable future, or will you adjust even more?

No, this is sufficient for my and your needs.

Gaia, what is the cause for the sinkholes in Louisiana and Alabama?

Yes, this is a natural event, Tom, not man-made. As I move water and other elements underground it will, at times, cause the ground to sink in certain places where the soil is not very stable. Naturally, if it affects humans, they have signed off on this to occur for their learning. There is a lot of movement underground, Tom, and this is just one demonstration or instance of this natural occurrence.

Underground Living

Gaia, I have a question regarding the 20-something societies that have chosen to live underground on Earth. Is this common for there to be many societies in the interior of planets, such as Venus, Mars, and our other planets?
No, Tom, it is not common. This planet has many attributes, or assets, if you wish to call them that which make life possible on this planet as compared to other planets in this solar system, and even in thousands if not billions of other systems in the Universe. The Earth is much more unique than you can imagine, Tom. Yes, there are a great number of other water planets in the Universe, but not with the makeup of the interior that this planet has. There are underground lakes and rivers and streams, which you humans know just a little about. There are large caverns in my interior with their own light—almost as bright it would seem as the sun, but less intense. So, the interior of this planet is just as attractive for life as the exterior is.

How many of these societies are humanoid, like the Lemurians?
Not very many, Tom. Just another couple.

Hominid?
Again, a couple.

Then I would assume the others would cover the gamut of possible life forms?
Yes, for the most part, Tom. Sorry to be a little vague here, but I'm asked to keep it vague by those societies who do not wish to be visited by humans based on your writings one day. You will be more widely read than you might imagine, Tom, in the future.

Are most of these societies living at the same level vibrationally as the rest of the Universe, as compared to Earth humans who are now close to 5.0, compared to the 5.3 or 5.4 for the rest of the Universe?
Quite so, Tom. I'm glad you made the connection. They are not taking part in the Earth Experiment, so they can be at the same level as their universal brothers and sisters, shall we call them.

Weeds and Their Purpose

Gaia, what is the purpose of weeds, and how do they serve our planet?
One important factor is that weeds do produce oxygen for the planet. They also signal to farmers and gardeners that spring is just around the corner, as many are the first to appear. Creator loves variety, may I remind your readers, and when you go to the stars you will see cousins of weeds. You will have discovered benevolent ways of directing these weeds to live in other places.

Can fairies assist in eradicating invasive weeds?
Fairies tend to assist in the growth of all plants and flowers. What appears to you as an ugly weed has beauty to a fairy. So, the answer would be no, but for gardeners and farmers, they understand what they wish to grow, so they assist in tending those crops of whatever nature they are. They gently urge these plants you call weeds to move to other areas where they will not be killed or eradicated. Still, if the plant wishes to grow there, they will not stop it.

Chapter 5
Oceans & Bodies of Water

Atlantic/Pacific Oceans

Gaia, why are the depths of the Atlantic and Pacific Oceans so different?
Perhaps this answer might seem a little simple, Tom, but it has to do with plate movements. As the scientists speculated, the continents were more a single landmass. The landmass needed to be split in order for the Earth Experiment to work, with different looking peoples sown, shall we say, on each landmass. The landmasses, which split forming the Atlantic Ocean, left a shallower ocean depth than that in the Pacific. It was always that deep, although the continent of MU existed. Its location you have. Nowadays, as the North American landmass moves to the west and the Asian landmass moves to the east, great pressure is brought along the Ring of Fire, as it is called, as each landmass moves farther into the Pacific Ocean. Those landmasses will slowly fill in the depths of the Pacific Ocean.

So, am I understanding the difference between the depths of the Pacific and Atlantic is because of the preexisting landmass?
That's correct, Tom.

Bermuda Triangle

Gaia, what actually caused the planes to crash in 1945 in the Bermuda Triangle?
A combination of instrument malfunction due to the magnetic conditions, along with pilot error, Tom. They became confused and flew in circles until their gas ran out. You still have much to discover about this area known as the Bermuda Triangle, and it will not be completely solved or understood

for several years, although certainly, theories abound. Therefore, I will leave this question of why the area reacts this way for those "ah-ha" moments for your scientists and investigators.

Gaia, did any of the planes or ships that disappeared in what is referred to as the Bermuda Triangle wind up in the Gobi Desert?
Absolutely not, Tom. That is a fanciful story and was actually used in a movie, should anyone wish to research it.

Speaking of the Bermuda Triangle, were any of the people who are listed as disappearing there ever been rescued by ETs, or would that break their soul contracts?
Exactly, Tom. Those who perished in that area of the world did so as part of their soul contracts. No one would be allowed to whisk them away. Otherwise, they would have to have another life.

Great Lakes

What is the importance of the Great Lakes Region?
As was noted by your questioner, it is a huge basin of fresh water, along with all the varieties of freshwater fish that live there. It is also so large it creates its own weather systems, so that the interior of the continent does not have to rely on those weather systems from the West Coast. Many types of farms thrive in that region—too many to list here. It also serves as a waterway for the transport of goods all the way from the East Coast. Overall, it is part of the ecosystem of the North American Continent.

Iron Ore Plumes

Gaia, what benefit are the iron ore plumes on the bottom of the South Atlantic Ocean?
That's an easy one, Tom, as there are many varieties of fish and plants that thrive on this. It also has the effect of settling the pollutants in the water from human wastes of all types.

Mapping the Oceans

Gaia, how long will it take to map the oceans, and can you give us hints of what surprises are in store for scientists? (Asked April 2014)
It will take, as you can imagine, Tom, many more years to map the ocean floor. There are only so many funds allocated for this purpose as space exploration is much more exciting to not only the general public, but to legislative bodies who allocate the funds. So, you are certainly looking at 20 to 25 years for this to slowly progress. There will need to be better mapping instruments developed, which can map large areas instead of the small areas you are able to today.

Regarding surprises, as these instruments come into use, scientists will be amazed at the amount of life that dwells deep in your oceans. They see little hints of this as they send submarines down to these deep depths, but there are many life forms that they have not yet been photographed— completely new ones not listed in any book on the subject. And there will be surprises in the topography where, let's say, certain formations exist not known before, such as land masses deep in the ocean that were once above the surface.

Plastic in the Ocean

Gaia, where is all the plastic in the ocean disappearing? Is it on the bottom, just dispersed, or are the fish consuming the plastic?
There are a number of scenarios as you can guess, Tom. Ships are encountering this garbage in even the most far-flung remote locations on the oceans of the world. Regrettably, the most plastic is consumed by many different types of fish that think it is some sort of food. Many are poisoned and die, while others are able to excrete the plastic as waste. And certainly, some of the plastic finds its way to the bottom. There are photos of this if you search. The majority of the plastic remains floating.

Quite some time ago I told you one day your scientists, or an inventor, will come up with a way of disposing of the plastic in the oceans. As I have told you many times, Tom, humans will solve your problems, so I allow. That's what you are on Earth to do: solve problems—to reinvent everything that other societies have invented before, but you will do it better, and you are here to solve the unsolvable problems of other societies.

115

That is your legacy as the Explorer Race.

Tarim Basin, China

Gaia, is there a huge body of water, a lake, under the Tarim Basin in Northern China?
Yes, this is just one of the places on Earth where I have large amounts of water existing, or stored, you might say.

Do any species of beings inhabit this underground lake either in it or beside it?
As they do not wish me to talk about their society too much, I will only say that there is intelligent life there, but not on the same vibrational level, so you would not see them should you explore this area.

Is it true that the lake area is larger than the Great Lakes?
That would be a fair estimation of the amount of water I store there.
Tsunamis in Egypt 2022

How high did the sea tsunamis affect Egypt in any of the three rises in ocean levels?
Each time, Egypt was partially affected. Keep in mind that the Mediterranean did not have the appearance it does today, since there was land in between the Atlantic Ocean and Egypt that took the brunt of the tsunamis up until MU sank, which was when they had flooding.

Was the Sphinx affected?
Yes. It was inundated.

Chapter 6
Spiritual Concepts

Ascended Masters

Gaia, will our ascended masters merge with us or make other choices?
A general answer will be that they also look forward to the merger, as they have worked also to assist in raising your vibrational levels. Don't forget that some of the souls having lives on Earth—10% already previously mentioned—were created by Creator. Those souls will have a choice of merging back with Creator or merging with you. Most will choose to merge with your souls, but a smaller percentage we see as wishing to return to their source. That may include an ascended master or two. All of these are choices fairly far in the future, so I am giving you probabilities here today.

Broken Heart

Gaia, what physical changes are there when someone's heart is "broken?"
Yes, there are definitely physical changes, Tom, as there is the grief of loss, somewhat similar to the grief of the loss of a loved one when they transition. The two can be somewhat compared for your purposes. The energy cords that connected two people may also remain, which is why we suggest you request the severing of those energy cords that are not in your best interests in order to assist you in moving on.

Depending upon how many times the two have encountered each other in past lives, this can feel devastating because perhaps they were married or in similar relationships in the past, but for this life their soul path is to find others, from soul groups they've worked with in the past, to mate with. And, of course, we cannot forget balancing since perhaps in a past life they broke someone's heart and now this time their heart will be broken for balancing purposes. So, there are many, many factors that can be involved in the separation of two people, with many of the times being quite complicated if you were to view the relationship from our perspective.

And, yes, someone can die of a broken heart if they do not sever these energy cords and move on. The heart retains these memories over many lives and the energy of loss can be devastating, Tom, for anyone who has experienced it. To go farther with this discussion, you would need to know more about the physiology of the human body, so let's end it here.

Compassion

Gaia, what is the purpose of compassion, and how do we, or should we prioritize?
Good question from your reader, Tom. Showing compassion in a myriad of ways helps to raise your vibrational level. If you ignore those in need you will actually take a step back in your development. So be compassionate to those in need, whether human or non-human. You will find a lightness of being over many years as you work, whether it is healing, or just sending a Benevolent Prayer to someone or something you cannot physically assist. And by doing so, you help the whole world to raise everyone's vibrational level.

Should you prioritize? Certainly, if you have strong feelings to assist another person, then that becomes a priority. Perhaps you are paying back an old karmic debt from another life when they assisted you.

We understand there are just so many minutes in a day, but that should not stop you from saying a quick Benevolent Prayer **out loud** for that person or non-human, just as you and Dena did on your way to Arkansas when both of you said a benevolent prayer for a homeless lady walking along the side of the road as you passed. That did assist her, we can assure you. In summary, the more compassionate you are, the higher your vibrational level will rise in this life, and you and other compassionate people will lighten the whole world with your brighter lights.

Connection to Source

Gaia, are we all connected to "source" and if so, what is "source?"
Yes, a heady question for today, Tom. Your soul fragments are all
connected together through an energy grid set up by Master Kryon for me
and for your souls so that all roads lead to Rome, shall we say. Your soul
fragments are connected to this grid and the grid is connected to an energy
soup, we shall call it, also known as "source," where all your souls
basically reside, and that are connected to all the other lives each soul is
having across the Universe, and even beyond to other creators who birthed
them. All very complex, Tom, but it does work.

Consciousness

Gaia, what is cosmic consciousness? Is it the consciousness of all souls?
You could say it is the consciousness of all souls within the framework of
this creation, Tom. This can have multiple meanings, depending upon the
person's beliefs. Keep in mind that all the planets and suns in this Universe
are also ensouled.

Gaia, where is consciousness located?
Your consciousness is located at the seat of your soul, Tom, is the simple
answer. It must be located there for you to exist in this world.

So, is that the heart chakra or somewhere else?
Yes, Tom. There you have it.

**Teilhard de Chardin predicted a singular unique event where all
human consciousness would come together. What is the probability of
this happening?**
There will be many events that would lend themselves to that description,
but not as that person imagined. Each time a great invention occurs, or
some revelation, mankind will think you've achieved a pinnacle of success
only to see another mountain to climb in the distance. I will add here that
you could include the event far, far, in the future when all our souls will
combine to become a creator.

Crystals

Gaia, do stones and crystals contain spirits or energies that contribute to benefit dreams, correct health problems, and enhance requesting Most Benevolent Outcomes?
Good question, Tom, although we have covered part of this before. These stones and crystals do contain energies, we will call them for your purposes, Tom. Certainly, their molecular structure can contribute to your welfare according to the properties of the stones or crystals.

That said, as I have mentioned before, there are books written on this subject that your readers can find at certain bookstores, which go into detail on the properties of the various stones. Let yourself be guided if you have an interest in learning more about these stones' properties when you go to buy a book. You'll know which one is right for you. Naturally, you can request a Most Benevolent Outcome to choose the book that is the best one for you.

Demons

Gaia, can you explain what demons actually are and whether they possess dolls and statues at times? Are they stuck here?
Here we get partially into beliefs, Tom. Demons were an invention of humans, just as humans invented Hell. Yes, there are negative entities that we have mentioned before, which is why we have you surrounding yourself with white light during these sessions. Those entities are different from demons, which are an invention of man.

Then, are these negative energies not stuck here, but are on some level of existence?
Yes, and again, we remind you that Creator loves them just as much as it loves you.

Are their numbers dwindling or are they a complete reflection of us?
Their numbers do not dwindle as some people have predicted, but they will not grow larger. When you send white light out, it does weaken their ability to have any influence.

Do you have an opposite negative soul operating negative Earth?
No, a good question, but I do not. Surrounding yourself with white light and sending it all over the world does reduce their energy.

What about the power of crosses?
Again, this is a belief that was invented by humans, so the crosses have as much power as humans give them.

Dreams

Gaia, what is the future for our understanding of dreams, or will they always remain enigmatic since each person has their own dream symbols.
Dreams will be more understood, Tom, in the future. As people meditate more, it will open up for them to ask questions about their dreams and receiving answers as to their meaning.

Should dreams be controlled, as when we have vivid dreams and know we are dreaming?
This is allowed for your learning, Tom. You're correct that there will be dreams where you have no control since these are necessary to give you messages from your soul, or when you are assisting others across the Universe.

Scientists study dreams all the time. Won't they come to more of an understanding of dreams and symbolism and our entry into the quantum area, I'll call it for lack of a better word?
Yes, but this will take many years, Tom. First, they need to accept the idea that you have multiple lives on Earth and can draw from any of them during the period when you are in the quantum state. And they have to come to accept that there are multiple timelines where you also will visit or draw upon those experiences your other selves are having. This is a giant leap for them, and it will not come overnight.

Do our soul fragments meet us in our dreams in airport settings?
Typically, airports are used as a dream device to signal that you are about to return to your bodies from wherever you have been during dream time.

You are the soul fragments.

Energetic Differences in Geography

Gaia, how would you describe the energetic difference between different mountains and different lakes?
Here we get into some of those four million souls we have discussed before, Tom, who assist me in running Earth. There are souls whose job it is to energetically inhabit perhaps a whole chain of mountains, or just one or two magnificent ones. And there are souls who love water and create the energy, which attracts various fish, fowl, and plant life both above and below the surface. The Earth is much more complex than your scientists realize, Tom, which is why early man and woman, named pagans later, worshipped the mountains, lakes, and streams as they could feel the different energies better than modern men and women since there are souls who do this work as part of their own learning curve, shall we say.

Energies: Positive and Negative

Gaia, is there anything between the positive and negative energies, and will they somehow be combined in the future?
They are just energies, Tom, quite separate at this time from each other. They will remain separate, yet not only you here on Earth, but all over the Universe beings will be able to use or utilize these separate negative energies. This is quite complicated and far beyond even your greatest scientists at this time. This knowledge will come far in your future, but it will come.

Gaia, I'm asked what is the difference between positive and negative energy?
Ah, such a question. These energies, we must use the plural form for both, as was explained before, are more than opposites, they are so different that even the best scientists, we will call them, across the Universe found it impossible to work with the negative energy, so it was ignored. Creator from the beginning knew this to be a fact in every other of the billions of creations. That's why it is so amazing, Tom, that humans were able to balance these two energies when no one else had. You made the impossible

possible. So, an explanation of comparing the difference between the two is so much more than night and day. Imagine the hardest rock in the Universe that can withstand any method of cracking or penetrating its surface and that is one small way of describing or using a simile.

Can you tell me if the following are positive energies? Electromagnetic?
Yes, positive. There will be huge discoveries about this energy in the future.

Crystal?
Yes, one of the positive energies that, like all energies, can be misused.

Gravity?
Yes, again, although it would not seem so on the surface (yes, a little humor there).

Dark energy?
Again, positive as it is not identified that way in the rest of the Universe.

Telepathic energy?
Quite so.

Energy that connects the planets and stars?
Yes, although its existence has only been speculated in a limited way by your scientists.

Gaia, is one of the negative energies entropy?
It is not.

What about dark matter or dark energy?
Dark matter makes up all the space in the Universe, which your scientists will learn much more about in the future. And the same about what you call dark energy, but it is not negative energy.

Is antimatter negative energy?
Not as asked here. There is antimatter in places such as black holes but is not considered one of the negative energies.

Gaia, are there different forms of negative energy as there are different forms of positive energy?
Quite so, Tom. That is a good question and good that you recognized the

possibility. Here we get into quantum physics, so let me just say that there are several forms of negative energy, and it will be many years before your scientists are able to identify the differences between negative energies and the different forms of positive energy. That is why everyone is confused when you and everyone else have had questions about how negative energy is completely rejected in other parts of not only this Universe, but others as well. There will be thousands of experiments done by your scientists in order to learn about these energies.

So, crystal energy is just one of the positive energies, is that correct?
That's correct, Tom. And as we have alluded to in the past, there was a different energy given to the Lemurians that will only be discovered by chance by a scientist. Yet, there are even more.

Gaia, why are there not an equal number of negative energies and positive energies?
Yes, you would think there would be a balance, but in reality, they do balance, as the negative energies are more powerful than the individual positive energies. That is a simple explanation, you understand, for you at this time. I must allow those humans in the future to have their ah-ha moments of discovery. It is so much more complex than you can imagine.

Can you give an example of one of the negative energies?
No, just a hint. Your whole existence is but one of the four negative energies. Yet, you work with the other three. How is that for a puzzling answer? That answer will puzzle scientists in the future for a very long time.

Previously I was told the Creator of our Universe decided to see if negative energy could be worked with, as it was explained that even though all these other societies were millions of years ahead of us technologically, they were stuck at around 5.3 or 5.4 in raising their vibrational levels. When we go out to the stars, we will introduce small amounts of negativity (.02% to 2%), and this will cause everyone to increase their vibrational levels.

Gaia, are there any of the 10 positive energies that we can call upon, or are we locked into working with only negative energies? Also, why

10 positive and four negative? Why not equal numbers? And finally, do we work with all the negative energies?
Yes, Tom, your souls agreed to work solely with negative energies in a negative world, with no access to positive energies. Keep in mind that these are simply energies, Tom. Negative does not necessarily equate to bad. They are simply energies that no one had been able to harness in the past. You have accomplished this, which is why so many are amazed that you were able to do it in such a short time.

Regarding the numbers of positive and negative energies, your scientists will have to slowly learn about these over the coming years. Until now, no one had an inkling—speaking of your scientists—that there were all these different energies. You and your readers have been told something that will be debated for hundreds of years.

Are negative and positive energies able to be seen in the physical Universe, such as black holes?
I will not give you too much information here, Tom, as I have previously told you there are revelations in the future for your scientists. Let's just say that you must keep in mind that the rest of the Universe consists of 10 positive energies. The black holes work within that structure, so in a way you are viewing one of the laws of these 10 energies.

Gaia, do we have the vocabulary to describe the four negative and ten positive energies?
Great point, Tom. You just do not yet have the words to describe these energies. This will come as your scientists discover more and more in the future, but as I said before, bravo to those who attempt to now. The list can be narrowed a little more, you could say. People have no concept yet—and I'm really referring to your quantum physicists—as to how much you do not know. When I previously said that you were in an initial stage of discovery, you could say that is an understatement, Tom.

Will science learn about these energies before or after we learn to portal hop across the Universe as other advanced societies do?
It will have to be before, Tom. That's a good question and gives you an idea of why you've been told previously that portal hopping will not have

a breakthrough until around 3250. The last part of the puzzle will not be discovered until after that spaceship departs for one of the planets orbiting a fairly close star, and which we have previously said will not be the greatest choice.

So, does portal hopping use one or more of these energies?
Let's just say there is an energy that connects all planets, suns, and galaxies, as we have noted before.

Gaia, would one of the negative energies we have spoken about before be the veil around the Earth?
No, not the way the question was asked. The veil just is. It works within the context of all the negative energies.

Would another possibly be the distortion of only seeing physicality?
No again, Tom.

What about the space-time continuum?
Yes, in a way, Tom. I know that your readers are working to decipher what the four negative energies are, and these questions are certainly reflective of this thought process. The space-time continuum is all part of the negative energy cocoon, shall we call it. Each of you not only lives within this negative energy, you are this energy. Otherwise, you could not exist for very long. That's why all the ETs that visit this planet must have protective energy suits, we'll call it, to protect them, and why they cannot stay long on the planet.

Negative Energies – the Existence of Four

Gaia, what is it about the four negative energies that make our solar system colorful?
It is simply their unique properties that cause this different hue. That's the best answer we can give you at this moment in time.

I was previously told that we would introduce only .02% to a maximum of 2% negativity to any society we visit when we start traveling to other planets. That's just enough to cause them to start raising their vibrational levels again.

Gaia, is there any negative energy leftover from the Indian-white man conflicts in the Denver, Colorado area that contributed to the school shootings in a narrow geographic area?
Yes, Tom. It was good that your reader put two and two together as that is exactly part of the reason those shootings took place. The land still carries the negative energy of what happened on the "Front Range" as it is called. There was blood spilled there as the white hunters and then troops invaded what had previously been the Indian's hunting grounds and where they spent the winters in the lower elevations.

I'm also asked if we can perhaps say a Benevolent Prayer to assist people who live there in this time period to live peacefully?
Yes, Tom. Do say a benevolent prayer, which we will assist you to compose. If you flood the area with loving energy, you will find fewer, much fewer—incidents like the three you were asking about—will happen in the future. Again, this is part of the adjustment to a new more peaceful energy.

I will also remind your readers, Tom, that each one of those three incidents involved soul contracts not only for the shooters and their victims, but for all the school children and their families who were affected by the shootings in any way. Those families felt the heartache and fear that they caused other families in a thousand wars of all kinds in the past. These events are much more complicated, shall we say, than they would appear on the surface to an average citizen.

So, let's say, this Benevolent Prayer: "I ask any and all beings to send loving energy to not only all living beings on the Colorado Front Range, but also to transmute all negative energy to that of love and compassion, thank you!"

Gaia, does playing a game where there is a winner and loser create negative energy?
Yes, it does in a way, Tom. I realize you are struggling with understanding positive and negative energies, but you do generate a negative energy with games. You create a yin and yang—polar opposites in a way.

Energy Cords

Gaia, is the energy cord between two people by soul contract, from other lives, or from some other entity or spirit?

These energy cords develop from their soul contracts, Tom. This is typically as a result of other lives these people have had together, and then they decide to have some sort of relationship in this life as part of their soul contract, you see. Their own guardian angels assist them, of course, in meeting if they are not family. There is an instant connection established that becomes the energy cord that binds them for the agreed upon time of their interaction and learning. When it is time to separate, many times this energy cord remains. It can be severed by requesting a Most Benevolent Outcome. Time is supposed to heal old wounds, but it is sometimes difficult if the energy cord is not severed.

For those not familiar with this procedure, you simply say, "I request a Most Benevolent Outcome for severing any energy cords not in my best interests at this time, thank you!"

Energy Waves

Gaia, what changes will be the result of passing through the energy waves? This includes your changes and human changes, and where did the energy waves originate?

The energy waves came from waves sent out from the center of the galaxy, Tom. That would be the easiest explanation for you and your readers. Nothing, you understand, is by happenchance, so this was conceived and planned long, long ago in anticipation of our passage through this part of the galaxy. It is all part of Creator's design as part of the Earth Experiment. There will be a boost in not only your energy, but mine and every single living thing on this planet. It will assist you in raising your vibrational levels in the Fifth Focus. Yes, there will be energy that will be difficult for those people who have a lower focus to live in, but that is part of progress; evolution is a better description. You will see many benevolent changes on Earth in the coming years, Tom. Younger people will look back at this time period in the coming years and will feel very disconnected to it, as their vibrational levels will continue to rise. That's enough for now.

Entanglement Theory

Gaia, please explain entanglement.

Entanglement is your connection to all the other souls on this planet, and that includes those having Earth lives and all those labeled Group Souls and even those Golden Light Beings people call guardian angels. Everyone is tied together, i.e., entangled, which sounds on the surface as not a good thing, but it is.

Eternity

How would you describe eternity?

Here we could have several answers, but in layman Earth terms, your Universe will last for eternity. Once it was created, few of the billions of universes are uncreated, but it has happened. Again, it is like a sculptor's clay, they can collapse a creation and start over, if they are not satisfied with what they have created.

Eyes as Windows to the Soul

Why are our eyes "windows to the soul?"

A very deep question in its own way. This occurs between two individuals who have had many lives together. Your own guardian angels make sure there is recognition on a physical level with the person you're seeing so that the connection is made. You've seen those eyes before many times, just with other people. Your eyes, your scientists will discover one day, are more complex than they can imagine.

Experiments

Gaia, are there other types of experiments going on in the Universe, and if so, what type?

As you were told before, the Earth is the major experiment. The other types of experiments going on at the present time have more to do with the ten positive energies, Tom, and are far beyond your understanding at this time.

Wasn't there supposed to be another planet working with negativity on the other side of the universe?

Yes, but again working with the 10 positive energies and not your four negative energies. You might say we flounder in describing it in terms that you can understand at this time as it is impossible for you to understand these energies when you even try to name them. Suffice to say, Tom, that the most important experiment in the Universe is the one with the Explorer Race working with the four negative energies. That will give your scientists a lot to study over the next several hundred years.

Fifth Force

Gaia, scientists say they have discovered a "Fifth Force." Your comments, please?
This is, but in a long line of discoveries about energies they are still unaware of, Tom. They are still only "scratching the surface," to again use that term. This discovery will, I might add, lead them to another energy, so they should keep working in this area. There is much to learn here.

Free Choice

Gaia, would one of the negative energies be free choice?
No, Tom. Nice guess, but free choice is not an energy so much as the ability each of you have been given should you decide not to follow the soul path you and your soul agreed would be the best path to follow, with the greatest growth in each life. As we have said before, your soul knows the crossroads, we will call them, and has a whole other set of challenges and experiences ready, should you decide to veer off the path, but the results will be having to adjust one or more lives in the future to experience those challenges.

Gaia, does judgment, blame, guilt and shame have anything to do with the four negative energies or perhaps illusions and fear?
They all exist in these four negative energies, Tom, but these feelings we will call them, also can and do exist in the ten positive energies. You can say they are amplified in the four negative energies, but are not the four negative energies, including illusions and fear. You have more fear because, without knowing your true connection with your souls, it is like jumping off a precipice.

Gaia, is one of the four negative energies separation?
No, it is not, Tom. Nice guess from your reader. In a way, all the negative energies are separate from the positive energies. They exist unto themselves.

Will scientists who study the four negative energies be social scientists?
No, Tom, I know where your reader is going with this line of questioning, and the four negative energies must be studied by quantum physics scientists, as this is much more complicated than just simply labeling. These are energies, just as the 10 positive energies are energies in their own right.

So, one of the negative energies is not competitiveness?
Again, all of your lives, Tom, work within the framework of these negative energies. You cannot label one competitiveness, or prejudicial, or racist, or deception, or greed as the questions posed by your reader asks.

Do all of those labels exist in the positive energies?
YES! Just not in the exact same way. It is much more difficult to accomplish anything while living in the four negative energies than it is in the 10 positive energies. Yes, you could describe it as moving through molasses. It takes great effort to live in the four negative energies. That's why those that volunteered for the Earth Experiment had to have great desire, along with a higher vibrational level. No one in any of the billions of universes believed that anyone could live within the confines of these four energies.

Gaia, do the four negative energies have names and what about the 10 positive energies?
Not so much names, Tom, as there is a recognition and understanding of what they do in the whole scheme of things. I know your readers seem to be stuck on names, but they simply exist. Up until the Earth Experiment, the four negative energies existed, but were shoved in a corner—like the stepchild no one talked about. Therefore, I cannot at this time simply assign some names to energies that have no names—they simply are— they exist. There is an understanding of how they work, but this is

something for your scientists to figure out in the future. I do appreciate your readers, Tom, wanting to identify these. I will say that every one of the four negative and 10 positive energies make up creation.

Would you call them building blocks?
Yes, that would be a good analysis of their function.

Gaia, are the four negative energies we work with physical or emotional?
They are physical energies, Tom. They just have not been discovered yet, and as explained before, will not be identified for many years.

So, they will be able to be measured in the future with the right equipment?
That is correct. This equipment has not yet even been dreamed about in this time period.

Frequencies

Gaia, explain the frequencies sensitive humans can feel.
Yes, most people reject these feelings as being too weird, but we do highly recommend working with these energies as it will be of great benefit to not only these sensitive humans, but to all. They can literally feel the heartbeat, we will term it, of the planet. The planet is alive as we've said numerous times, Tom. And these energies are working constantly. The ability to tune into them is a unique gift and should not be rejected.

What about wave energy?
Again, part of the energies. It's as if they feel the waves of an ocean, but it is the pulse of the Earth.

Where do the "dull energies" originate?
There are many types of energies, and this is but one of them. It is not created by outside sources I can assure you, but is simply one of many energies. One can learn to block this energy, but there are ways it can be used too. That's part of exploration. You can tune into the energy when you feel you need rest.

Would feeling a benevolent energy-being be your guardian angel or an ET?
It can be either depending upon the circumstances, although most of the time it is your guardian angel sending its love and letting you know it is there to protect and guide you, should you allow it to. That's where requesting Most Benevolent Outcomes assists them in their job. Surround yourself in white light when you feel that presence to be certain, but more than 90% of the time it will be your guardian angel. Every so often it will be your main guide who is also from your same planet sending love your way, but your guardian angel is much stronger—their energy—so you tend to feel it more.

What percentage of the population can feel energies?
It's much higher than you would think, Tom, but in a normal time period most humans just ignore these frequency shifts. So, the answer would be over fifty percent would notice these differences in frequencies.

Harmony/Disharmony

Gaia, can you touch on harmony and disordinance or disharmony?
Yes, Tom. You can tune yourself so that you do harmonize with your surroundings and even the Earth itself. You can also tune yourself to harmonize with all you meet or encounter. By the same token, you can be in disordinance—it is all up to you. This is all part of raising your vibrational level, and the higher you raise it, the more in harmony you are with not only the Earth, but all those that are attracted to you. It's that light in the darkness concept. By the same token again, you can go the other direction and be in disordinance or disharmony with all those around you. This is why we ask you to send white light and love to the planet each day as it not only raises the vibrational level of the planet, but also for you. You can also surround yourself in a bubble of white light if you feel you are in the presence of people who are unharmonious—that discordance referenced above.

Helping Souls Cross Over When We are Dreaming

Gaia, if a disaster occurs while we are in a dream state and we are

133

there, how do we comfort those people transitioning or are we just there to observe?
No, you take an active part in assisting with their transition. You help create a feeling of love and compassion and assist the transition angels in their work as there may be hundreds or even thousands transitioning at the same time. You may think they cannot hear you or respond, but it's the energy that you bring. If this happens in the future, and there will be many times all over the planet this happens, and you find yourself in a lucid dream state, concentrate on sending beautiful white light and love. You will assist in making the transition that much easier for those souls.

Honeycomb Cells and Energy

Gaia, does energy run through honeycomb cells held over someone's head pass benevolent energy and healing through our light body?
Let's just say that there needs to be more work and study in this area, Tom. There will be revelations should more study be done.

Can you combine colored lights with honeycomb cells to amplify the effects?
Special wavelengths of lights do heal. Again, we must remind you that there is much study for those interested in the ancient art of healing with lights, as the Atlanteans did. You are just now reaching that time period when you will start using these healing lights again.

Does the size of a honeycomb make a difference or just the shape?
Again, we must allow those working in this area, as soul contracts are at play here.

And last question, should these cells be made solely from organic material?
I will only say that this is an area where there should be experiments. We must allow scientists to have their "ah-ha" moments of discovery.

Human Imagination

What is human imagination? Does it already exist?

It does exist in all of you. It is your connection with your upper timeline selves, your guardian angel, and guides that constantly assist you in your daily lives and of course your soul. You are not alone—it just feels that way because you are veiled.

Human Face Templates

Gaia, do we repeat the same face template in a number of lives, or is it just that there are a limited number of templates so we cannot help, but use the same one many times or several times?
Yes, it is the latter option, Tom. Most soul fragments have 600 to 800 lives, as we have mentioned many times, and as there are less than 150 templates, it stands to reason one or more templates might be used several times, but normally the same template is not used more than, let's say, 10% of your lives. An interesting, thoughtful question.

Hunches

Gaia, do all our hunches come from our guardian angels or guides, or do some of them come directly from Creator?
Yes, all of the above. If Creator wants you to know something, that thought or feeling, or whatever you wish to call it, is sent in a split second through your guardian angels and guides—you understand everyone that is connected to you personally, including your own soul. Creator is a hands-on creator when it comes to the Earth Experiment. You might call it Creator's baby. Otherwise, your hunches and suggestions are sent to you based upon your soul contract.

Imaginary Friends

Gaia, are "imaginary friends" just a vivid imagination by a child or what?
It can certainly be imaginary, but quite often it is simply their main guide who takes on the appearance of another child. Some children are much more apt to see an image than others. This, as is noted, normally fades in time, but some children are more closely connected to Spirit at an early age. Seeing a ball floating around might be disconcerting to a child, so the

guide is able to take the form of another child. Parents should just accept the imaginary friend as long as it is a benevolent relationship. They can always surround the child with white light to make sure the child is protected.

Kauai Special Powers

Does Kauai have any special energetic powers such as Mt. Shasta or Sedona—especially Kalalau and Polihale?
Yes, Kauai is a special place that even those who do not understand energies appreciate. This dates back as you will understand to Lemurian times, but the energies of the aforementioned places on Kauai do have great energy and act as beacons of energy. This energy was pronounced, again, back to Lemurian times and was honored by those who understood such energies. Meditations can be heightened if one is nearby.

Kundalini Energy

Gaia, is there a Kundalini energy that moves from continent to continent over time?
Yes, Tom. There is this energy that permeates the Earth. It's energy that I send. Just as your bodies have a living energy, so does mine. This is a good question, Tom, but can have a very complex answer. This energy does not necessarily move over time, but connects the continents in a subliminal way, you see. It is another way for my body to energize itself thanks to the links with the Sun and other planets in this solar system and the Central Sun Alcyone in the center of this galaxy. You will find in your studies—and, yes, I mean everyone here, Tom—that life has many energetic connections. You just have to discover them. Obviously, these connections will be more on higher dimensional focuses but are even able to be detected in the 3rd dimension with the right instruments.

Life Flashing

Gaia, does life flash before your eyes before death?
Yes, in a way it does, Tom. Your memory cortex, we will call it, is stimulated, and memories flood your mind.

Light Energy over the Dark

Gaia, is light winning?
Keep in mind, Tom, that the Explorer Race's advancement is not always up, up, up, but can zig zag a little. Overall, you have made great advancements. May I remind your readers to send love and light to the planet each day. They, along with others, will assist in raising the vibrational level. And may I remind everyone that you signed up to be on Earth at this time to assist in bringing light to Earth. So do what you came to do.

Love

Gaia, is love the most powerful energy in the Universe?
Absolutely, Tom. The Creator emits love, and you can see it in the tiniest forms of life. There is the old saying, "Love conquers all." There is great truth in that statement.

Would we say that love is faster than light?
Again, absolutely. When you send love to anywhere in this Universe, it is instantaneous. Love has its own pathway.

Would it be faster than thoughts?
Thoughts are instantaneous too, Tom.

Would it be classified as more powerful than gravity?
Quite so, Tom. Love is the most powerful force in the Universe.

Lower Vibrations

Gaia, when I send white light to all those of lower vibrations that are Earthbound, does it ever help any of them, or does it just send them away?
Good question, Tom. Yes, it has aided many of them that the light reaches. It's not, let's say, an immediate jump up and head to their light, but sort of a simmer effect where as you send the light over and over throughout the weeks and months, there is finally a tipping point as you would imagine

where their own guardian angels, as they are termed, are able to cajole or urge or welcome them and they are off with them.

Some soul fragments, as you might imagine, Tom, are so Earthbound due to quite negative lives they led that it can take a long time to recover, but as you know there is no time here, so they don't miss out on anything, shall we say, but to answer your question, yes, send and continue to send them light as each time you do it lightens just a tiny bit and you, along with others who do the same, eventually do make a difference, so please continue your efforts.

Meaning of Life

Gaia, what else is the meaning of life for us?
That is such a broad question, Tom. Your soul's desire to be a creator one day. For you, that is the meaning of life. The meaning of life can be different for different soul fragments, but as far as the Explorer Race goes, that is the motivation, to raise your vibrational level as fast as you can, and I will add you are doing a good job to accomplish that.

Merging into Creator

Gaia, what will be the catalyst for us to merge into a Creator?
When it is deemed by this Creator that your combined level of knowledge is sufficient to do the job—to handle the trillions of decisions per second and not be overwhelmed. Part of that will be a collective understanding and use of the four negative energies, along with the 10 positive energies. They must be, and will be, integrated throughout this Universe—not just a few thousand planets in this galaxy. Many of you, especially after the end of the Earth Experiment, will continue to pick Creator's knowledge of why this is so and that is so. Still, Creator believes you will accomplish this steep learning curve, and your souls are determined to reach that level of knowledge and understanding. For me, it will be like old friends suddenly becoming one.

Most Benevolent Outcomes (MBO)

*Regarding MBOs, you request them for **specific** things for you. If you're about to drive to work, you request a MBO for a safe drive to work. Then you drive and find the drive is easier than before, or perhaps there is a wreck that you pass by, and you think how "lucky" you were not to have been five minutes earlier. Or you see the police have just pulled over someone before you passed. You learn to **trust** in requesting **Most Benevolent Outcome**s for the mundane things in life and you slowly expand to all the important requests, which typically take much longer, so you have to remain patient.*

Is saying a benevolent prayer for others multiple times good or is it similar to a MBO request where you say it just one time?

Keep in mind that the MBO requests are specifically for you, and only need to be said one time, although as we have said many times, you are not penalized if you say them multiple times. Benevolent prayers are a little different. Many times you are saying Benevolent Prayers for people all over the world in dire need, and these Benevolent Prayers, as we have said before, have a crescendo effect as more and more people say the same Benevolent Prayer. Each time you say a Benevolent Prayer that adds to the energy. You not only raise the Earth's vibrational level by being compassionate towards others, but you also raise your vibrational level too. You can never say a Benevolent Prayer too many times. And finally, please say these Benevolent Prayers for forgiveness each day as you touch your lives in all time periods—past, present, and future that are all going on at the same time.

Is there any difference if Most Benevolent Outcomes and Benevolent Prayers are said with a lot of background noise?

Not one bit. Your verbal voice cuts through these sounds.

Gaia, why aren't Most Benevolent Outcomes available to humans in all our lives?

Even in its heyday, we will call it, in Atlantean times, only one million out of several million used this simple tool to lead easier lives. Younger souls like to be told what to do, instead of taking charge of their own lives. They don't believe they have control. It takes a little older soul in terms of lives on Earth to realize how much easier their lives can be. As you say in your blogs, Tom, people can't believe it is so easy, but it is. More people will be attracted to The Gentle Way in the future. It will not disappear as it did in the Atlantean times.

Gaia, are we at cross purposes with you if we say Benevolent Prayers for rain to put out forest fires?
It is better to say benevolent prayers for the safety of people and all the inhabitants of the forest, Tom. As I have explained before, forest fires allow the forests to regenerate with new growth.

Gaia, can people request Most Benevolent Outcomes for less destructive and more constructive use of your energy?
This may be a little difficult to describe to you, Tom, but the answer is yes and no. There are times during which you can request a change in energy from what seems malevolent to more benevolent, but there are times when I must release this energy in its purest form as it may seem malevolent to you, but for me this energy is sucking out negative energy from my body and releasing it into the atmosphere. And keep in mind that your souls have approved this release of energy as, say, a tornado, hurricane, or earthquake for the experiences they must have to finish their work here. So that is the reason for my fence-sitting answer. You can request a change in the energy, but whether I can answer your request extends up to your higher selves.

Gaia, I'm asked how does everyone or at least a number of people saying the same Benevolent Prayer work?
Yes, Tom. This would be difficult to explain to even a quantum scientist, so perhaps just a little more this morning. When everyone says the same Benevolent Prayer it sets up a very benevolent vibration in the Universe—yes, not only this planet, but the Universe. And I and many other souls contribute and respond to this positive vibration, if you will. When enough people say the same prayer then you raise your vibrational level and all those all over the Earth, not, let's say, just in the United States.

Therefore, you are tapping into a universal field when these prayers are all said together or within a short time period together. They have a crescendo effect. Violence has its own vibration and cannot occur if enough people say the same prayer. It blocks the vibration of violence. Let's let everyone "chew" on that for a while.

*Let's all say this Benevolent Prayer **out loud**: "I ask any and all beings to assist in bringing peace to the world, and may this occur even faster than we can hope for or expect, thank you!"*

Gaia, does praying out loud activate the throat chakra, or does talking in general do the same?

Yes, your throat chakra is in constant vibration, shall we say, but when you pray it reaches a whole other level, especially when certain notes are reached and, needless to say, in conjunction with other throat chakras emitting the same sound. We have suggested that much more study remains here, and we will not take away the ah-ha moment of discovery.

Does our saying the Forgiveness Benevolent Prayer each day help the other timelines that do not?

Obviously not as much as them saying the Benevolent Prayers themselves, but yes, there is a radiant effect both down and upwards to the other timelines. But sending them white light and love to these other timelines does have a significant effect on them. So, for those sending white light to the planet each day, there is a cumulative effect.

Negative Spirits

Gaia, do negative spirits have a form like our guides do?

Yes, a portion of negative spirits can form globules, we will call them. Still, they are affected by sending them white light to scatter away, while losing their power. Good question, Tom.

Gaia, please explain the purpose of negative spirits. For what purpose did the Creator of this Universe create them or were they attracted to this creation?

The Creator did not create them, Tom, but welcomed them with open arms as part of the negative experiment. You might say they anchor the negativity. And, as was said before, their numbers are not increasing nor decreasing. As your positive energy grows, theirs does not grow to counteract this energy.

Theo has told me he does not like these negative spirits, or are they whole souls?
They are not whole souls. Their actions are irritating to say the least. This is why you are asked or told to surround yourself with white light each time we do these sessions.

They are allowed to exist even around humans, so how do they try and influence us?
Ah, a good question. They try and influence people to actions that are negative for their mind, body, and spirit, but when you surround yourself with white light, they can have no influence over you whatsoever.

Gaia, I feel like I'm missing something here, am I?
Yes, there are more questions to ask, but you or your readers must ask them. I can only answer what is specifically asked. Those are the rules.

Gaia, are dark energies mirroring us?
No, Tom, they exist but are not mirrors or opposites of you. They are separate entities but are there to take advantage of those whose energy fields are low. The stronger your aura, the less effect they can have.

So, forgiving someone would have nothing to do with releasing any dark energies?
It certainly lightens your soul, but we're talking about apples and oranges here. We realize this whole subject is confusing, but you will have more questions on the subject in the future as your readers come up with questions.

Gaia, what can people do to be permanently free of negative spirits?
Yes, this can be difficult for some people, Tom, who have attracted negative spirits either through illness of various sorts to addiction to drugs, and even being in the presence for long periods of time with people who have their own negative attachments. As we have recommended in the past, you can request a Most Benevolent Outcome to sever all energy cords not in your best interests. This brings your guardian angel into play and

becomes a mighty force for you.

Then you should surround yourself with white light each day and breathe in the white light in a meditation. This should be done without fail each day. Then, if a person still feels threatened, there are those that will assist in clearing negative entities such as your friend Richard Sutphen. We must also mention that belief systems enter into the picture. If a person believes strongly in negative entities, then that helps in attracting them to that person. They must change their thinking so that they understand that their guardian angel is a whole soul with tremendous powers should they continue to call on it to provide protection and root out any negative attachments. Your GAs are much stronger than any negative attachment, we can assure you.

Are negative spirits limited in their vibrational level?
They are basically at one negative level but can feed on a human's negative level to grow stronger.

Do they exist in all universes?
Good question, as yes, when any of the billions of creators create a universe, there are remnants of the fabric that is left over that your scientists will not discover for a very long time. These remnants are pieces of the fabric. They are sent love. In human terms, it would be like the canvas of a painter, or the clay that an artist uses to create.

Number of Souls Needed to Inhabit a Planet

Gaia, I've been meaning to ask if Earth is the only planet in the Universe with such a large contingent of souls—four million I believe I was told—involved in the operations of a planet, correct?
Absolutely, Tom. The Earth Experiment required a large contingent of souls to assist me, including all of the group souls of all the beings living on Earth. There are many other ways in which Earth is unique in the Universe, but certainly the number of souls involved here would be at the top of the list.

Older Souls

Do older souls have higher vibrational levels than younger souls?
Yes. Each time you cross from one quadrant to the next in younger, medium, and old souls in terms of Earth lives, your vibrational level rises. There is a larger jump with your move from say the younger soul category to medium, and likewise to the old soul four quadrants.

Planning our Earth Life

Gaia, how far in advance do our souls preplan our lives, and are there any changes just before birth?
As we have explained before, Tom, your souls are much more than even you can imagine, although you've come a long way in your understanding. When the Earth Experiment was being set up, you could say, they chose the time periods well over a million years in advance, and the type of lives they would have in those time periods, along with coordinating with other souls who would be having their soul clusters in those time periods. As you might imagine, this is a great planning process far beyond your understanding at this time.

Regarding changes prior to birth, yes, there are tweaks in the soul plans and soul contracts. And, as we have said before, you are also constantly rewriting your pasts and futures as you experience these lives and grow and raise your vibrational levels. Your memories of the past adjust too.

Positive Energy and the Explorer Race

Gaia, after the Earth Experiment finishes in 7,000 years or so, and the Explorer Race goes back to our home planets, will you switch to positive energy, as I've been told in the past that Earth will become a place to visit and enjoy the beauty?
Not precisely, Tom, but by then the amount of negativity will be so small it will not bother anyone, as keep in mind you will be introducing negativity to all the rest of the Universe. Therefore, it will not bother any of the beings who come to Earth on vacation.

Orbs

Gaia, does the consciousness of the photographer affect what is seen of orbs in photos?
Not really, Tom. They do like to be seen for a variety of reasons, so they may appear to remind you that they are present, or even to remind you that they exist.

Does the aura affect photos?
No, but the number of lives you've had on Earth will affect how experienced are the orbs you see in the photos.

Do the orbs give the photographer any information on an unrecognizable level to the photographer or the people in the photographs?
Yes, because on another level you understand the difference in colors and the details of the orbs themselves. Remember, in the past I told you that someone in the future will study orbs and what the colors and rings and such mean.

Are the orbs ever lit by our auras?
No.

Do any of these orbs merge?
No, they remain separate entities.

Does taking of photos increase our vibrational level?
Only if you study them and realize you are assisted in your life—but just a bit, not so much.

Are large orbs typically your main guide or what?
A main guide certainly will have more intricate detail, but there can be other orbs that are your guides, or someone else's guides that appear in the photos.

Gaia, are birds and animals attracted to orbs for healing?
Tom, they are attracted to orbs for a variety of reasons. They are much more able to see them, but they can also feel them. The more complex orbs can also leave healing energies animals can feel. And the orbs do this

knowing in advance, having been advised by the group soul.

Gaia, are most orbs non-human?
Typically, there are one or two guide orbs around most people, but that pales in comparison to the large number of soul fragments you term "orbs" that are headed for staging areas each day.

Plant Communication

How can we tune into plants?
You can send them love. You can say benevolent prayers for your plants. Give them love and they will flourish. You can also communicate with them, should you desire. They are open to communication anytime.

Possession

Gaia, please explain more about possession.
Yes, we have touched on these negative spirits before, left over from the creation of galaxies, suns, and planets. They have an energy that is waning. On other worlds they have no power at all, but in the Earth Experiment, when working with the four negative energies, they do have some power, although it is slowly waning now. As we have commented before, various forms of substance abuse can open the door for what you term as possession. And, yes, mental illness can also be an open door too. Then great amounts of white light are needed to break this possession. Wrapping yourself in a bubble of white light is transformative. Prayers said out loud for those affected does bring in their guardian angels to assist. This is a learning experience for everyone involved.

Predictive Dreams

What is the purpose of predictive dreams since we normally cannot interfere or are given enough information to keep an event from happening?
Your soul fragments are all interconnected, Tom, and keep in mind that your souls all sign off on these catastrophic events. Most people ignore these dreams, which in many cases are symbolic in nature, such as the

dream you had of a Delta-shaped aircraft crashing prior to the Delta airlines crash in the 1980s at the DFW Airport.

Some can be warning dreams as you had when you dreamed of the bomb and changed your schedule away from Manilla, and some are simply to let people know so that it is not such a shock to their system when the event occurs. You have many predictive dreams in each of your lives—and I'm talking about all of your readers—but most do not record their dreams as you and a small percentage do. If they did, they would see symbolic dreams of challenges in their future along with great successes. It takes work to record your dreams each night, but the results are quite gratifying.

Are dreams part of anchoring an event?
In a way, yes, but not as asked. There is the planned or problematic event and then comes the dreams.

Sending Light

Gaia, when we send light to the world does it actually help those people who have secrets to reveal?
Yes, an interesting question to begin the day, Tom. When you send light, and there are many others in the world who send light to the world too, you all have this great cumulative effect of literally lighting the world vibrationally to assist those who carry burdensome secrets to reveal them in the light of day, shall we say. So, yes, you do assist those people to reveal secrets of activities not in humanity's best interests.

Gaia, how can we raise our vibrational levels?
It will go even faster if all of your readers start sending love and light to the planet each day. Only a percentage of your readers do this at the present time. They have not learned how big a difference they can make, even with such a small number as compared to the overall population.

What response can you give those who say they can't see a difference they're making in sending light and love to planet Earth?
As humans, Tom, you doubt everything. Saying a prayer—sending light and love—is done on faith that you can make a difference in assisting in

raising the vibrational level of the Earth. Many people do not send light and love, and that is your choice. It just means that it will take longer for you as humans to raise your vibrational level. Thankfully, more and more people are sending light and love, or in some other way saying a prayer for the planet you live on.

Again, the choice is yours. You can sit on your hands and do nothing your whole life, or you can take an active part. Perhaps it is not sending light and love, but in some other way you work to make Earth a better place to live, and that does contribute to raising society's vibrational level and with it the planet's.

*All you have to do is each morning say **out loud**: "I send white light and love to every single continent, every single island, all the rivers, lakes and streams, the oceans and seas of the world, and I release this light to light up the darkest parts of Earth, thank you!"*

Soul Contracts

I'm asked if great wealth, longevity, good health, and even wisdom are all things we will experience on Earth before our Earth lives are finished?
Certainly, Tom. And you can add to that list hundreds of other conditions, including: poverty, sickness, short lives, ignorance, just to name the ones that are opposite of what your reader asked. Nothing is left out of your Earth Experience by the time you all move on. I will add here—you will be the leaders of the Universe one day.

What about free will as it relates to soul contracts?
Certainly, you all have free will, Tom, and I understand there are many misconceptions, even though this has been explained before. Soul contracts are what you and your own soul decides is the path you will try and take during any given life, to be the perfect life for learning for the benefit of your soul. This does not mean that you will be wealthy, or healthy or any of the possibilities we mentioned above. It simply means that you are trying as best you are able to follow that path.

But you do have free will and that will lead you off that path, which you and your own soul or higher self wishes you to take. In many cases it is quite a bit worse result than had you remained on course. And I will mention this for your reader and others—a great big hint—Most Benevolent Outcomes keep you on your soul path or contract. That is perhaps not the only way to achieve this, Tom, but it is certainly the easiest way to remain on your chosen path.

Gaia, what percentage of free will do we have in our predestined lives?
As we have explained before, each of you has a soul contract that you and your soul agreed would result in the highest learning in this life. You, your soul, and your guardian angel and guides all work to try and stay on that soul path during your life on Earth. But because you do have free will, as part of being veiled, you can stray off that path, and then there are another whole set of challenges already prepared, should you do so. But they do not result in as much learning as you and your soul hoped for. We have advised you to request a Most Benevolent Outcome to stay on your soul contract, and that will keep you on your chosen path.

Gaia, how many lifetimes does it take to understand "seizing the day?"
It can be just one, or many.

Does this living life to the fullest depend on soul contracts or free will?
It typically takes a number of lives to take what one has learned so far and put it to good use—to be a success in life. One gains this knowledge over a number of lives in a variety of roles. One must learn to adapt. Free will, as we have explained before, can mean that you go off on a path where you learn less than had you stayed on your soul contract. Each time you return, you vow to stay on your soul contract in the upcoming life. That is another reason we remind your readers, Tom, to request Most Benevolent Outcomes constantly, as they do just that—keep you on your soul contracts.

Unconditional Love

Will we in any way introduce the unconditional love we experience

from our dogs and cats, and other pets to other planets?
That is a nice thought and question. These pets are here to teach you unconditional love. When the Explorer Race goes to the stars, starting around that period of time in 3250, you will be bringing that negative energy with you, which will again raise their vibrational levels, making everyone you encounter more loving. So no, you will not take your pets along, but they will have accomplished their goal on a soul level to teach you to love all those you encounter equally.

Will we bring all four negative energies to these other planets?
Yes, they cannot be separated. Each energy has its own purpose, as you will one day learn.

Will these other planets be required to accept? What about the Vegans and Lyrans?
All will understand that Creator wants them to accept these negative energies and begin to grow again. A society can be billions of years old but still has much room for growth.

Vibrational Levels and Predicted Events

Gaia, I'm still trying to understand why there are changing of predicted events. Would one thing that enters the equation be the changing of energies, and is that not the same as our vibrations, or is it something different?
Ah, Tom, you are continuing to explore, and I like that. Yes, certainly changing energies does affect whether an event will occur or not. And, yes, part of these energies, and I should say the majority, would be your change in vibrational level. This is more important than you perhaps realize at this time.

Your energies are evolving, shall we call it, so fast these days that many on this side are astounded, but very happy and pleased for you. Naturally, a part of that is your work and others too, Tom. Although your numbers may seem small, remember that it takes only a small percentage of people to change the world for the better. And, yes, there are people even who read your writings that say these benevolent prayers and it does change the energies involved for the better. As I have told you before, I must allow you to see your successes, Tom, so I do change events based on the change of energy that you request. So, it is not some energy that I have not mentioned to you before, but the energy your own people that follow your writings invoke.

But then we do get into the probabilities don't we, which leads us back to the same point of how can we trust the probability of any event you tell me is basically 100% when it is not?
Yes, I see where you are going, Tom, but there will be events where they happen exactly as predicted and others change as the last two did. The equation as you call it is not set in stone but can be ever changing based on all sorts of energies.

Vibrational Levels Variance from Life to Life

Does our frequency change from life to life as we have good guy-lives, then bad guy, then good guy again?
During these lives your vibrational level can go up and down. When you rejoin your soul, there is a cleansing in preparation for the next life.

White Light

Gaia, is visualizing and sending white light and love the best way, or is there something better?
I know you must ask these questions that come from your readers, Tom, but most of your readers know the answer to this one—requesting Most Benevolent Outcomes and asking for Benevolent Prayers out loud. You still have those who doubt the enormous effect of using sound. This will be proven by science one day, but in the meantime, I highly encourage all of your readers who have not yet begun to use Most Benevolent Outcomes and Benevolent Prayers in their lives to start experimenting.

For those doubters, look on this as an experiment, just as you did many years ago. They will be amazed, just as you were, that this truly works. So, keep sending white light and love, as, yes, that works, but you can triple and quadruple the effect if you and perhaps your friends say a Benevolent

Prayer for whomever you are sending love and light to. I guarantee it.

Gaia, what response can you give those who say they can't see a difference they're making in sending light and love to planet Earth?
As humans, Tom, you doubt everything. Saying a prayer—sending light and love—is done on faith that you can make a difference in assisting in raising the vibrational level of the Earth. Many people do not send light and love, and that is your choice. It just means that it will take longer for you as humans to raise your vibrational level. Thankfully, more and more people are sending light and love, or in some other way saying a prayer for the planet you live on. Again, the choice is yours. You can sit on your hands and do nothing your whole life, or you can take an active part. Perhaps it is not sending light and love, but in some other way you work to make Earth a better place to live, and that does contribute to raising society's vibrational level, and with it the planet's.

Is there an actual increase in far-right thinking?
Here we return to the young soul's experiences, just as there are those who would be considered far left. Both ends of the spectrum are learning—gaining experience.

Chapter 7
Metaphysical Tools

Astrology

Gaia, please explain the benefits and limitations of astrology.
Ah, a good subject to begin the day, Tom. Astrology has many benefits, but some limitations. Astrological charts of a person's birth can be a great help not only to the parents of a new baby, so that they can guide him or her in their formative years regarding different interests the child will have or should be introduced to, but can act as a guide for the young person who by the time they reach their teen years have completely forgotten their previous lives on Earth, and wander around wondering what they should do in life.

Then there are the transits of the planets, Moon, and, yes, even stars, as to how they affect each human in different ways. There are times to "make hay while the Sun shines" and times to wait and just take care of what you must. The 12 houses each play a part in a person's life as the Moon, Sun, and planets revolve around the Earth, it seems from an astrological point of view. You used an astrological forecast to become the first tour operation in Dallas to ever run a trip to the Superbowl for Dallas Cowboys fans. Naturally, you had to be open to that possibility, but you took advantage of that to boost significantly your tour business. And then used the transits to choose the best times for the ski club parties. These are just a couple of examples of how astrology was given to the Explorer Race as one of the tools to use while you are veiled on Earth.

So, why don't more people utilize this tool, Tom? Naturally, there are religious sects that preach against it as the work of witches and dark souls. The yin and yang or positive and negative opposites in any Earth life. Yet, as you have noticed, over the years, Tom, astrologers can see a transit where there are squares, oppositions, and conjunctions of the bodies in their relation to Earth but are not able to accurately predict what the results of these transits will actually have on your population. They now have the ability to look back at the same transits over the past couple of thousand years, but this only gives a hint of what will play out. Astrology will become a little more accurate in the future as astrologers will have more history at their fingertips. The best astrologers will also combine numerology into the equation to make more accurate predictions. Until then, there will be limitations on what they can predict with any accuracy.

You have said previously that astrology shows divine intent in the planning of lives prior to birth. What other benefits can you list?

Tom, each individual chart shows a person's aptitudes and weaknesses. It gives you a blueprint of what you can work on in this life while reminding you of the planning that goes into each life on Earth. Astrology can also give you information about relationships—those that will be beneficial and loving and those that are diametrically opposed in their thinking or actions in comparison to yours. Everyone should learn more about astrology and have their own individual chart done. You will see your connection to past lives and what you need to work on in this life.

Gaia, have the astrological signs shifted with the reported movement of the constellations?

There has not been a significant shift in these constellations over the last few thousand years since astrology was invented. It would be considered minute. It will take many thousands of years more before there would be a noticeable difference. Astrology was and is one of the tools made available to humans for you to learn more about yourselves and your personalities and a little bit about your futures as you continue.

Gaia, will a new planet being discovered cause a new sign to be added to the Zodiac?

No, Tom, it will simply help your astrologers to be more accurate since the planet does have an influence on your bodies and minds.

Gaia, is it correct that the North Node in the 12th house represents a spiritual life and the South Node in the 12th house is a sign of one's

last life on Earth?

Certainly, the North Node in the 12th house can represent a spiritual life, but is not the only indicator, just as the South Node in the 12th house can accompany one's last life but can have other meanings as well. We will leave it to your astrologers to debate that point, as they cannot see the whole set of lives. They will find this placement in multiple lives, not just the final one.

Gaia, if ETs gave astrology to all the races, how far back does the study of stars and planets originate?

Far, far back, Tom. Don't forget that those same societies that introduced astrology to the races looked up at the stars and their planets and moons in their solar systems millions and, yes, even billions of years ago. Their sophistication is well beyond your abilities to interpret transits and placements because you have not yet discovered even all of the influences in your own solar system. This will come in time, but to answer your reader's question, it dates back to as long as there have been intelligent beings in the Universe.

Were the races given a star map or did we have to create one ourselves?

No, here they were given help to basically explain the constellations and planets. They were not allowed to give you everything, so they provided the basics. And, yes, those figures drawn of the appearance of the constellations were to help you in identifying those clusters of stars. It was as if you connected the dots for a picture a child would understand.

Gaia, you said in the past that ETs taught astrology to both the Mayans and the Chinese. Did they teach astrology to all the races seeded, or did astrology migrate from, let's say, these two centers?

Good question, Tom. No, this knowledge was given to all the races including the Egyptians, Atlanteans, Lemurians, and Caucasians. Some chose to use this tool more than others, but this tool was given equally to all. It was one of several tools given to try and assist you in dealing with hard lives on Earth. Then, individually, people decided to use this tool or reject it as nonsense and go about their lives without the benefit of knowing more about themselves, others, and transits of planets, the Moon, stars, the sun, and so on. The Gentle Way falls under this, in a way, as some people benefit from its use every day and others reject it as hocus pocus or some other such nonsense. Each person has their own soul path in each life.

Gaia, did the proclamation that Pluto is not a planet affect astrological charts in any way?

Not in the least, Tom. Pluto does influence you and everyone else, just as the so-called planets do. These are astrological bodies, and some have more influence on you than do others such as Jupiter and Saturn, simply because of their immense size.

How will the new Planet 9 affect the astrological charts?

The discovery will simply fill in a gap as to how you are influenced by the planets, Tom. Those who are professional astrologers will see how this dark planet, we will call it, affects and influences you.

Is there anything on Pluto we are not meant to see?

None, Tom. All these planets in this solar system are available for you to explore in one form or another. This is part of your training so that when the Explorer Race goes to the stars you will be able to instantly recognize other similar planets. You will find similar planets throughout the Universe.

Celtic Necklace

Gaia, what is the story on the ancient Celtic necklace?

Yes, an interesting necklace, Tom. As they have deduced, it was worn in various ceremonies of the time and was infused with this energy. It would be like comparing it to a recording of images and feelings of that time period. They should allow a sensitive person, perhaps even someone with psychic abilities, to unlock more of its secrets. A good sensitive should be able to do that for them.

Crystals

Gaia, can crystals at home be charged using commonly available

resources?

Yes, and no. Another one of those answers, Tom. The resources are commonly available, but how they would be utilized has to be rediscovered from ancient Atlantean times. In modern times people have resisted on a subconscious level, as we have spoken about before, due to fear of repeating their misuse. That will never happen again. Soon there will be those who rediscover this free energy and this will change the world, bringing energy to remote villages that have no electricity or running water.

Gaia, did the Atlanteans and/or Lemurians ever put crystals into water in order to charge it or change it for healing purposes?

Yes, but as you're thinking, Tom, there was more to it than that. The crystals were charged before placing them in water, so there was truly a dynamic change in the molecules. Your scientists will learn how to recreate this in the not-too-distant future.

Were different colored crystals used for different illnesses?

Quite so. But, again, we will state that without charging these crystals little will be accomplished.

Fingerprints

Gaia, why do the Adam and Eve-model humans have fingerprints?

You have already seen why as they are used for identification purposes. There was great thinking that went into this part of your body. As it was decided upon one body and not multiple ones such as many species of animals have, you needed some type of identification. You would term this divine design. There is also the message that each one of you is unique in the eyes of the Creator. That's a powerful yet subliminal message to each of you.

How does that tie in with Palmistry?

It's just an expansion of that idea. Not only are you unique, but the lines on the palm of your hand, although not as unique, let's say, can reveal much about yourself and your soul contract. There is still more to learn in this area.

What about reading Tarot cards?

This has more to do with learning to read messages sent from one's higher self. The subject cuts the cards, aided by their own Guardian Angel. Then that person's guardian angel whispers in the ear of the Tarot reader messages that go beyond the face of the cards. It is simply a way to send messages from the guardian angel to the person when they are not open to meditation.

I assume that Astrology is somewhat similar?

Yes, this is another way to show the person that they are unique and have a soul contract. It shows them there was planning on this side for the exact minute they were born. All of this is by divine design, although it is not recognized on the surface as being so.

Guardian Angels

Gaia, what purpose or desires do our guardian angels have if not to meld with us to become a creator?

Tom, not everyone in the Universe wants to meld into a creator. I will be perfectly happy to remain the soul of the Earth thousands of years into the future. I enjoy my work, just as those souls you call Golden Light Beings enjoy theirs. When the Earth Experiment is over, they will have many opportunities to use their knowledge in thousands of ways. And when your souls meld and become a creator, I'm quite sure you will call on them for assignments. Your path is extremely unique, but it is your path, not theirs.

Golden Light Beings

You are a quantum master. What do Golden Light Beings, such as Theo, aspire to?

Over eons of time, they will continue to raise their vibrational levels—just not as fast as the Explorer Race volunteers. Those Golden Light Beings that are taking part in the Earth Experiment are quite happy with their jobs. They have never been so busy, and it is quite exciting to handle hundreds of thousands of soul fragments in all of their lives on Earth all taking part at the same time. After you eventually meld into a Creator, you have the option of creating a new job for them—and I might add there are many options. We will all have to wait to see what you, as a creator, will create yourself.

Do you or Theo ever give us false information, and if so, why?
As you have been told many times, Tom, no human is 100% perfect in receiving this information we give. You override the answers we give, which you have experienced many times. Then there are times we are asked about a specific event, and if we give you the correct answer it will interfere with one or more soul contracts. We do our best to avoid answering those questions. I have explained to you in the past that, let's say, someone's soul contract is to experience a tornado or earthquake. If we were to say that it will take place at this minute or that minute on such a day, there would be a number of people that would leave and not have that experience. So, the answer to this question will be that it all depends on soul contracts.

Numerology and Sacred Geometry

Gaia, how does numerology and sacred geometry fit in with the Earth Experiment? And is this used in the rest of the Universe?
They are used extensively in the rest of the Universe. On Earth you have a long way to go in understanding and being able to use numerology and sacred geometry. These are great tools and should be studied. We have touched on numerology in the past as one of the tools to help understand such things as your soul path, but numerology is much more complex than is even known today by thousands of people who study it.

Will it help or hinder our understanding when we convert to the 12 number system?
Yes, it is like you have only a portion of the numeric system used in the rest of the Universe. Regarding sacred geometry, this gets into why pyramids were built on ley lines. Much more study lies ahead for your mathematicians and scientists.

Will we know much more about all this in this century?
You will begin "filling in the blanks" in your understanding, but it will be the next century, or at least the end of this century, since this is not seen as

a priority to study.

Gaia, do paintings of sacred geometry symbols have a powerful effect on people who see the paintings?
They can if they study the paintings, as compared to someone just looking at the painting and moving onto other paintings, let's say in an art gallery. If they can breathe in the painting, then they will receive messages and images associated with that particular sacred geometry symbol. These paintings should be exhibited in a calm location where people can absorb the symbology.

Other Side

Where is the Other Side? Is it away from the Earth?
Yes, and no, Tom. Keep in mind that when your soul fragment leaves your body upon your transition, in the dimension you exist you can be everywhere. That is so hard to understand that you are in or return to a quantum state. Even the best minds have a hard time understanding this, so don't think I'm avoiding the question, but your soul fragment returns to exist in another dimension.

Palmistry

Gaia, is palmistry a valid form of prognostication, or simply messages downloaded to the palm readers' minds having been sent by their GAs?
Here we can say, Tom, that palmistry is connected to the messages one receives from spirit. All prognostication comes from spirit—it is not separated from messages from spirit and simple prognostication. There is no such separation whether the message seems like a simple forecast or a more complex message, its origination is the same—it all begins with spirit. Then it depends upon the knowledge and sophistication of the palm reader as they interpret what they see.

Gaia, did humans have the ability from the beginning to read palms?
It was later, Tom, as that was the least of their concerns at that time. It took thousands of years for them as they discovered the differences between

humans to see that their fingerprints were different from each other, and that the palms held keys to their existence. Naturally, these revelations were given to those whose soul contracts were to receive these messages from spirit.

Was it a particular ET race that suggested or contributed the lines?
It was a combination as they collectively knew you first needed the subliminal message that each human is unique through fingerprints, and that your own palms could reveal your length of life and much more about your personality.

Why are the left and right palms somewhat different?
That's for those who study palms to have that inspiration.

Is there much more to discover about our palms?
Yes, there is more to discover. Those that read palms should request Most Benevolent Outcomes to learn more about the science of palmistry—and, yes, it is a science that your scientific community has ignored thinking it is a bunch of folderol. Each part of the human body has a purpose, and the palms are just as important in their own way as fingerprints are.

Do the lines on our feet provide unique information about us as do the lines on our hands?
Yes, but it will necessitate a great deal of study by someone to ascertain subtle differences.

When will the lines on our feet be completely decoded or understood?
Quite a long time, Tom, as this is not a priority for most people.

Power Animal Spirits

Gaia, do we have one or more power animal spirits as our guides?
An interesting question, Tom. This is where your beliefs enter the picture. If, as an example, you are an indigenous person that believes in animal spirits, then one can be attracted to that person, or to a whole tribe. Generally, most societies of the world do not have this belief, so they do not have an animal spirit protector. The only exception to this would be

their beloved dogs who remain with them for a time after their transition before moving on.

Premonitions

Gaia, where and how does premonition originate?
These are events that one becomes aware of. You begin to feel these as a high probability through your pineal gland, acting as an antenna. Your own guardian angel can be sending these messages to you, especially if there is danger involved. Your guardian angel wants you to stay on track, and some event could result in injury or death, so your guardian angel signals you what is coming.

Psychometry

Gaia, is psychometry another form of telepathy, or does it work differently?
You can say it is a form of telepathy but relies on other initial receptors that still feed in through the pineal gland. Your scientists are just discovering the organ in the body just below the layers of skin. Amazing, isn't it, that given as many dissections of the human body have been done that this was not discovered before. And, yes, there are many more discoveries ahead for those in science as we would not want them to be bored now, would we? So, back to psychometry. The information is conveyed from the fingertips up to the pineal gland where the images are then seen by the person adept in this procedure or work. It is but another ability that can be increased, again, with a lot of practice. It is something that can be taught, or through practice with certain objects of, say, different ages. It takes concentration and practice.

White Light

Gaia, how much good does it do for one person to send white light and love all over the world?
Quite a bit, Tom, even more than you can comprehend, as humans are quite powerful. And when you get several thousand people doing this—and I'm just speaking of your group—then you make a tremendous difference. You

shine light and love on places where some people think there is no love. It truly acts as a catalyst for change. Slowly, more of your people are beginning to join in and say the Benevolent Prayers, and in doing so you accomplish almost miraculous things. Even the rescue of the Thai boys would not have gone so smoothly without those Benevolent Prayers your group said. There would have been more loss of life, since there were soul contracts standing in the wings, shall we say, for exits. You helped create a great feeling of love worldwide, so don't sell yourselves short. Send love and white light together each day and doing this will be multiplied, energy-wise, many times over.

Gaia, is there a difference between white light and gold light?
Tom, I know that you know the difference between gold and white light, but for your readers, white light is the strongest and purest light in the Universe. Gold light is strong, but white light is the purest of all. That's why we have you establish a bubble of white light first, then a bubble of gold light on the outside as an extra added protection. We want your reception to be as perfect as it can be on Timeline 6.

Gaia, when we surround ourselves in white light, how long does it last?
Good question. Typically, this is controlled by your own GA, and allows it to subside if not needed.

Gaia, what is the difference in sending white or violet light to someone or something?
For the present time, stick with white light, Tom. You can't go wrong. You will learn in the future that there are times to send a different colored light, depending upon the situation. I am being just a tad vague here, as this is something for the population to learn and understand as you study how colors are used in healing. That understanding is not too far in the future.

Gaia, how is gold light different from white light?
White light is the purest form of light there is. Gold light comes in second and adds properties that your scientists have yet to discover but will in the coming years. Therefore, I can only comment just a little. One must think, "How does this light affect me compared to white light?"

How does it protect us?

Again, it's the properties contained in the light. We have suggested to you to surround yourself in white light, but then also a bubble of gold light. We would not have done so if it was just something to do. It diffuses the dark properties prior to encountering the white light. That is the best explanation we can give to a person not educated in quantum physics.

Chapter 8
Souls

Age Levels of Souls

Are most hardline conservative politicians in that same younger soul mold?
Quite so since they come from the fundamentalist religions.

Are there equal amounts of genders in young, medium, and seasoned souls?
Yes, almost equal.

What place in the world would be considered to have the most seasoned souls?
Again, there is no place on Earth with a preponderance of seasoned souls. You would think it would be some place such as India, but in reality, seasoned souls choose lives to further not only continuing to raise their vibrational levels, but also to assist others in doing the same. It is the old saying of "one for all and all for one" as they know they must assist in raising or they will never achieve their goal. That's why you keep coming back, Tom, as you keep pushing people along.

Would you say that rural areas are mostly populated by younger souls where life is a little slower than in busy cities?
Yes, Tom. Mostly younger with some older souls mixed in to provide lessons to the younger souls. There has to be some sharp cookies to teach the younger ones lessons and it can be souls who need lives where they are considered the bad guy.

Will there be a time when young souls are a minority and medium and old souls a majority?

Yes, but not for some time, Tom. The world population has to reduce, and that is slowly happening by people having fewer children, plus the normal experiences such as the pandemic and other Earth events. So, when, you ask? Yes, well over 1,000 years—more on the order of 4,000 or more years, Tom. There will be young souls in every time period. A variety of learning is needed, and just as people these days go back in time for needed lives, so they will go forward. When many young souls today have had only 100 to 300 lives, they need many more lives to reach that average of 600 to 800 lives.

Is it by design that many of the harder "bucket list" experiences seem to be during the young soul period of time?
Yes, many more mistakes are made by young souls. By the time one reaches the medium soul category, you've had time to correct many of the bad decisions you made as a young soul, when you got off the soul path or contract. Imagine your path as being in a zigzag where in some lives there was little growth, and in others a straight line, or with just a few curves.

Gaia, would you define "younger souls" as those being from 100 to say, 200 lives or would you say we should include those that we have referred to in the past as being "newbies" with fewer than 100 lives?
You can define them any way you wish, Tom, but as a general rule I would define "younger souls" as those being under 200 to 225 lives of experience. It all depends upon whether that soul fragment will eventually have a total of 600 or the higher number of 800. Then a soul with, let's say, 200 lives with a top end of 600 lives will have had many more learning events than the person at 200 lives who will have around 800 lives. In a way, it is like comparing apples and oranges. You have to know the top end of each soul fragment's number of lives, so we use very general numbers when discussing Earth lives. Hence, my advice is to keep these numbers as a general guide, while knowing each individual soul may have less or more experiences at any given time.

Then what we would call a younger soul could have lives at any given time period dating back as far as or even farther than the days of Atlantis and Lemuria?
Quite so, Tom. They would have lives at or during any time period when

needed. As we pointed out before, they may flounder in those lives, but at the same time, would learn a great deal.

I was asked why my future granddaughter would not have a life back with her family just a little farther up in time.
But she is having or will have a life during this time period with members of soul clusters that she works with time and time again. That does not preclude her from having a life, let's say, back in Germany at virtually the same time period after this one. We remind everyone, again, that you cannot think linearly. She could even have a life after this one back in Germany before her last life. There are many options, and it all depends upon what experiences and learning a soul fragment can gain from a particular life. As was mentioned before, she has had previous lives with your daughter, so obviously she will be having a life with several soul clusters she has had lives within the past.

Is it wise to have so many young souls on Earth at this time?
Again, we repeat what you were recently told. The young souls can make rapid advancement in a more modern time period. This, you might say, allows for even greater advancement in this century. You have not advanced as far as you think you have.

Gaia, how many of my readers are young or medium souls?
There are very few of your readers who have reached the stage of a medium soul, Tom. Their souls look at you to teach them and give them tools for living and having much more productive lives. You truly lift them up to be able to handle these lives on Earth and be more successful.

Gaia, since all of the souls having lives on Earth are at a set limit, what percentage of the people we meet and interact with on Earth in this life are new to us?
Yes, as you are thinking, Tom, it depends heavily on how many lives you've lived. So, let's take a life where you already have 300 to 400 lives on Earth, the percentage could vary depending upon your work. If you meet and interact with people on a daily basis, then it might approach 50%. It could be much higher if you typically only interact with your family and a couple of friends. So, there can be no one answer. It can range to almost

100%, depending upon the circumstances, to less than 15 to 20 percent.

Does Africa suffer because of so many young souls?
In a way, yes. A huge continent where many young souls reside. As your overall population has reached its peak, Africa will begin to see an increase in people being born in the higher quads of young souls and more medium souls. Everyone must have lives on all the continents, so people having lives in Europe and the United States, as just two examples, will begin to have lives on the African Continent.

Is it wise to have so many young souls on Earth at this time?
Again, we repeat what you were recently told. The young souls can make rapid advancement in a more modern time period. This, you might say, allows for even greater advancement in this century. You have not advanced as far as you think you have.

Gaia, do old souls incarnate on a faster timeline than young souls? Is imagination used across the Universe to solve problems?
You use your imagination, Tom, much better because you are veiled than the souls who are not veiled. If you recall, by being veiled you come up with, and will come up with, unique inspirations compared to those who are not veiled. So, there is imagination throughout the Universe, just not to the extent it is here. That's why you have been given so many problems to solve that all the other societies have not been able to solve.

Gaia, are young, medium, and old souls divided into fours or threes?
Yes, Tom, a quadrant is by definition a fourth. There was a slight misunderstanding there on your part. We knew you would correct it in time.

So, when you change quadrants there is an uptick, you previously said.
Quite so. You might call it a bonus for each milestone the soul fragment reaches.

What do we pick up from gentle old people—aura of old age or the life they lived?
Life is a series of experiences, Tom. They can beat you down, it may seem,

but you bounce back up. You draw from not only this life, but from previous ones too. If you send light to the world, that light will come back to you a hundred-fold. You radiate this love for life and all those who have joined you in this great experiment.

Animal Souls

Gaia, did the souls of the animal kingdom on Earth easily volunteer for the Earth Experiment or reluctantly, and will more souls withdraw from the Earth Experiment?
Yes, they had a great curiosity of what the Creator was trying to do, so they agreed, but not every soul you understand on those other worlds are taking part. They asked for volunteers and with love there were those souls who in many cases have been contributing for thousands if not millions of years. And, yes, there are some souls withdrawing and others that will take their places to ensure that the experiment continues. This is all part and parcel for their learning too, you see.

Gaia, do animals, such as dogs and cats, have soul contracts to assist humans, even when it cost them their life?
This is controlled by your own guardian angels, Tom. Dog Soul and Cat Soul, just as two examples, understand their part in your lives. They also know that they will return for another life with you, whether it will be in the same life or a future life. So, you could say their soul contracts are to do whatever needs to be done as part of your family. They have great love for you that transcends time. Subconsciously, they recognize your souls just as you do theirs.

Does assisting humans raise their vibrational levels?
In a way, yes. Again, may we remind you that all of the souls taking part in the Earth Experiment were at the very top of their vibrational level when Creator asked them to be part of the Earth Experiment? They were already operating at a high level, so assisting humans, you might say, in any way, was part and parcel of their agreement with Creator. There will be millions of decisions you will make when you meld into a creator, and some of them will be regarding these Group Souls. Will you perhaps find other duties for them, after the Explorer Race leaves Earth forever?

Gaia, you've said in the past that Dog Soul and Cat Soul each have approximately five young souls assisting them. Are these souls actually involved in guiding the soul fragments to staging areas or is this handled by volunteer human soul fragments?

Both, Tom. You thought that it was possibly just the young souls spread out guiding the soul fragments to the staging areas, which they do, but are assisted by volunteer human souls as part of their learning. It is a massive job that goes on 24 hours a day, as we've said before, that it does not just take place at night. You could say that the young souls act as managers to keep everything humming along.

Gaia, can I assume that Chicken Soul created chickens first and then they laid eggs?

Excellent observation, Tom. Chicken Soul has the ability to create chickens, just as many others of what you term Group Souls created their species. And there was testing that I allowed in order to achieve the perfect species of each animal, insect, etc.

Gaia, when Creator asked for whole souls to volunteer to ensoul animals that would be used for food, what were they promised? And how long before the world will stop eating meat?

Please understand that souls can say no, but this is such a unique experiment in the billions of universes, that many volunteered, but relatively few were chosen. They were told that their vibrational levels would rise too, just not as fast as the levels would rise for the souls who volunteered to be humans. They were also told that over a span of time fewer soul fragments would be needed to be eaten by humans. And they all understand the circle of life.

With that said, regarding your question of how much longer humans will eat flesh, it will still be a few hundred years. That is not so long, when you consider how many thousands of years have already passed. Better plant foods will be developed. As just one example, people are working on the taste of plants to mimic the taste of hamburger meat. They are quite close, and more and more people will opt to eat these instead of beef, but it is a slow process.

In the meantime, more humane ways of slaughter will be mandated by law. More ways to provide protein for the body will be discovered. So, my final advice would be to honor and bless all your food you consume each day, wherever it originates.

Gaia, is Snake Soul from the Reptilian Galaxy?
Quite so, Tom.

Were reptilians mostly created there, or were they created all over the Universe under Creator's wishes?
There are reptilian worlds all across the Universe, Tom, but a higher concentration in one galaxy.

Then Snake Soul volunteered for the Earth Experiment long before there was the war between what is now the Federation and those from the Reptilian Galaxy?
Quite correct, Tom. There was wide knowledge of what Creator was doing and planned to do with the Earth Experiment. That's why your idea worked of offering to include them in the experiment too. More reptilian souls wished to participate, just as your soul and many others did, in order to raise your vibrational levels.

Gaia, do dog and cat soul fragments follow us from life to life?
Yes, Tom, if there is a great connection there between the human soul fragment and those fragments of his or her dogs and/or cats, yes, they will each be attracted to the other in numerous lives on Earth. That is another reason for the close bonding some people share with their pet family. It happens because of the love each has for the other. The dogs' and cats' Group Soul honors this by bringing them back together again.

Gaia, what can people do to promote the ethical treatment of all beings?
Obviously, Tom, it starts with each of you. Then you can begin working on all the other people that call them "dumb animals" and such. Great strides are being made in this area, Tom, and greater recognition of just how intelligent these beings are in their own right. This will accelerate in the future, you see.

Each of you must follow your passions, and as long as you honor all beings on this Earth, as your Creator loves variety and loves every one of these creatures—these beings—equally, you should strive for that too. You can assist in so many ways that as an individual you must choose your passion.

Gaia, can puppies or kittens be ensouled after birth, and how does it work when someone requests a Most Benevolent Outcome for the return of a favorite dog or cat, and they next adopt one that is say, one or more years old?

To answer the first question, Tom, yes, the puppies and kittens can be ensouled after birth if need be. It all depends on when the group soul of the cats and the group soul of the dogs wishes to ensoul them, as it is not needed at or before birth as humans.

To answer the second question, which you already have a hint of an answer, as there is no time limitations the group soul can simply assign that soul fragment to a puppy or kitten one or two or, yes, any number of years in advance of the person adopting the dog or cat so that their beloved friend returns to them for another life. The thing to emphasize here, Tom, is that they must request the Most Benevolent Outcome to be reunited in order to ensure the return of the soul fragment. Yes, it does happen without the request, but it is much more of a certainty if you request it.

Archangel Souls

Gaia, would an archangel be compared to the soul of Jesus? Are not the beings we call archangels larger in size than the soul who produced Jesus, or are they the same size, or can you describe it in terms everyone could understand?

Yes, Tom, an archangel, as we have described before, is simply a large piece of a creator than the soul who produced Jesus. That soul would be a normal size soul, but it gave a larger piece of itself to have an Earth life as Jesus. An archangel, on the other hand, produces many souls.

Was the soul of Jesus created by an archangel?

Yes, in a way, Tom, you could say that, but not an archangel that would be considered closely involved with the Earth Experiment. The soul who

172

had a piece of itself live the life of Jesus was attracted to this Universe out of love—to teach love. That is its major soul interest, just as your soul fragment has a main interest in religions, its main interest is to teach love—unconditionally.

Gaia, did Creator birth Archangel Michael or did another create Michael?
No, Creator did birth Michael, Tom. Michael and the other Archangels all have a multitude of duties in this creation, not just including Earth. Creator created them out of love, as you have been told numerous times.

What will Michael do when our soul fragments all merge into a creator and take over running this Universe?
Michael and the other Archangels will return to Creator, as their job will be done. Yes, that is correct, Tom. After the merger, you will have many, and I cannot emphasize this enough, decisions on how to run your Universe.

Placement of Souls

Gaia, is there a soul for each country, or is it simply that groups of souls are attracted to have lives in certain countries?
There you have it, Tom. There is no "group soul" for each country. Groups of souls as part of their planning millions of years ago chose to have lives in multiple countries for their soul's growth. It is quite difficult for you to have the understanding at this time of how this time frame works so that all of your lives are going on at the same time. All your lives past, present, and future are all taking place right now and all of your lives affect the others. Each is important in its own right.

Do you contact the souls for each country about upcoming events, or do they contact you, or since you are all in the energy "soup" that you described, are all of these events known thousands and millions of years in advance?
There are certain major events mapped out, but many events are connected to probabilities where the souls decide the timing according to the progress your soul fragments are making. Your souls also work within a framework

of major Earth events whether they be earthquakes, volcanic eruptions, weather, and so on.

Appearance of a Soul

I saw an artist's depiction of a soul. One thing that intrigued me was the tentacles. Do you have what would appear to be tentacles coming out of your energy body that connect to thousands of things, such as the other souls assisting you in running this planet?
Quite so, Tom. Some are just for less than a second as I communicate, and others are what we can call, for your purposes, Tom, permanent connections.

Artistic Clouds and Their Soul Creators

Gaia, how would you describe the souls that form artistic clouds? Is that all they do?
Yes, an interesting question, Tom. You would have to describe their soul interest as art in all its forms. Forming clouds is just one of their interests. They would best be described as having a fragment of themselves forming artistic shapes while other parts or other fragments are having artistic experiences throughout the Universe. You are, or were, correct in thinking that they can be multipurpose. They do these shapes with great love. Many humans would not recognize a shape they're not familiar with, but someone on another planet would recognize them. So do take time to look at their creations any chance you get.

Gaia, what was the odd pink swirling effect over Mesa Verde, Colorado recently?
One of the cloud angels or souls was trying out a new artistic look. It was not an ET craft, Tom.

That brings me to my next question—why do some people see them, and some do not, and are they aware of one or more humans looking at the clouds so that they can show off or display their work?
Oh, yes, quite so. As any artist, they enjoy someone taking interest in their work and will put on a demonstration at times if a person relaxes and sits

outdoors enjoying watching the clouds. You can also request Most Benevolent Outcomes to see some unique cloud formations and they will try and oblige, depending upon the prevailing winds, moisture in the air, and so on. There has to be the right conditions for them to paint their pictures, shall we say. So don't give up if the first one or two times have no results; persevere and you will see some beautiful art—just not permanent. There are many artists today—humans—who make or create art that they know will not last such as those who make sand or ice sculptures.

That does bring up the question, are the souls forming the cloud shapes having fragments experiencing Earth lives?
No, but a good question. These souls have chosen to be artistic without having physical lives. Tom, that you exist as energy, and energy never dies—it just exists in another form.

Characteristics of the Soul

Gaia, I have a question about souls. I understand that souls are balls of energy, correct?
Quite so, Tom.

Therefore, does the average soul have a certain dimension regarding width of this energy? Could you say that a soul is 3 feet wide, 10 feet wide, etc.?
Yes, Tom. A soul does have a dimensional width, but it can vary according to how long the soul has been in existence. Therefore, a "newbie," using your words, would not have the dimensional size of a soul birthed long before it.

I would assume, but correct me if I'm wrong, that a soul would top out at a certain width?
Yes, you could say that, Tom, but it is up to each soul how large it wishes to be according to how much energy it absorbs. And of course, we have not discussed the light they emanate according to their experiences. You already know your Theo emanates a golden light, but of course that would indicate that different souls emanate different colors in light spectrums far

beyond what colors humans recognize today. I'm not trying to avoid your original question, Tom. I'm trying to explain that one size doesn't fit all when you speak of souls. Each soul has different interests and experience, but all souls try to vibrate at a higher level.

Still, billions of souls are probably still birthed each day, I would assume?

Quite correct, Tom. Each creator creates souls for the creator's learning and to pass the information along as needed to whatever creator or soul needs it. All of this is so much more complicated and complex, shall we say, than humans can comprehend at this time, but as all of you raise your vibrational levels you will ask more and more questions and receive more and more complex answers—especially the Explorer Race where your vibrational levels are increasing at such a fast level compared to other souls in any of the billions of creations. You are one of a kind, which I will remind you many times over your life, Tom. Souls on Earth have no other souls to compare themselves to, but I can assure you, compared to other souls you are increasing your vibrational level and therefore your energy level exponentially.

Gaia, do our souls have just one interest and series of lives like I seemed to have as an amphibian on Nommo, or multiple and different lives on more than one planet?

Here we get into soul interests of trillions of souls, and yes, you understand this, but I'm saying this for your readers. The majority of souls have one soul interest, but then there are souls who wish to express themselves in multiple forms. You might say they were given dual or twin interests.

Are there any souls in the Earth Experiment with dual interests?

Of course. The Earth Experiment attracted many diverse souls—most with one interest, but a few with more than one. They can have complicated lives on Earth, having had multiple types of lives on other planets. Don't forget that Creator loves variety.

What do the 90% of souls not created by Creator have in common to take part in the Earth Experiment?

All the souls that volunteered for the Earth Experiment, as you have been told before, had reached a vibrational level that was in the top tier of all those on their planets. We called it many things in the past for you and your readers, Tom, but it all boils down to a vibrational level reached that puts you on a level with the highest vibrational levels of those on other planets. That is the main reason that some planets had a number of souls that could apply while other souls on their planets could not, since they had not reached a high vibrational level. Even then, there were souls that did not wish to volunteer.

Gaia, how do souls choose the time period that their soul fragments live in, when this was done so far in advance—was this 10 million or just one million years ago?

As you might guess, Tom, this could take hours to explain in detail. Simply put, all the souls were able to see and work on each time period, yes, 10 million years ago. They were and are able to see the probabilities far in advance, having the knowledge of how all their own societies progressed over millions and millions of years. Needless to say, great thought went into these stages of development, recognizing that it would not be just a straight line. This was done rapidly, but again with great knowledge, and allowing for the old saying of two steps forward and one step back. Still, no one was sure if any of this planning would work within the confines of the four negative energies. They did not do this all by themselves, as naturally Creator had great input, as Creator could see all the possibilities—every single one. So you could say it was Creator's framework and they planned all of this with Creator's great scheme.

So was it the souls, or was it Creator who set this up?

You cannot separate the chicken and the egg, Tom. It is just too complex. If you were to see this creation from my viewpoint, as keep in mind I was involved too as the soul of the Earth, Creator laid out the Earth Experiment and the souls filled in the blanks, you could say. Again, this was and is still a highly complex design far beyond what we could explain in just a few short sentences today. Even the other planets in the solar system had input, along with all the societies taking part—not just the souls whose soul fragments would be having all of these millions, and, yes, billions, of lives on Earth.

Gaia, do souls feel what we feel and hear what we hear?
Not in the same way as your physical forms do. All the information about your lives is instantly available to your souls, so they have the ability to experience and feel all of your Earth lives that are all going on at the same time. Only you are veiled. We have stated before that your souls can be having a half million to over one million lives going on across the Universe for the soul's learning. That is extremely hard to understand for most people, Tom, as most people have never thought of themselves as simply a fragment of a soul contained in your bodies. This is too hard for most people to grasp, because you are veiled, and it would seem to you that each body contains the whole soul.

It is even harder for people to accept all these other hundreds of lives you will have, and have had, on Earth in order to fast-track the raising of your vibrational levels. To use some old terminology, your souls are "go-getters." They do not wish to sit around as most souls do and slowly raise their vibrational levels. Again, may I remind your readers, Tom, that the end goal is to meld together and become a Creator, which has never been done before by any group of souls. You will then take over this Universe allowing the Creator to go to another level itself.

I have previously been told that we can imagine souls as electro-magnetic balls of energy—tremendously more powerful than we can imagine—able to have 500,000 to one million lives going on simultaneously across the Universe for their learning.

And we have the same guardian angel (GA) in each of our lives that are all happening at the same time (and don't forget each life has twelve parallel lives). Even when we become mad at our GAs and "fire them," they simply take on a different personality, and when we transition, we all laugh about it. Theo is taking care of over 17,000 souls with six to twelve soul fragments in each cluster and their 12 parallel timelines each having 600 to 800 lives on average all going on at once. That just leaves me breathless thinking about the work involved!

Gaia, where there are multiple transitions at one time, are the soul fragments able to see each other, including the soul fragment(s) who

caused their death or are they contained in what has been described as a tunnel of light?
This is an excellent question. Yes, at times they can see that person or persons, but this is when those whole souls you call angels (and we have suggested you call them transition angels) take over and, shall we gently say, forcefully direct them into a tunnel of light. If they are soldiers, they still feel they should be continuing to combat those who caused their deaths, but this only lasts for a short time as the transition angels are quite adept in directing them away.

Those that are killed in a terrorist attack are quite confused, but again the transition angels transmit great love as they gently direct their charges. They are also assisted, may we remind you, by their own guardian angels whose job was to have them there at the right second so that their soul contract to transition at that very second is completed. They do not just stand on the sidelines, but assist the transition angels, so there are many times the person transitioning sees two angelic forms or more if that person's beliefs warrant it.

So, am I to understand this is somewhat a division of jobs or are we separating something that should not be separated?
There you have it, Tom. We are all connected on this side of the veil, which is quite hard for humans to understand, but we all have different tasks we have volunteered for and there are those souls whose soul mission is to assist thousands of soul fragments all transitioning at the same time, for whatever cause—violence, sickness, or old age—back to their own soul group or cluster.

I think there may be some confusion here, mixing timelines with multiple lives in different time periods going on simultaneously. There are 12 timelines for each person's life with 12 "yous" all having different experiences and making different decisions for the learning of each whole soul.

We have been told previously that in the quantum dream state you do look in on other lives and even other timelines. This might be done because there was a lesson learned or a similar experience in one of your other lives. That's why I encourage all of you to have a notebook and penlight next to your bed to try and remember your dreams each night. Sometimes I don't remember any and the largest number of dreams I've recalled in one night is nine.

Connection of All Souls

Gaia, our souls have not already melded together in the future, have they?
No, but again a good question, Tom. Elsewhere universal time is observed instead of the space- time continuum you experience on Earth. Therefore, many thousands of years will go by before the melding takes place.

Will it not be just a melding or joining together again, since we basically all came from the same birth mother, shall we call the Creator of Creators?
Yes, but in a small way. Keep in mind, Tom, there are billions of creators, so some souls were created at far different times, I will call it, in 3D terms for you. All will have had tremendously different experiences and lives by the time this happens, far in your future.

Creation of Souls

Gaia, how was our Universe filled with souls? Did the Creator put out a call to other creators asking for souls, and I might add, is this a common practice of creators, or was the call answered by souls already created, but had not found a purpose or a universe?
This is a good question, Tom, and you could answer all of the above. Yes, creators do put out a call, which is instantly received by other creators, and this is immediately acted upon by those who are interested in taking part in a new creation as the details of the creation are instantly received too. They in turn, you might say, pass the information along to those souls who they know would have an interest in that particular form of creation, keeping in mind that there are creations far beyond your understanding and imagination at this time. So, perhaps millions of creators would know that this or that creation would not be of interest to the souls they had birthed and would decline the offer. Others would accept, if the creation

were of interest to them.

That leads me to ask, has the Creator of this Universe supplied souls to other creations?
Yes, of course it has. And it does so in order to broaden it knowledge and understanding. Again, this is a very common practice. One creator might have billions of souls in other creations. As I mentioned before, Tom, and Theo has too, the Creator of this Universe would be ranked quite high among its peers for what it is doing with its creation.

Are all the new universes magnets to souls to experience?
There are always souls who have been created but have yet to find purpose for their existence. As Creator of Creators births new creators, they then create new universes and attract souls to them, according to what those creators wish to do with their universes.

Creator of Creators

Gaia, I have been asked to ask you several questions about the Creator of this Universe. How was the Creator created?
The Creator was created, Tom, as we have spoken about in the past, by the Creator of Creators. It was birthed along with billions of others with great love.

Where does it exist?
It permeates every single cell of creation, Tom, and it exists in all dimensions. This is hard to explain to you, Tom, in 3rd dimensional terms, so we'll say its main energy crosses all dimensions known and unknown.

Why did it come into being?
Again, Tom, It was created out of love by the Creator of Creators.

Gaia, someone makes the argument that Creator does not exist; rather he is existence itself. And, if he is existence itself, there can be no others. Comments?
A nice theory, Tom, but just that, a theory. There is space, which your scientists have a long way to go to understand—it will literally take

millennia to understand the 14 different energies, and the actual fabric that makes up this creation—this Universe. Would you deny that a beautiful painting just exists—that there was no painter who created it? That is a simple explanation for those who would deny the Creator, who created this Universe.

The energies Gaia is referring to are the 4 Negative Energies we all live with, and the 10 Positive Energies the rest of our Universe and all the other universes work with. Scientists will not discover these for several hundred years. Obviously, scientists have a LOT of research ahead of them. I'm told they don't want the scientists to be bored!

Has the Creator decided what it will do next—go to a higher level, I was once told?
That is correct, Tom. It knows from seeing this occur to only a handful of other creators that have moved on. It is quite mysterious in a way, so the Creator is quite intrigued, you could say.

Then when that happens will the Creator have any more involvement in running this Universe of ours?
No, he will have trained you to not need IT by that time, Tom.

Defining What the Soul Is

Gaia, explain the difference between a soul and a spirit?
These are interchangeable words for the most part, Tom. But we have discussed in the past that there are negative spirits that are remnants of the creation of the Universe. These are not souls. Other than those, all the rest are what you would term souls, or larger fragments of creators, or of course, Creators'.

What is the Holy Spirit in the Bible?
Again, another name for Creator.

What is the ego and what is meant by eliminating it?
Here we get into beliefs, Tom. They are simply referring to reducing our self-importance that many build up in their work.

Dreaming and Working with Other Souls

Gaia, how many souls are involved in dream time, not counting each person's own guardian angel as we call Golden Light Beings?
It would be a little over the one million souls that are Golden Light Beings. They have not yet achieved that status, shall we say, but working with your own guardian angels, they are able to match your soul fragments to a desire for answers from all over the Universe. It is quite complicated, as the souls of those people seeking answers to problems must be matched with your soul fragments in sleep time.

We have spoken before of how you are the great problem solvers of the Universe. Even a soul fragment in what we have called a first quadrant young soul can already solve many problems. Naturally, the more lives you have the more difficult the problems you solve for people, while at the same time mixing in other timelines and past, present, and future lives. This is but another reason to write your dreams down when you remember them. There will be occasions when you remember being in strange places that do not appear to be Earth.

Fragments of Souls

Gaia, would a soul, having one of its fragments having a life on Earth, substitute another soul fragment (what we call a walk-in) to use a special gift?
Most of the time, Tom, the soul fragment's soul contract covers that life aspect. We have covered walk-ins before, and these are normally done because the soul fragment does not have the tools to cope with certain situations and the soul does not wish the fragment to be subjected to more of a situation it is not capable of handling.

Why would one of its other fragments be more capable? It would seem that although there are differences, they would not be so great.
Au contraire, Tom. There can be great differences, as a soul fragment might have had to handle that problem in several lives, while this is the first time for the other soul fragment. So, it inserts the other fragment, and another life is set up for further learning, so that the fragment learns how

to handle that problem. There are or can be great differences as we have noted in the frequencies of the soul fragments and their interests and abilities—again to obtain the greatest learning and experiences for the soul.

Would a soul insert, let's say, a larger fragment of itself for a significant life—good or bad—or are all of its fragments the same size, or is this an impossible question to answer because I'm asking it to be described three-dimensionally?

Yes, you are much closer to the answer there, Tom. All of a soul's fragments are capable of having significant lives, and when your questioner mentioned someone such as Hitler, his soul fragment was really no larger than his brothers and sisters, you could say, for an analogy.

So, using Hitler as an example, how many soul fragments were or are there in that soul's cluster?

Yes, it would be on the lower end of the averages as you guessed, Tom— more on the order of six, but whether a soul fragment is part of a cluster of 6, 8, or 12 fragments, there is little difference. It may seem on the surface that a soul fragment would need to be larger to handle a significant life, but it is more on the order of vibrational levels the soul chooses for each fragment, so that each has its own interests and is not a duplicate of the other fragments in the cluster.

Gaia, how do souls fragment themselves?

The same way creators do. Souls have the ability to fragment themselves into thousands of pieces, if they so choose, but with attached energy cords, we will call them here for your purposes. As explained before, your souls may be having a million lives going on across the Universe, at the same time your soul fragments are having lives on Earth. Each fragment of a soul can be given a different soul interest by the soul for its learning. There is this energetic connection that you have not yet discovered.

Is it these energy cords that we have connected to our heart chakras?

Yes, that is exactly the connection, like beautiful tentacles from your souls.

Gaia, do soul fragments ever have lives on other planets besides Earth

and our home planets?

Generally not, Tom. Keep in mind that your soul was attracted to have lives on that planet because it fit your soul's interests, and that includes the form it takes on your home planet. You join other souls with almost exactly the same kind of interests. The difference between you and the souls of your home planet that chose not to have lives on Earth is the desire to raise your vibrational level with the goal of melding into a creator. They have no such desire and are happy to have life after life doing the same things or having the same experiences life after life. That's why they are stuck at the same vibrational level and are not growing.

It won't be that long, in universal years, that you will be going to the stars and sharing little bits of negativity with all these other planets, and they in turn will share with others, and those others will share with others and so on until not only this Universe, but eventually billions of others will do the same. At this point you cannot imagine the effect your lives will have on the Universe and others.

Gaia, can one lose a soul fragment through experiencing great trauma?

Yes, in a way, Tom. When a person experiences great trauma, a portion of the soul retreats for a time depending upon the severity of the experience. The fragment of a fragment detaches for a time until the soul itself reattaches the soul to the rest of the fragment. This may sound complicated, but it happens numerous times, as the soul wishes the fragment to continue its life and too much trauma might cause the soul fragment to take its own life too early and not gain from the experience. After a time, the fragment is reattached, sometimes with the help of a professional, and the soul is able to process life better.

Your soul fragments, as I have mentioned before, and Theo too, have many more capabilities than you can imagine at this time and juncture. Just the fact that your soul fragment is capable of splitting itself into 12 separate fragments in order to experience lives on 12 timelines should give you an idea that your soul fragment is much more capable than most people think. Perhaps in the future you will think of other questions to ask regarding your soul fragment's capabilities and I, or Theo, will be happy to explain.

Do all soul fragments have significant lives, and if so, how many on average?
Your first question is an easy one to answer, Tom. All soul fragments have significant lives no matter your soul interest. How many you have is really up to each individual soul and is partly based on how many lives in total you have on Earth. There is no one answer. We can use a very general answer here of 10%, but again, it is up to each individual soul how many significant lives their soul fragments have.

Gaia, why do some soul fragments start their lives in modern times instead of long ago when it was very primitive?
Yes, there are so many souls wishing to have lives on Earth that sometimes it is easier with all the billions of people living nowadays to be placed in families where the majority of the souls are all fairly new. There are still many places on Earth where the people live almost primitive lives, so it is not so much a stretch in those conditions.

Where it is more difficult is when they are placed in modern cities where they are overwhelmed, but the tradeoff is that they learn an enormous amount in a short time. As I have said before, it's as if they are thrown into a lake or pool and told to sink or swim. Some, a majority even, do sink, but not before gallantly trying. Keep in mind it is normal for people to learn much more in a failure than they do in successfully accomplishing something. You learn from your mistakes. The souls who have clusters of fragments just beginning lives are quite aware of where the first lives will be but grab any open spot they are able to find.

Do all the soul fragments in a cluster join together for lives back on the home planets they originated from, or are they still the soul fragment they were in the cluster on Earth?
Yes, they are still the fragments from the cluster of souls sent for Earth lives. They do not meld together for a life on the home planet. That is quite obvious when you look at Antura having a life on your home planet where he is still the fragment but not split into 12 parts for the timelines as you are for an Earth life. So, you could say those 12 parts are the whole fragment again.

Gaia, at what point in their development did our souls decide to fragment?
When they volunteered for the Earth Experiment, they knew they would have to have thousands of lives going on at the same time for their learning.

Does one soul know, or receive guidance on when, how, or where to fragment?
This is deep seated knowledge, Tom. It is always there. No need to ask anyone.

Can we, being incarnated in this life, have conscious contact with one of our other soul fragments?
In a meditative state you can, as you do with Antura, and in times past, Reveals the Mysteries. They are, after all, fragments of your soul.

In our next life, does soul fragmentation continue the same way?
There is no change, Tom. Your path of incarnations continues on whatever path your soul has set up for you to gain knowledge needed in the future.

Can we direct our soul fragment?
Your soul directs your fragments, not the other way around. Yet, as we have spoken about before, you do have freedom to not stay on your soul contract, but that is to your detriment not to do so. It lessens what you can learn in one life. That's one of the reasons we have spoken about before to request Most Benevolent Outcomes—it keeps you on your soul contract, which you want to do for the highest learning.

As Gaia has explained previously, only about 10% of the souls taking part in the Earth Experiment are fragments of the Creator of this Universe. The rest came from worlds that were originally populated in this Universe by souls from other universes, which were attracted to this Universe to express themselves.

Gaia, what percentage of soul fragments having lives on Earth have adventure and exploration as their soul interest?
Yes, Tom, it would be less than 1%, as keep in mind there are many, many

soul interests we have yet to touch on. So, it is less than 1/100 of one percent that would have that specific soul interest.

What types of adventures would they choose on other planets?
Tom, you can see from what Antura does. They have an interest in seeing the differences between what they are already aware of, and what is different not only in their own solar system, but far beyond in other galaxies and, yes, even other universes. They all contribute to the knowledge of other planets in their solar system, but also to the planets in their Federation of planets. You would think that with societies that are over a billion years old there would be little left to explore, but I can assure you there are still billions of things still unknown about this Universe, and billions of planets where they will be surprised by what they discover.

Would these soul fragments be considered a "jack-of-all-trades?"
Over their many lives they will gain knowledge, but that can also be a hindrance, hence the reason you are blinded here on Earth. There is a stagnant mentality as to how they go about exploring. As you go out to the stars, you will do things differently. Earth humans will certainly be the "jack-of-all-trades."

Are they heroic in soldier lives?
It all depends upon their soul contracts, Tom. You all must have what we might call negative lives to balance the positive ones. They could be the worst of the worst soldiers, or, yes, they could be the best of the best. There is no one description that would fit those soul fragments with this soul interest.

Are they natural story tellers?
Not really. Again, it depends. You cannot lump all of these soul fragments in one neat description.

Are they still able to have lives with depression and anxiety?
All lives must balance, Tom, and since you are human, those are part of the human experience.

Would a time traveler in the future have adventure as a soul interest?

Yes, there will be a portion of those anthropologists in the far future with that soul interest.

Would any of these souls with this soul interest ensoul an android in the future?
Yes, but they would tend to be younger souls.

Gaia, can you put a percentage on what part of a soul has lives on Earth?
This varies so much from soul to soul, Tom. Some souls might only have, say, 100,000 lives across the Universe and other souls several hundred thousand—yes, even up to one million lives. So, the percentage, even with the lower number, would be small, but again I say that these lives are by far the most important as you might make more decisions in a day than some societies make in a lifetime. That is how intense you could say these lives on Earth are, compared to elsewhere.

So, would all these lives be going on at the same time, or is there an ebb and flow variation in the total number, or do they remain constant in number?
Again, we get into soul choices, Tom, and there can be unlimited answers to this question, all depending upon the soul choices.

Do the human soul fragments do this forever—the length of the Earth Experiment—or are they replaced at certain times by other human soul fragments that wish this experience?
The soul fragments do this forever—yes, the length of time all of you are here having lives. It is part of their soul interest to perform this work while also having human lives. Meanwhile, the young souls assisting the group souls are also learning and are quite happy to have a job to do. Creator has thought of everything, Tom.

That leads me to the question, besides the four million souls assisting you in running the Earth, do you have soul fragments of yourself doing certain work, or guiding these souls?
Excellent question, Tom. To use a human expression, I have my hands in everything. I don't just bark out orders. I must make millions of decisions

each second. When long ago you were told that you were only seeing the tip of the iceberg, now you are seeing just a tiny bit more, Tom.

Gaia's Soul Fragmentation

Gaia, you said you had your hands in everything. Does that mean you fragment yourself, and if so how many fragments?
Yes, using the word "hands" is just a metaphor for the thousands, and, yes, millions of fragments of myself overseeing and running this living being that you call Earth. It is one I enjoy and trained extensively for millions of years in order to achieve a certain level of perfection. Just our conversations require a fragment of myself to answer the questions your readers ask. You are not the only one I communicate with. I'm quite capable of having 10,000 conversations going on at the same time. I'm glad you asked these questions as it expands the general concept and knowledge your readers have about me, along with you, Tom.

Guardian Angels

Gaia, what is the highest probability for the number of whole souls we call guardian angels melding with our souls to become a creator?
The highest probability, Tom, would be fully half will desire to accompany you in the melding as you term it. They have become intimately involved in all of your lives on Earth and communicating with your souls on a constant basis. Some, of course, will go on, attracted to other creations.

What percentage of our souls will decide to merge?
Yes, we have spoken once before that a small percentage of the souls actually created by the Creator of this Universe will decide to merge back when this Creator goes on to a higher focus, but other than those soul fragments, few if any will choose not to meld.

Helper Souls

Gaia, how many souls are in your cadre of helpers: one million, millions, hundreds of thousands?
Well over one million souls, Tom.

Is it over five million?
No, but close to that number.

Over four million?
Yes, but not too far above that, you see. Again, they do have multiple duties so there is no need for more than this.

Yes, but it seems that number is extremely high. Am I receiving you correctly? Over four million souls are your helpers?
Yes, quite so, Tom, as keep in mind that this is a training ground not only for the Explorer Race, but also for newer souls who wish to learn how to take care of a planet, so that one day they can move on to ensoul their own planets. Don't forget that there are multiple timelines so that they are actually taking care of 12 planets at the same time. Creator knew this is such a unique place in the Universe, he wanted to make sure I had plenty of assistance with such a complex assignment, shall we call it. The souls are able to deal with different frequencies all at the same time. The learning curve, you could say, is steep, but the souls, which assist me, enjoy the challenge, and naturally we are all there to assist each other.

I assume that's why there are, and were, various peoples on Earth, which recognized there were souls of plants, trees, mountains, and lakes, which they prayed to.
Yes, quite so. Those peoples were more attuned—much more I will add—to the Earth than are the societies of today, but we understand that too.

Besides the multiple frequencies, Gaia, are the souls also spread out over the whole space time continuum, as we are, or have they been in this time loop?
Yes, again your readers, Tom, are being given a slight understanding of the complexity and uniqueness of this planet. There is no other like it in the Universe.

Mars or Maldek and Soul Fragments

Gaia, did our soul fragments have lives on either Mars or the planet Maldek that blew up before our Earth lives?

A few of the souls had soul fragments that had lives on those planets, but not all. There were other soul groups that had lives on those planets for learning. As was said to you in the past, your souls had to reach a certain vibrational level. Some souls used lives on those two planets in preparation for this life, but that was only a percentage, not everyone, but that was a good question. There will be many discoveries made by those in the future who will explore Mars, after they discover Mars was inhabited by an intelligent race. There will be many ah-ha moments.

Gaia, I had perhaps assumed this in the past, or perhaps I forgot that I asked, but are our individual soul clusters all from the same planet, or are they made up of soul fragments from different planets?
Yes, the soul fragments in a soul cluster all originated from the same planet where they may have had thousands of lives before their vibrational levels increased to the level needed to begin these Earth lives. Therefore, your clusters will have 600 to 800 lives on average per soul fragment. And, as we have stated before, these are general numbers since a person could have 634 and another person 817. And, of course, they may have several lives back on their home planets mixed in because when they gain knowledge, they wish to share it with those on their home planets who chose not to fast track their vibrational levels.

Middle East Souls

Gaia, are most of the soul fragments having lives in Syria and Iraq and even Afghanistan considered to be young souls in the number of lives lived on Earth, and if so, what would be the average number of lives—under 50, or more?
Yes, Tom. There you have it. The average number of lives would be 50 or even just a little under. These lives are necessary for a soul fragment's experiences of being in a war as a refugee or even starving to death due to being surrounded by hostile forces. So, yes, the majority of these souls are quite young—even less than five lives—as these lives have to happen and can be during any time period dating back thousands of years. So do say Benevolent Prayers for these young souls, Tom, as this does help them cope with their situation, and for help from outside sources such as relief organizations and governments.

*Here is a Benevolent Prayer for these young souls to say **out loud**: "I ask any and all beings to assist in bringing aid, comfort, nourishment, and peace to the citizens in Syria, Iraq, Afghanistan, and the surrounding countries, thank you!"*

Mountain Ranges, Trees, Plants, and Souls

Gaia, are mountains and mountain ranges ensouled, or do they just have a connection to you?
I do have souls that assist me with large mountain ranges and the mountains that make up the mountain ranges. We have not discussed this at length, so you may wish to work up some questions for me here.

Do you have less or more than 25 souls assisting you with this work?
Just a few more, Tom. There are vast mountain ranges all over Earth. They enjoy the work as don't forget they could be ensouling an asteroid as I did for millions of years. Here they get what you could call "hands-on training" for one day being assigned a planet. They are my apprentices.

Gaia, back to your mountain apprentices, what is the exact number, since I would think there would be many more than the 25 you mentioned. And would an individual mountain such as Mt. Everest have a soul, or would it just be part of the Himalayas?
Let's take up the number first, yes, as I told you there are more than 25.

Are there more than 50?
No, just below that figure, Tom. It is more in the mid-40 range. Go with the figure of 45. Regarding individual mountains, these souls, don't forget, are much more capable than you might initially think. There is one soul taking care of the Himalayas, but a fragment of itself takes care of Mt. Everest. It is visited by thousands of people each year and the most sensitive of those can feel the soul's presence. It is, in its own way, a living entity.

Gaia, I've been meaning for a while to ask you about the ensoulments of mountains, trees, and anything else you can add.
Certainly, Tom. Yes, many inanimate objects are ensouled. Why, you may

ask? Because all souls need this experience.

So, are these whole souls or just fragments that ensoul trees and mountains?
Yes, Tom, they are fragments. The souls do not need to be completely within, as I am within the Earth. So, they will have fragments of themselves to have this experience. And like all souls, as I have mentioned before, they are experiencing hundreds of thousands of lives across the Universe all at the same time.

So, how small do we go with these ensoulments—pebble, bushes, grass, and so on?
Yes, even the smallest piece of sand that washes up on shore is connected to a soul.

Gaia, checking with all the GAs, what percentage of people in the world believes that all animals, plants, and trees are ensouled?
Perhaps a little larger than you have imagined, Tom, but not huge. Let's go with the number 40% of the people in the world believe all you mentioned are ensouled. That leaves a lot of people that do not, but that will slowly change over the years, thanks to people like you.

I would have thought it higher, after thinking about it, as some religions do have that as one of their tenets.
You've included all living things, Tom, and some might believe animals are ensouled, but do not include plants and trees, you see. Part of your soul contract is to widen these people's understanding of life on Earth. We will see that your book reaches a wider audience than you can imagine at the present time as, don't forget, it will still exist after you have transitioned. You have been told many times that much of what you write is for future generations.

Gaia, are tree fragments warned in advance if they will be cut down, or destroyed in a fire or tornado, or some other calamity?
Certainly, Tom. The souls of the trees and plants know from the time they first begin to grow how long they will last. This is not a surprise. These souls are able to see the future, just as human souls can view all time

periods.

Gaia, why would tree souls agree to lightning strikes that potentially would destroy the tree?
Good question, Tom. When the various tree souls agreed to come to Earth, they completely understood they would have to live by and in Earth conditions. That not only meant having some of their trees be struck by lightning, but to have whole forests die in forest fires, and others swept away in floods. As I have told you before, Earth is a living thing, and all those souls that take part in being here completely understood the rules in a microsecond when Creator asked them to assist in populating the planet, but they are also given great freedom to grow their trees anywhere on Earth that can sustain them. And they agreed to provide wood for your fires and lumber for your homes. They are all part of an ecosystem and do their part as part of the Earth Experiment.

Gaia, do plant and tree soul fragments have staging areas too?
Yes, they do, Tom. All soul fragments that are not in human form have these staging areas. We knew you would get back to clarify that, and now we have.

So, they don't always return to the same area they were in before the tree or plant died?
Not always, Tom, but most of the time there is that comfort level and these plant and tree souls need the fragments in whatever part of the world they were in before.

Do the fragments have any say?
Yes, quite a bit, you see, as they were attached to the other trees and/or plant fragments they grew with. There is a balance, but also these souls have their own learning and communicating with other tree and plant souls through their fragments adds to their knowledge in many ways beyond what you understand at this time.

Gaia, do trees feel pain, such as when we trim or even cut down a tree?
Yes, in a way they do, Tom. When a tree is trimmed, the tree knows it is normally in its best interest to do so. All trees have a group soul, and all

feelings are passed back. When a tree is cut down and/or dies, again, there is this connection. The reverse is true if the tree is allowed to stand in a forest untouched. It enjoys humans and can recognize you as you pass by each day. Be kind to trees and they will be kind to you. Trees are imbued with their own form of personalities and there are those trees who prefer human contact and those that do not.

Gaia, has the Explorer Race had lives as a tree prior to our lives as humans in the Earth Experiment?
Quite a few of you have, Tom. It is a way for many of you to experience and appreciate the contributions that trees make in this world.

So, what percentage of souls taking part in the Earth Experiment have had lives as trees?
A high percentage, Tom—let's say over 80%. In the scheme of things, these were brief lives—30 to 50 years.

Are any souls still doing this in this time period?
No, this took place several million years ago.

Gaia, do trees communicate with other trees and perhaps other forms of life? How would you explain their awareness?
Trees are able to communicate on a certain level with not only other trees but, yes, flowers, grass, shrubs, or bushes and even to welcome birds and other creatures. In the future, humans will learn to communicate with trees. They even have their own personalities. And they do communicate telepathically on what I will describe as a channel most humans have not tuned into, except for those who love forestry and can "feel" the energy of the trees. This is something humans are capable of developing, should you desire.

Past Life Experience of Current Souls

Have the millennial souls being born during this time period had more lives on Earth or about the same as the other time periods?
Because there is more peace in the world, although it may not seem like it at the present time, there are a number of souls lined up and already

arriving who are more seasoned souls of every type and persuasion you can imagine—especially the arts—as they need times of peace to be able to create. There will always be a mixture of young souls who are having lives during peaceful times in order to work on family dynamics and there will be those younger souls who have to experience such things as wars and major Earth events. So, to summarize, more older souls in terms of Earth lives are having lives at this time. You will see great progress over the next 100 years as you were previously told.

Soul Cluster

Gaia, can we tell the difference between a person we meet from a soul cluster we often work with and one that has a good aura?
Most people cannot, Tom. That's the simple answer, but so much more happens below the surface. Almost every person you interact with, even in a small way, you have interacted with before or they have interacted with you in the past—there is a slight difference there. There are thousands of soul clusters and millions of soul fragments, and as we have said before, some you interact with all the time, and others only sporadically. This is a complex orchestration, Tom, for all your souls' learning. One's aura can change from life to life, depending upon not only your health, but whether you are playing the part of what is considered a good person, and one that is a thief, robber, rapist, or murderer. Then you get those warning signals from your GA. Pay attention—don't discount them.

How many random people do we meet from soul clusters we work with in many lives?
That is impossible to answer, Tom, as in one life you may live in a remote location and encounter few people in that life, and in another where you are in a busy city and meet random people each day. They may be random, but again, your lives have probably touched before.

Soul Contracts

Gaia, what are the soul contracts of people who have the money and ability to travel, yet stay close to home?
As you might guess, this occurs quite often with younger souls. Many

make a good living, but where they grew up is quite comfortable to them. There are those who have prejudices—real and imagined. They fear the unknown. Many times, these are set-up lives for lives in the future with those they are close to. As you can imagine, there can be many reasons for sticking close to home.

Gaia, was there a group soul contract for the firefighters who were killed in Arizona fighting the forest fire?
Yes, certainly they all had soul contracts to perish there, Tom, so you could term it a group soul contract, although all of the firemen were from different souls—none were from the same cluster, you see. So, they were able to balance lives where they had burned buildings and such, which resulted in the destruction of men, women, and children. People tend to forget how much violence there is now and was over the years, Tom, until something like this occurs. There are many images even on film of soldiers setting fire to buildings, huts, houses, to force people out to shoot them or if they stayed in the houses, they were burned alive. All those lives have to be balanced at some point. I can assure your readers those firefighters were happy to balance those previous lives while doing something honorable for their fellow citizens.

Gaia, how does a drug overdose correspond to a person's soul contract?
On everyone's bucket list there is a life where one experiments with drugs to the point of addiction. There are many types of addiction, and it can range from too much alcohol to drugs, to eating, to any number of other addictions. A drug overdose can very well be on a person's soul contract, or it can be free will. Naturally, if the person dies it is part of the soul contract that a death by addiction was part of the soul plan for the further education of their soul.

Are these typically younger souls?
Younger to medium. As they become more seasoned, they avoid these addictions. It is as if a person burns their hand in a fire. They become much more cautious after that.

Gaia, what were the soul contracts of the victims and perpetrators of

the atomic bomb attacks on Nagasaki and Hiroshima?
All the people who died in those bombings, just as other bombings in the Second World War, had taken lives in other conflicts, including Atlantis and Lemuria and even other wars before records were kept or were destroyed.

Gaia, what is the probability of the use of A-bombs or similar devices in the future?
They will never be used again, Tom. You have raised your vibrational levels to a point where that will not occur again. So therefore, the probability is zero.

Gaia, do some people's soul contracts call for side effects from the vaccines, including medical complications and even death?
Yes, of course. These complications are definitely on their soul contracts. It is all part of your learning. The hospitalizations and even deaths can be a way of balancing another life. As you were previously told, your souls are very creative in balancing bad guy past lives. May I remind everyone to request a Most Benevolent Outcome each time you leave your house or work to avoid anyone who is ill.

Gaia, regarding the Boston bombers, why would it be in their soul contracts to plant the bombs and kill what on the surface appears to be innocent people?
Yes, a complex question, Tom, with a variety of reasons. First the "victims," as we will call them, all had soul contracts to either die or be injured in the explosion, as in past lives they had caused explosions which maimed or killed people literally over thousands and thousands of years. So, it was balancing, but both the bombers and their victims knew on a soul level that this would bring about great passionate feelings of people all over the world, and that one event will raise, and has raised, your vibrational levels just a little more, as even rivals showed compassion and togetherness. That is important, as some people take being rivals to the extreme, expressing hatred just because another's ball team is not theirs.

An event such as this wipes away this façade and brings out the humanity in men, women, and children. So even the bombers knew on a soul level that they would be contributing to the greater good, even as they planned their dastardly deed, shall we say. So many of your readers will be able to step back and look at not only the pain and misery of those affected by the bombing, but also the great compassion this created, and will continue to create in the future.

Gaia, will there be healing for the Canadian Aboriginal population from past injustices, and what is their most probable future?
Tom, the old saying "time heals everything" does apply in this case of injustice to native people. Yes, there is still animosity and prejudice towards them, but this is dissipating and in the next generation or so, these will only be stories as these native peoples will be much more accepted. They are the fulcrum of this land, but there will continue to be integration of these people into society, just as has happened in most parts of the United States.

They will find gainful employment, although there will be those holdouts for some time who wish to follow the ways of their fathers and mothers. So, the highest probability will be acceptance and integration over a period of time and the injustices towards these native peoples will dissipate and eventually will be nothing but stories and not perceived insults and other displays of antagonism.

May I also remind everyone, Tom, that these are soul contracts to experience this as they have been on the other side of the fence and have been the antagonists in prior lives. This is how there is balancing.

*Here's a Benevolent Prayer for everyone to say **out loud**: "I ask any and all beings to assist in protecting and healing all the Aboriginal people of the world who are suffering any racist and inhumane policies and may this take place even sooner than we can hope for or expect, thank you!"*

Gaia, is everything that happens in life part of our soul contract?
Yes, in a way, Tom. Certainly, there are Plans B, C, D, etc., that come into being according to how many times a person does not follow their original, and I'll add best, soul plan. But your souls are able to see every possibility, Tom, and simply adjust the soul contracts to try and make the best out of

the situation.

Gaia, why do the people of Haiti have soul contracts to experience such misery from earthquakes, pestilence, and hurricanes? Is it because they are quite young in terms of Earth lives?

Quite true, Tom. These souls chose to check off several things on their bucket list as you and other people call it. Most of the souls having lives there are quite young in terms of Earth lives—under 100. So, not only do they experience these severe events, they also learn how to cope with poverty, constantly rebuilding and learning reliance that they can survive and rebuild their lives over and over again if need be. It gives them a firm base to know that if they can handle all of that in one life, they can handle anything they will encounter in other lives.

Gaia, why is it on so many soul contracts for adult children to live with their parents during this time period?

So many of the souls that are the parents of adult children incarnated during this time period to work to anchor the raising of the vibrational levels, so they would be considered on average older souls in terms of Earth lives. In many cases, their sons and daughters had taken care of them in other lives, so there is great balancing here as the parents of today do the same for their children. Another reason is that a number of children have taken on circumstances where they are unable to take care of themselves and on a soul level their parents now agreed to take care of them during these more difficult lives.

Do they generally have an internal struggle of feelings of independence?

Those feelings of a desire for independence are always there, no matter the circumstances, but the care is given with love in most cases, and it is, but one life that is needed to balance, or it will be balanced in the future when the children become the caregivers. So, please understand that there are millions of circumstances for adult children to live with their parents. It can be medical, economic, and of course being the caregivers for their parents. You cannot make a sweeping statement that all adult children should live independently.

Soul Interest

What percentage of our lives on Earth are spent working on our soul interest?
Pick a number, as it varies from life to life. You might be working on relationships a higher percentage in one life than another. In other lives you may begin working on your soul interest even in your earliest childhood years. Just look at the child prodigies who start at barely past the toddler stage. There is no set number, only the person being interested in subjects in school more than others or seemingly not interested at all. The more mature the soul, the easier it is for their guides and GAs to communicate with them.

Do people with more technological soul interests have more lives later in more technologically advanced times?
It would seem that way, but there are many time periods where one must learn the basics and add knowledge. People tend to forget that the Atlantean people existed for 50,000 years before they destroyed themselves and the Lemurians even a little longer. Both became very technologically advanced—there just are no records. There were plenty of opportunities for people with various technological interests to gain experience. They did not need to cram hundreds of lives in this and future time periods.

Gaia, how far in advance do our souls preplan our lives, and are there any changes just before birth?
As we have explained before, Tom, your souls are much more than even you can imagine, although you've come a long way in your understanding. When the Earth Experiment was being set up, you could say, they chose the time periods well over a million years in advance, and the type of lives they would have in those time periods, along with coordinating with other souls who would be having their soul clusters in those time periods. As you might imagine, this is a great planning process far beyond your understanding at this time. Regarding changes prior to birth, yes, there are tweaks in the soul plans and soul contracts. And, as we have said before, you are also constantly rewriting your pasts and futures as you experience these lives and grow and raise your vibrational levels. Your memories of

the past adjust too.

Soul Sign-Off

Gaia, how does the need for a soul sign-off agree or work within the structure of our soul contracts to exit at a particular time and way?
Yes, before you are born, Tom, there are certain sets of probabilities in place regarding how the world will operate—I'll use that word. These probabilities can include, depending upon where you live, the probabilities of hurricanes, tornadoes, and earthquakes. So, if your soul contract calls for you to experience one of those events, or others I have not mentioned, then it is up to your soul and your guardian angel to adjust your schedule so that you are there when a particular probability does manifest.

All of your futures are fluid in a way, Tom, and it is quite easy for your soul and your guardian angel to adjust to specific timings chosen for large Earth events such as the ones I mentioned. It may seem complicated on your 3D/5D level, but your souls have done this thousands of times for all of your lives on Earth.

So, what does that tell us, everyone? If you suddenly hear about friends that have to suddenly travel to or from the West Coast—basically a lot of movement in any direction, that might just be a clue to a coming event.

Gaia, am I correct in stating that all souls affected by earthquakes must sign off before you cause it to happen?
That is correct, Tom. All souls must sign off.

What if 99% of the souls sign off and one percent does not. Can it be arranged for their people to be away and not affected, or is that just part of the equation too, that on certain people's soul contracts they are not to be directly affected by the earthquake—only on the periphery, shall we say?
I leave it to each soul to either experience the earthquake, and or tsunami, or not experience it according to what they need on their "bucket list" as you call it, Tom. So, the people, let's say, in the immediate affected area, Tom, may have a soul contract to experience it and possibly be injured or

lose their life. Another group of people may have it in their soul contracts to experience the earthquake but miraculously survive. Then another group may have their soul contract read to be on a trip and are only affected in that their home is destroyed. Then there are the "first responders" who have soul contracts to find the dead and injured. Others affected can be medical doctors and nurses to treat the injured. Then another soul group has their contracts read to assist in rebuilding the damaged area.

And finally, there is the soul group that is not affected directly but shows compassion for those directly affected. Obviously, the first two or three groups are the most important, shall we say, but again, they all must sign off on the event. I work closely with all of the souls involved. They are all nearby and we are in instant communication with each other.

Twin Flames

Gaia, I asked this years ago, but perhaps a better explanation on twin flames in the present time? And can a person incarnate into two different bodies in their next life?
What people call twin flames, Tom, are in actuality soul fragments from the same soul cluster. As we have discussed before, it is very rare for this to occur, since the soul wishes its fragments to have separate lives for the greatest learning. The term can also apply, due to a lack of knowledge, to two people from different clusters, who over and over again incarnate as husband and wife, wife and husband, or lovers. Over time, this becomes a deep connection—hence the term, twin flames. Yes, and even homosexual relationships if that is called for, to experience in one or more lives.

Regarding incarnating into two different bodies, no, but again as we explained before there can be overlapping lives. Still, they are considered separate lives and can take place one right after the other, or 40-something lives down the way, such as your life going on right now working in the Pentagon, in preparation to be a close advisor to the U.S. president starting in 2032.

Walk-Ins

Gaia, are "walk-ins" still common these days, as we have heard little about these recently?

Not so common, but, yes, there are still walk-ins, Tom. This was quite prevalent at the time when you were getting close to the Harmonic Convergence and your souls were assisting you in getting over the hump, so to speak. It was quite noticeable to those people—family and friends—who interacted with the person. Suddenly, they seemed like a different person—different personality—and they were. This has been discussed in detail in such books, as by Ruth Montgomery—just a little explanation for your new readers, but these days things are more settled, you could say. So, yes, to answer the question, walk-ins still occur, but not in the numbers that occurred in the 70s and 80s.

Whole Souls

How can whole souls develop if everything is known or constant?

That's one of the reasons for the Earth Experiment. Over a very long time—eons you could say—the souls raised their vibrational levels to a point where they would not rise anymore. Something had to be done, and this Creator decided to use the four negative energies as a catalyst. No other creator had been successful, so it is quite an achievement that Creator's experiment worked.

Gaia, do soul fragments remain close to Earth after transitioning, close in the galaxy, or can this not be explained in 3D terms?

Good question, Tom, from your reader. Yes, soul fragments return to a dimension much more than a location. Naturally, that is not so far away in your terms, but yet completely removed from any influence the Earth might have.

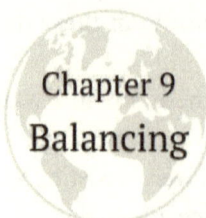

Chapter 9
Balancing

Avalanche Death and Balancing

Gaia, is being buried and dying of carbon monoxide poisoning in an avalanche balancing a life of poisoning others in a past life?
Your reader hit on one of the many ways one can balance a life where you poisoned others. As with many answers you have received before, Tom, there are many ways to balance harming and/or killing another person on Earth. It does not have to be a repeat of the actual act as your souls are very clever in having you balance past actions in other lives.

Drug Use and Balancing

Gaia, does there have to be balancing in a future life for the use of drugs, or is it one of those experiences that people must have on their soul contracts for one or more lives?
Yes, it is one of those experiences, Tom, but balancing must be done if they affect other people, such as their families, friends, and others they encounter with their drug use. They might induce someone to try drugs, which causes them to become an addict too. Then balancing must be done. And they will have to experience a family member who becomes addicted to drugs and the hurt and problems it causes families.

So typically, an addict does not live in a vacuum, and there will be balancing done in the future, as you must experience all the Earth has to offer and see everything from all points of view.

Explanation of Concept of "Balancing"

Does balancing go on until the very last life on Earth?

As we have said before, by the time you reach your last life, all must balance at the end. There are things that you can balance even in your last life on Earth. After that you can return to your planet and be considered the wise old soul to lead and guide others who either chose not to volunteer for the Earth Experiment, or whose vibrational level had not reached the level where they could volunteer.

Is there no form of balancing in the rest of the Universe?
Not as there is in the Earth Experiment, Tom. They are not veiled and can look back thousands of lives should they wish. Keep in mind they are at a little higher vibrational level than are you, and that does make a difference. Most, and I'm being very general here, do not have to make the hundreds of decisions you have to make on a daily basis.

Family Members' Actions and Balancing

Gaia, we don't have to balance actions of our families, do we?
No, not unless they were involved with the family in doing something together that must be balanced. Keep in mind that whole families can reincarnate together to balance deeds done as a family in the past. So, you see, Tom, that there are millions of possibilities here, but as a general rule everyone must balance their own actions.

Historical Figures and Balancing

Gaia, would you say that Bill Clinton, HillaryClinton, and Donald Trump will have an equal number of balancing lives in the future, or will one have more than the others?
Good question, Tom. Yes, all three will have about the same number of balancing lives. Each will be different according to the actions taken in this life. All three will carry over to other lives as these are all learning experiences for their souls. They will not have to have the number of balancing lives leaders such as Assad will have to have to balance his actions, along with a few other leaders from the 20th and 21st centuries. Those three you mentioned are certainly not in the category of leaders who order the killing of thousands of innocent people.

Gaia, what is the highest probability for Mrs. Clinton in this life, and what is the probability for her returning in the future to be the leader of the USA or another world leader?
Yes, the highest probability in this life is that she will immerse herself in programs to aid women not just in the United States, but all over the world. This will be a significant contribution on her part to women's equality. She will return again in another life and will be a world leader. There are hundreds of years in your future and having a woman lead the United States will come about, although Mrs. Clinton will not be the first woman to break the "glass ceiling," as it has been called. A dynamic woman will appear on the governmental stage, we will say, that will be a dynamic leader, without the baggage Mrs. Clinton has borne.

Gaia, Stalin ordered the execution of 22,000 Polish soldiers at Katyn. How can he balance that in his future lives?
He started, Tom, by having a life as one of those soldiers. Then he will also have lives in government where he will be hailed as a great and benevolent leader, but he was also responsible for millions of other deaths, so like such people as Hitler, the number of balancing lives is over 100.

Hunting for Food Balancing

Is there any balancing to be done by those who hunt animals to feed themselves and their families as compared to buying the meat in a store?
None. The animals hunted have agreed to be food for humans. The slaughter process can be very stressful for the animals, but again we have covered that the demand for red meat will dissipate over time until eventually your diet will be plant-based.

I assume the cattle ranches will have to change to produce other food, or they will go out of business?
Yes, and this will happen even sooner than most people expect. The government will step in to absorb these lands, and various animals will roam free.

Indigenous Americans and Balancing

Gaia, what balancing did American Indians have in order to experience genocide?

That's an easy one, Tom. Just look at the many times even in recent history when people lost their lives to genocide. All those lives where people took other peoples' lives have to be balanced whether it is in the past, present, or future. Those that take part in genocide must have lives and that can be multiple lives where they must experience being slain too.

Karma and Balancing

Gaia, does Earth have karma? How long will the drought in California and the Southwest last? Will parts of the Earth not be inhabited in the future? Is this part of a plan to move people off the coasts? (Asked July 2021)

The Earth does not have karma. Karma—or balancing—is for those taking part in the Earth Experiment. I, along with your souls, control these events, such as earthquakes or volcanic eruptions as part of your learning.

Then we would assume that the drought in California and the Southwest is part and parcel of our learning?

Yes, Tom. I do have cycles and that area is experiencing a drought for your ability to learn how to exist with little water, and of course this is a bucket list item. The drought will continue for several more years but will come to an end. There will be much learning in the meantime.

Is this part of your way to move people off the coasts and away from an area subject to earthquakes?

There you have it, Tom. I have to move these tectonic plates and the fewer the number of people that live there the fewer who will be affected. There are always multiple reasons for my actions. I'm using forest fires, lack of rain, and smaller earthquakes to give a big hint that this part of the country is not a pleasant place to live. Some people refuse to get the message.

When, during our sleep time, we have been told that we are solving problems across the Universe—why doesn't it create good karma for us?

On Earth, you assist people out of the goodness of your heart—your being.

It's the same way when you assist people all across the Universe. Your souls are thrilled to be able to help someone solve a problem. And it is not just a one-way street—your souls are also learning as part of your preparation to one day meld into a creator yourself.

Murder and Balancing

Gaia, regarding a deranged person who murders a number of people, would you say a soul volunteers its soul fragment, who is already scheduled to kill three or four people as part of balancing, to expand the role to add in others who need to balance too even though they had done nothing to this person?

Yes, Tom, in a way you could say that the soul volunteers a fragment for this duty. The soul knows that on a wide scale this will affect many people with compassion, which assists in their growth, as you can see by the hundreds and, yes, many thousands of people who pray for the families, leave flowers and other tokens of remembrance and so on, to people who on the surface do not seem affected but are. This has a ripple effect on thousands and thousands of people across the world. It generates love.

But what about the deranged soul? Doesn't it affect the soul fragment, which in turn affects the whole soul?

Again, in a way, Tom, but not as badly as you might think. The soul volunteered and there will be great love given to the person who is the mass murderer, and the soul fragment will be given lives where friends and relatives are killed and they suffer the same heartache, plus there will be physical problems such as heart attacks to balance. They will also have lives of great service. The soul gains much from these balancing lives it needs as part of its learning. The soul fragment is not scarred forever as all your lives must balance at the end.

Natural Disasters and Balancing

Gaia, what percentage of accidents or natural disasters are balancing compared to bucket list items?

Certainly, a large percentage of "accidents" are assisting in balancing— use the number of 90 percent for your purposes. Ten percent would be to create opportunities for caregivers of all types.

I would have thought the number of bucket list experiences would have been higher.
Young souls make many mistakes, Tom, and accidents are one way of assisting in balancing. It does not have to be an eye for an eye.

Obesity and Balancing

Gaia, did starvation in past lives result in obesity in this life, or are there other explanations?
Certainly, that is one explanation, Tom, and a major one, but there are other explanations, such as having ridiculed or done harm to an obese person in a past life. When someone does that, they balance by living a life as an obese person to understand what it feels like to be obese. Of course, the obese person can be learning how to control body weight and learn to exercise to show how you can change your body weight through exercise and portion control. Therefore, there can be one reason or several for obesity in this time period.

Gaia, if a person is obese, but says the Daily Benevolent Prayer, must they stay obese for balancing?
There is no "must," Tom. Certainly, there are choices one makes prior to this life, but saying the Daily Benevolent Prayer is a great step as I have said many times. You just have to say this on faith.

Then beyond this starting point let's call it, certainly there are many things you can do, but some obesity cannot be corrected by just dieting and must be done with the assistance of a good doctor as there might be something internally out of kilter, but to answer your reader's question, obesity is a very complex subject and no two people are alike. You can say they are, but each person brings their own past lives' baggage with them, we will call it, so, yes, there is balancing to be done, but one of the answers is to love yourself for who you are.

This is really difficult for many people. It can be a past life bleeding over, or it can be from childhood where the parents or parent told the child they were no good for anything. So "love thyself" should be one motto to live by, and love others unconditionally. When you request a Most Benevolent Outcome to be led to the best treatment for your condition, you do open the door to controlling your weight in whatever form or method you are led to. Just know you are totally loved on this side of the veil by everyone, and I do mean everyone, Tom. Take that to the bank, shall we say.

Parenting and Balancing

Gaia, do we balance being a parent an equal number of times, and what about the number of children?
It all depends upon the soul interest, Tom. Most souls greatly enjoy being a parent and assisting children to grow, but others have a different focus and prefer to have as few children as possible during their many lives on Earth. Still, in order to have lives on Earth they must experience everything a parent must experience during their several hundred lives.

Popularity and Balancing

Gaia, how do people balance lives as a popular person?
In some lives you are a leader, and in other lives you are a follower, Tom. These are all bucket list items, you could call them, but a strong personality can be good in one life, and the next to sit back and just be part of a group, or even be shy and introverted. There are many personality traits that are chosen for particular lives.

Pulmonary Fibrosis and Balancing

Gaia, what are people balancing when they experience pulmonary fibrosis?
It balances lives where they have snuffed out the breath of someone or more than one person. They choose this life to balance taking the life of someone by taking away their ability to breath. Your souls are very creative in finding ways for you to balance, just as you balanced bringing grief and heartache as a German soldier by experiencing congestive heart failure in this life.

Racism and Balancing

Gaia, why does it seem that the Black race is looked down upon by the other races?
Certainly, on the surface it has been the case that so many people from that continent have been enslaved, along with the fact that so many have remained in spartan villages with seemingly no desire to advance. This is now changing. There is a change, albeit very slowly, for them to raise themselves out of poverty, thanks to many innovations such as bringing power to remote villages, and with it, computers. This will open the floodgates for the education of the masses.

Was this part of Creator's or the ETs' plans?
Yes, to a certain extent. There had to be one or two races that would lag behind in development. You can include the Chinese here because for many centuries, and even still today, there are many remote villages that live the same way they have lived for thousands of years.

But as I mentioned before, there is great wealth beneath the surface in Africa, including needed minerals that you have no knowledge of as yet. There will be great stories in the future of whole villages living in poverty that suddenly become billionaires. That's how dramatic it will be.

Were there or are there problems that other planets could not resolve regarding differences in race?
Yes, and there you have another reason. There are planets where one race will look down upon others, so as part of the Earth Experiment you have taken on this problem as one of those you will solve. Each race will be looked upon for its unique talents, but as acceptance grows, so will the integration of the races until finally there is only one Earth race.

Gaia, I'm asked will the Black race learn of its true history in the future, and I'll add, will this come from our ET friends?
Yes, Tom, they will learn they are truly one of the originals and why the color of their skin is Black as part of the Earth Experiment we have discussed before; and, yes, this knowledge will come from ET sources as there is no other way for them, or for that matter, any of you to learn your

true origins.

Why are Black men killed so often?
Certainly, this has to do with poverty in cities, Tom, since the Black population has fought to overcome the stigma of having been slaves not only in the United States, but in other places that raided Africa—and, I might add, with the assistance of Africans themselves—to put people into slavery. There was a vast native population living in Africa that unscrupulous individuals took advantage of. With that came balancing, you understand, where they had to spend lives as slaves themselves. This goes on to this day, as has been in your news of children being taken to the Superbowl to be used as sex slaves. This will change over the coming years, Tom, as everyone learns their true histories. The Black race is one of the oldest on Earth and they will take pride in that fact. Once you give pride to someone, it is a gift that can be a great motivator.

And race will not be an issue one day?
Again, this will happen over hundreds of years, Tom, slowly, but surely, and, yes, you can see this almost every day on the streets of your cities, you see mixed race couples. There will even be a Superbowl ad featuring a mixed race couple this year. As this happens, the skin colors will be blurred, and eventually there will be only one skin color for all Earth humans—a light chocolate brown.

Speaking Ill of the Dead and Balancing

Gaia, do we have to balance speaking negatively about a person who transitioned or in some way tarnished their reputation?
Yes, in a way you do, as you open yourself up while still alive to criticism and for others to think less of you, whether that person had those defects or had made mistakes or not. You can also say something nice about them. Then you are raising your own vibrational level.

Spy Career and Balancing

Gaia, I was previously told that being a spy was on our bucket list of things to experience on Earth. Was it just one life, or did this crop up

multiple times?

It all depends upon your soul interest and contracts, Tom. Normally it is just one life but can be multiple lives if a soul wishes the excitement, danger, and terror of being a spy. There also has to be balancing. So that if the spy takes another life or lives, certainly those have to be balanced. That, along with being spied upon, so that one knows what it's like to feel betrayed by someone you admire, like, love, are friends with, or a family member, etc.

Which country has the most spies in other countries? Would it be the United States, Russia, China, or another country?

No, Tom. You named the big three. All three have approximately the same number of spies around the world with different tasks, shall we say. It is not always political espionage, but also economic, and that includes scientific espionage. There are many types of spies, as anyone watching television can see from dramas, but also those who are caught, and their captures publicized.

Technology Interests and Balancing

Do people with more technological soul interests have more lives later in time—more technologically advanced times?

It would seem that way, but there are many time periods where one must learn the basics and add knowledge. People tend to forget that the Atlantean people existed for 50,000 years before they destroyed themselves and the Lemurians even a little longer. Both became very technologically advanced—there just are no records. There were plenty of opportunities for people with various technological interests to gain experience. They did not need to cram hundreds of lives in this and future time periods.

Trauma and Balancing

What balancing do people with transgenerational trauma have?

Good question. These typically are balancing lives, where they live in fear, even though the probability of being assaulted or killed is much less than for their parents or grandparents. They were perpetrators in one or more previous lives, and they need to feel how it affects generations down the line.

Trophy Hunters and Balancing

Gaia, how will hunters balance the taking of lives of animals for sport?
Yes, they will have to balance lives where they hunt just for trophies. A hunter that must provide food for his family or as income certainly is a different story than those who hunt for simply the thrill of a big kill. Those people must balance by caring for animals so that they appreciate what animals do for you, or in some cases become the hunted; as an example, an escapee from prison or a slave being hunted down. Then they feel the fear the poor animals feel just before their deaths. Again, all lives must be balanced before the Explorer Race departs Earth one day.

Gaia, we've covered this a little before, but what types of balancing is there for a person who trophy hunts all their lives, hanging heads of their trophies in their houses?
As we stated before, they have the option of becoming an advocate against trophy hunting, or they can take care of wounded animals, giving their love to them. They can also suffer the grief of a favorite dog or cat being killed, so that they experience grief. And for the extreme cases you mention they might also be the hunted, to know the fear the animals feel as they are hunted down. Upon their transition they are all shown the error of their ways and vow to do better next time, and they do, and they themselves set up the circumstances for one or more upcoming lives, Tom.

Gaia, please explain the soul contracts of trophy hunters.
They have had past lives as hunter-gatherers and in this life, they have the urge to do so again, but this time their egos get in the way as a desire to conquer all. Obviously, these are young souls that have yet to learn to respect and love all life on Earth. They will have future lives where they will work hard to conserve the very animals they are killing for sport this time around. And, yes, as you thought, they will have lives where they will lose their lives to wild beasts.

You can even see this balancing in the present time as there are those who fall victim to all sorts of wild animals, from reptiles to bears to lions and so on. Those are balancing lives where they live in order to atone for past lives when they simply killed with no other thought, but to add another head on their wall.

Let us say this Benevolent Prayer: "I ask any and all beings to assist those who hunt for sport only to come to love all of the animal kingdom and assist in its conservation, thank you!"

Twin Towers Death and Balancing

Gaia, since you previously said that our souls are very creative in balancing lives, how will the terrorists who destroyed the Twin Towers and killed 3,000 people balance these lives?
All have already had lives where they perished when the towers collapsed, and we might add, Tom, more than one life, including those who were first responders—the firemen. They've also had lives or are having lives as those who are family members who have grieved over the loss of their loved ones. Their soul fragments are learning from every phase of the destruction—even those who searched the rubble for days and weeks.

Then there will be other balancing lives where they will be victims of crimes in very random ways, and either will pay with their lives, or spend many years in prison, many with harsh conditions since, don't forget, that they can have lives in the past along with the present and future. Most will have lives cut short as the result of wars, both ancient and in the 20th century. Plus, they will be given hints that those lives will be cut short. All will have lives as passengers on those planes who were simply innocent victims.

Gaia, is it possible to create a loop in time to learn something like art or some other skill?
In a way, this can be done in a meditative state where each time one meditates you take on the same problem or skill, and in this altered state you work singly on it. You slowly but surely improve. This takes great dedication, and most people in this time period do not have the patience this requires.

Twins and Balancing

Gaia, is it a soul benefit for twins to impersonate each other? Or must they balance in the future?
Being a twin is one of the lists of experiences on Earth. How you handle that experience depends upon whether you will need to balance or not. If you use that to take advantage of anyone in any way, then there is balancing that must be done. Being a twin means that you have an Earth life with someone closely tuned.

WWII and Balancing

Gaia, I'm asked if did Japan's participation in WWII had anything to do with their nuclear disasters and earthquakes and tsunamis?
It would seem so on the surface, Tom, but in reality, these are individual past life deeds that are now being balanced. Many people are attracted to the same continent or islands to have multiple lives there. Certainly, there are a number of people having lives in Japan now who were soldiers in World War II. Their lives were cut short by being a soldier and now they are balancing those actions taken at that time. But again, I harken back to my previous statement that all souls need to experience everything this Earth has to offer in one or more Earth lives. If balancing past lives can be part of the experience, then you've taken care of multiple things on your internal or soul list.

So, Japan as a nation does not attract nuclear events?
I did not say that as, in reality, the remembrance of a nation of such historic events can keep that event closer, shall we say, than letting it fade away. You attract what you fear.

Gaia, was there any balancing done by the crew of the Indianapolis for delivering the first nuclear bomb that would be dropped on Japan in WWII?
No, Tom, but an interesting question. All the members of the crew had the sinking of their ship on their soul contract. To be eaten by sharks did balance lives from the past where they had people killed by wild animals of many types. As we have said before, there are many ways to balance. It

is the end result that matters.

Women Who Tortured Male Babies and Balancing

Gaia, when will the balancing be over for women on the planet who tortured male babies, or have we already balanced that?
There is still some balancing you are doing for those souls, Tom, but by and large, the greatest part of that challenge is over. Yes, there are still females that are harmed, but then there are males who suffer abuse too. This is all part of raising your vibrations to the point where there will be no abuse at some time in the future—and I might add, not that far in the future. Your scientists will discover that there is part of the DNA strand that can be adjusted for those who have a desire to abuse females or males. I will add that your DNA strands are the most complex ever in the history of this Universe. What was once considered "junk DNA" will all be found to be connected to desires, traits, etc. Much of this will be discovered during the next 100 years—but not all. To reiterate, in a way you are still balancing that as one of many things you are balancing for other planets, but you are doing this on a level that they were never capable of doing.

Zetas and Balancing

What about the Zetas, who abducted Earthlings, searching for DNA and the Draco reptilians?
The Zetas—at least that part of their race—were dying and were desperate to find DNA that they could combine with their own. At that time, they were not violating the Earth Directive and were initially allowed, since the people they chose could balance abductions they had done in past lives. Still, it got out of hand and that was shut down, but not before they had enough DNA to create their hybrids.

The Dracos DNA is such that they are wired to aggressively invade other star systems to take over other planets. Creator has allowed this knowing this will change when the 10% of souls having lives on Earth that are reptilian return to their worlds with small percentages of negativity which you live with on a daily basis. Remember, the Explorer Race is going to change the whole Universe, raising their vibrational levels too.

Chapter 10
Past Lives

Antisocial Personalities and Past Life Influence

Gaia, are people with antisocial personalities mostly young souls?
Not always. It depends upon when their souls wish to experience a life with an antisocial personality, but generally we can say that these are experienced as a younger soul. May I remind your readers, Tom, that in many cases these are considered bad guy lives and the soul fragment having that life assists in the growth of other soul clusters that they work with life after life.

What about those with mental conditions?
Again, these are bucket list items to experience in one or more lives and assist in the growth of the other soul cluster fragments. Caring and administering to these people gives them the opportunity for great growth, or the need to balance if they treat these people inhumanely.

Auras Influenced by Past Lives

Gaia, how many lifetimes does it take for someone to seemingly have an aura about them that is charismatic, friendly, and instant rapport?
Depending upon the circumstances, we can say they are typically at least in the first quadrant of being an old soul, but this can vary dramatically if their soul contract is for them to become some sort of leader. There are very devious individuals that project this aura as part of their soul contract to be the "bad guy" this time around to teach their friends, and others in soul clusters, lessons. So, this is not something—a rule—that one must be an old soul to have this aura. It is all part of their soul contract to broadcast to others. They can be having a significant life serving others, or the reverse—they can be the honey that attracts the flies for nefarious means.

It is up to each person to learn to judge whether these are wise and good people, or charlatans. It's all part of your learning, and quite necessary I might add, for you to learn to trust your instincts about people.

Bleed-Throughs

Why does one tend to outgrow the ability to see bleed-throughs?
Children's perceptions have not yet hardened for their present lives. There is still much to learn for your researchers about children's early years, which also includes memories of past lives that slip into the past as they age.

Drowning and Past Lives

Gaia, am I correct in my understanding that everyone must experience drowning in at least one lifetime on Earth, and if so, what percentage of people living on Earth today have never experienced drowning in a past life?
You are correct in your assumption. Fire is another, being killed by another person is yet another, illness is a quite common one. So, percentages— let's see if you can receive this—fully 75%, yes, that high—have never drowned in a past life. I know that number is amazing as you thought it would not be higher than 50%, but, yes, it is quite high. That brings us to the present time where your souls are learning to have these cataclysmic events in order to check this off their bucket list. Even if the probability of this event goes to 100%, there will be many who will not be affected by the flooding that will take place, but, yes, millions will.

Gender Transitions and Reincarnation

Gaia, is it challenging for our soul fragments to transition between male and females over different lives?
Definitely. You might have two or three lives in a row as one gender, but the average soul fragment, don't forget, is living all these lives at the same time, so you are constantly influenced by all your lives, both male and female. The switch is easier than you might imagine.

How do we change genders from one life to another?
Keep in mind that the soul has no gender. It can lean in one direction or another, but for lives on Earth, it is simply setting up the DNA for a life as a male, female, or something in between, according to what the soul needs for growth. It is all in the design of the DNA for each life. Good question.

Jesus and His Past Lives

Gaia, was Jesus aware of his past lives?
Yes, he was quite aware, although he did not dwell on them. As we have said before, his soul fragment was larger than any other having a life on Earth. That statement may sound a little empty since you have nothing to compare one soul fragment with another, but to give you a perspective in human terms, yes, you could say that his soul fragment would be fully double and, yes, even triple in its capacity. That is a huge difference. If all of the soul fragments on Earth had the same capacity, there would be no wars, and you would have already achieved everything in a short time, but that's not what the Explorer Race came here for. You came to raise your vibrational levels in a comparatively short period of time. Jesus showed everyone the correct way to live, with love for everyone. You have been trying to achieve that ever since, and you will, one day in the future, I can assure you.

So may I gently remind your readers, Tom, to love everyone unconditionally. Yes, you may despise their actions many times but just remember that those people are being the antagonists in this life to assist each of you in your growth as long as you respond with love. Even the simple act of sending white light to a person or persons you dislike or despise creates a beautiful energy far beyond what you can imagine. So, when we say shine your light upon the Earth, we do mean send white light every single day somewhere to someone and you will create the loving Earth in which you wish to live.

Gaia, when Jesus healed the blind man, he was asked if the parents were at fault, or was the man, and he said neither. Was that his actual response?
No, Tom. As you guessed, the church twisted what he said to fit what they

wanted. He actually responded that the man was balancing a past life. It was not in those words, but in words that everyone at that time could understand. You can come back and ask that question again, but that was the gist of what he said.

Keeping Knowledge of our Past Lives

Gaia, do we keep the knowledge we have built up over our past lives on a subconscious level or do we start over each life?
Certainly, many people tap into the knowledge they have built up over many lives. Examples of that can be seen in children who can play instruments from an early age, but there are many, many more than that. What most people cannot see is where that knowledge came from. We have gone over many times that Creator wants you to solve problems and make advances without the knowledge of how you handled a certain problem in a past life. Only by you being veiled can this be accomplished, and your souls, I might add, completely agreed.

Reincarnation Removed from the Bible

Gaia, was reincarnation ever in the Bible, then removed?
You could say it was in more than one of the books that comprised the Bible, but those references were removed prior to the actual book. This was fought over for many months at the Council of Nicaea. There was a faction of the men who comprised the group, who wanted this in the Bible, but the majority voted—yes, voted—to remove these references. As you were told previously, they wanted people to feel they had sinned and would offer money to the church and would not understand balancing. They wanted people to focus on this life, which is fine, but it does not explain why some people are born into poverty and others into lives of wealth. Yet, the Bible says all are created equal.

Tom's Past Lives

Gaia, I'm curious as to how we communicated back in my life with the king in the 1800s. Did I do as I do now, was it someone who asked the questions, or how?

Yes, Tom, you went into what was called at that time a trance and the future king would ask questions, or whoever was there.

How did I discover that I could do that?
It seemed to happen "by chance" and, as you know, it was not that by any means. You were slowly awakening from sleep, and suddenly you were given a message by us, using the collective now to relate to him, which was important.

So, it did not happen as a child then?
No, although you did have your fantasies, and you had a great imagination. So, you, yourself, were aware that you were a little different from other children. You could sense things similar to what you did at an early stage in this life, but the breakthrough came with your friend.

After that, did we just make it up as we went as far as my being in a trance?
Yes, you had heard about mediums and visited a couple of sessions to see how they went into a meditative state. It was just that you were much better when you tried it.

Do you see a time in this life where I will do this in public, or will it be better to continue as we do now?
That is your choice, Tom. You are capable of doing that now, but just as you read about your friend, Steve Rother, you are reluctant to do so.

Gaia, of my 1,005 lives on Earth, did that include all the lives where I was not a Homo sapien, or just the lives as a Homo sapien we've referred to as the Adam and Eve model?
Yes, Tom, this did include all of your lives from the very beginning, millions of years ago.

Then how many lives did I have as a Neanderthal?
Very few as you guessed—under five.

So, just enough to get a taste for cannibalism (pun intended).
Yes, I know you could hardly wait to use that, Tom.

What about as a Cro-Magnon?
A few more, as those lives were good preparation for your Adam and Eve lives. There were 10 of those. After that, it was all as a Homo sapien, although you did have some earlier lives in humanoid form back millions of years ago, as you were told in the past.

Gaia, did I have a life as some sort of monk living inside an extinct volcano?
Quite so, Tom. There are such arrangements, shall we call them, with the monks in the Himalayas and this was a life of contemplation and spiritual awakening, shall we call it. You were again exploring religions of the world, and you and your brother and, yes, even sister monks would meditate for hours connecting with people all over the world telepathically. You and your fellow monks tried to assist in bringing peace to the world.

How long ago was this life?
Several hundred years ago, Tom. You were able to develop your abilities in that life, which carried forward even to this life and, of course, beyond. That was a significant life for you.

How was I chosen?
Ah, an age-old mystery perhaps? The monks were quite adept at communicating with spirit and were guided to you at a young age to begin your training. Your parents had a number of children, so it was one less mouth to feed.

Gaia, what sort of lives did I have in Asia?
As you did not have just one life in Asia, but many, it is impossible to just cover one incarnation. You've had lives in several religious orders of religions that were born in Asia. You would have to read more about these religions in order to comment further.

What about the Shinto religion?
Oh, yes, you would not have missed the beginning of that religion. Again, you can read more about this religion and others for Asia so that you can ask specific questions.

Gaia, when you started saying "God speed" was it simply to help me remember that past life in England, or was it somehow to connect us?
Good question, Tom. Yes, to both questions. I wanted to remind you of a significant life where you greatly contributed to helping the people of the world raise their vibrational levels by banning slavery, along with other accomplishments you had a hand in. And I knew that you would learn more about that life which would inspire you to attempt to achieve the same in this life. Emulation can be good at times.

In 2001 my wife and I and two other couples went to Sedona on vacation. This was where I saw my first UFO coming out of Boynton Canyon, but also one night my wife awoke and saw several lights hovering over me. So, I asked about this. Why were the lights over me while I slept in Sedona during our trip there in 2001?
Yes, those were some friendly ETs prepping your body in ways your scientists will not discover for hundreds of years, Tom, in order to raise your vibrational level high enough to perform this work for your fellow man and woman.

Gaia, exactly who was Apollonius of Tyana, and did I ever know him in my life either as Strabo or Salome?
Yes, your paths definitely crossed several times. Unlike Strabo, none of his writings have survived, so his life was only recorded by a biographer.

Was he an older seasoned soul?
Oh, yes, quite seasoned by that time. And, yes, he did influence a number of people.

But he was not on the level of Jesus?
No.

Gaia, was I one of the 10 first Popes in a past life?
Yes, you were, Tom. A bad boy, we'll say, but that was your soul contract for that life, and I might add you played it to the hilt, shall we say.

So, was I one of the first five Popes?
No, Tom. I know you thought you might be one of the first five but try

seven for the number.

So, is it seven.
Yes, Tom. Seven is the correct number.

When I go into a meditative state, I have surrounded myself with white light and then with gold light. Does that make any difference, or should I just stick with the white light?
No, Tom. Continue as you are doing, as, yes, you can separate the light, and it never hurts to have too much light protection. It also helps us to adjust to your vibrational level a little more easily than with just white light.

Gaia, did I or did I not have a family that went with me to Egypt in the Gentle Way life on Atlantis?
Yes, and no, Tom. How's that for an answer? You had no immediate family, as your work kept you very focused in that life, but you had distant family, we shall call them—cousins and such—that accompanied you to Egypt. You do have to be very specific in your questions at times, Tom, but in this case, there was no immediate family.

What sort of balancing lives did I have for the bad-guy lives on Atlantis and Lemuria?
We have touched on some of these lives in the past, Tom. Since you had over 160 lives on Atlantis alone, many lives would be similar to what people are having today, where you would have balancing lives on Atlantis, since many of those lives were as a younger soul. And that was the same with Lemuria, where you only had 65 lives or so. Then we covered the balancing of the life you had there where you were one of the perpetrators who lead to the destruction of that continent, and spent over 80 lives balancing that one, including lives where you were on both Lemuria and Atlantis when they sank into the sea.

Regarding a spirit "gathering itself together," it is constantly connected to all its fragments having not only lives on Earth (all at the same time), but also the 500,000 to over 1,000,000 lives going on all the time to learn about our Universe, for when it is time to take over.

World War II

Gaia, what was the total death toll in WWII, as much as 100 million, more or less?
Less, Tom, but not by too much. As is being demonstrated in Ukraine, many civilians are killed by indiscriminate shelling of civilian areas. And like other wars, the current one is one where there is balancing. If a soldier in WWII killed civilians, they might balance that by being a civilian in Ukraine that is killed in that war. And I might add, since we have lives both in the future and past, if they kill civilians in Ukraine, they might very well have their next life back in World War I or II as a civilian who is killed. All lives must balance.

How big was WWII compared to others in Earth's history?
At least you did not destroy yourselves as you had done previously. We have repeatedly said there will never be another world war. The Ukraine war will be the last in Europe.

Chapter 11
Timelines

Introduction to the Concept of Multiple Timelines:

So, are we having 12 parallel lives?

In a way, yes. Your soul wishes to experience all the potentials of this time period so there are 12 of you to make sure the experience is complete.

That's a lot of expression. Somewhat disconcerting. Not exactly, but unsettling to know that there are so many aspects of one's soul running around somewhere. Since we made up the game as The Group channels through Steve Rother, did our souls set this up in agreement with All That is?

Yes. He—it—was pleased by such a wonderful game, and of course he could see all the potentials and all the learning that would result.

Why would there be a need for parallel lives in modern times?

Again, on this timeline you cannot see where there would be differences, but each timeline is at a different frequency, so there is a large difference between timelines, with the upper timelines having easier lives, and the lower timelines having more difficult lives. We have previously mentioned that you died a number of years ago on Timelines 1 and 2, just as one example.

Are soul fragments equally divided between timelines?

Yes, although the soul fragments for the lower timelines must be hardier in order to exist in the lower frequencies.

Gaia, anything about timelines that I have not asked you?

Timelines are a natural part of creation for your lives there on Earth here. You set up the timelines for your soul's knowledge. Those points you already know. I just wanted to reiterate them before proceeding. Timelines are not straight. They weave in and out and that's why they cross sometimes. Each timeline is focused on a certain element or a certain focus on a mass response, a mass mind set–here you're not receiving well—a mass consciousness—yes, that is correct so that decisions by the individual soul fragments fit in with that mass consciousness. So, you have an overall setting that each soul fragment works in conjunction with—sort of the rules of that particular timeline. It is a structure that the soul fragments work within. A big house you would say.

How can we pick up ideas and concepts from these timelines or dimensions?
This is done through conscious concentration on those timelines and tuning into them. You will learn the processes in the coming years as you learn more about them. You will be able to access those ideas and concepts through a form of meditation that is not unknown even today mostly by yogis in India. They have crossed those thresholds many times as they discovered how to move their bodies from one place to another. It is simply tuning one's body to another vibration.

Gaia, regarding timelines—are we the primary aspect or concentration of our souls or is each of the 12 aspects equal or are they just potentials after ours?
Each of the timelines are separate aspects of each soul. Each is an equal personification or piece of a soul.

Gaia, are our birthdates and times of birth identical on all timelines?
Quite so, Tom. It might vary just a tiny bit, but your souls wish to have everything as even as possible.

Yet, we all seem to have different exit points and possible exit points along the way.
Yes, here it depends upon whether you have been able to stay on your soul path, or "wandered off the reservation," as Theo amusingly terms it. That's the first criteria, but there are also others. You may have one exit point, but your soul sees you are handling that life well, so you get an extension. If you are just existing and not taking up challenges and learning, then that

exit point is used.

Ascension Timeline

Gaia, were we somehow pushed off the ascension timeline and if so who or what did this? Are there multiple collapsing timelines or is this another way to describe probabilities?
Remember, Tom, that we have said in the past that your vibrational levels as a whole dropped back a little. You were not pushed off, as it was more a retreat through human actions. Yes, there are multiple probability timelines we have discussed before. These probabilities drop away until on a daily, monthly and, yes, yearly basis, you choose the probability you as a human race wishes to experience. That's why we ask each one of you to say that Benevolent Prayer and send white light each morning for peace on Earth as it does contribute to raising your vibrational levels to allow everyone to choose the highest and best probability for you.

This is what some people call ascension but is actually simply raising your vibrational levels and not going backwards. Each person needs to send out love each day and that means being compassionate. That is happening these days with young and old treating people better, and with love. You are making a big jump. It took a worldwide pandemic, but it has greatly aided you in being the loving beings you are at heart. These times allow you to demonstrate your love for those less fortunate.

The Beatles and Other Timelines

What happened to the Beatles on the upper timelines? Was John Lennon assassinated?
No, he was not. He continues to live, and he recorded and wrote many more songs.

George Harrison?
He lived a little longer than he did on your timeline, but his soul contract was to leave.

Did they stay together longer on the upper timelines?

Quite so—all the way to Mr. Harrison's death. They did not have the clashing of personalities as happened on your timeline.

Changing Timelines

What milestones have to be met to change our focus from third to fifth, and then to the seventh?
Here it does get complicated. We have previously discussed that humans as a whole raised your vibrational levels in 1987 to a point where you will never destroy yourselves again, as you had previously done during Atlantean and Lemurian times. Then you continued to raise your vibrational levels to the point where Earth as a whole was able to change your focus from the 3rd dimension to the lowest level of the 5th dimension—which had never been done before in this Universe or any other while everyone was living on the planet.

Here is the complicated part that will be explored in the coming years. There is a part of your soul in the 7th dimension, which would take too much time to discuss fully today. That part of you is at a much higher level and sends love and light to each one of you on a daily basis.

Was that part of us on the Fifth Focus before moving to the seventh focus?
No, it was always there as part of your whole soul. And that makes all the difference in the world as to having a gentler life than you would have had you not rediscovered MBOs.

What about the degrees of difference between the timelines?
Very minute, but very large when you think of existences being separate, but there are those who can move back and forth between timelines.

Are these people able to move between all timelines or just a couple?
Some can move through all of them, but not many. More can move between just a couple or three. It takes great training and perseverance to do this. Yes, yogis are some of the people that can accomplish this through their training, and different shamans in different countries. One must learn how to tune oneself to a different channel, so to speak.

Is it not true, Gaia, that it is almost unheard of for people to cross timelines?
That's quite correct. There have been a few reported instances, and a few more that were never reported where there were holes or a merging of timelines. When there is a merging for a short period of time, there is great work done so that everything appears normal. When someone accidentally plops into an adjacent timeline, the souls in charge of maintaining the barriers spring into action to return the person back to his or her timeline and repair the breach.

Does anyone ever stay?
No, that cannot be allowed.

I have reported before that the Zetas would bring someone back to almost the exact time, or close to it, in which they were abducted. This included the women who would be impregnated and lived on the spaceship for nine months (later, four months as they improved their methods) and then put back at or very close to the time they were abducted.

Contact with Other Timelines

Gaia, was my reader in contact with her other timelines or past lives and if so, how?
Yes, Tom, she has been in contact with her other timelines—not so much past or future lives. Normally this is done much more during your sleep time as you compare notes, shall we way, but she allows herself to go into that Alpha meditative state during the day and communicates with her other timeline selves. The main thing is she does not reject this communication as most people would. If you think something is impossible to do, then it is for you. The reverse is true too.

This is part of the growth you will experience—and I mean everyone eventually—as part of the Fifth Focus. The barriers between timelines will seem to be thinner, and of course, they are. There will still be 12 of you on 12 different timelines, but you will be able to ask how to handle a particular problem and it will not just be your guides and guardian angel helping you solve it. You can call on your other selves to assist you too, and that also works the other way, especially with the lower timelines in the denser frequencies where you can assist them to have easier lives. So, look to hear more about this happening over the next few years, Tom. This will not be the only time, just the first.

Crease In Time

Gaia, how did the phone conversation my wife Joanna had with her brother suddenly repeat the first three minutes?
Yes, this is difficult to describe in layman terms, Tom. Putting it simply, there was a crease in time, a slight anomaly in the fabric of time. Certainly, this is quite a rare occurrence, but she is not the first person to experience this. There is what we have described in the past as a fabric of time and sometimes there are little ruptures.

If you recall, in the past we've discussed there is this fabric of time and space between timelines and there are souls assigned or who volunteered to constantly repair these separations, and sometimes things fall into and out of the 5th timeline, and the reverse is true for them. It does not happen so often with timeline 7 as there is a little greater separation between timelines 6 and 7.

Death on One Timeline

Gaia, I've been told there are 12 aspects or fragments of my soul on 12 timelines. When each one transitions, do they become aware of the others?
No, not immediately. Each is treated as a whole separate entity as far as they are concerned. It is only a little later do they become aware that their soul has had other experiences—other parallel lives as some people call them—on Earth at the same time. Then they are able to meld and study together to understand where or how each handled certain situations differently and are reacquainted with the complexity of life on Earth. You set up a wonderful game for yourselves with each soul having 12 game pieces as it were. Each goes around the board of life and stops different places and has different experiences and makes different decisions and draws different experiences to them so that your souls can truly understand

how that person reacts to all situations during its time on Earth. It's a wonderful game of experience that results in the Creator of All That Is learning more about itself so that it can move on to the next level of its experience. It's just a far more complicated game of experience when you reach the level of knowledge that your Creator has.

Determining the Timelines

Gaia, how many degrees of separation are there between timelines or how are they calculated?
An interesting, good question, Tom. They are calculated on a vibrational level and the separation is not too great between them, which allows the timelines to merge or cross, as the timelines basically are of the same degrees, but are separated almost physically. Needless to say, there are large numbers of angelic beings that handle and work on these timelines to keep them repaired and separated. They look for tears or possible problems in a timeline, so that it remains whole as these events are all taking place simultaneously. A good question, but difficult to describe in words that you and others can understand.

Then it still seems to me that the timelines are at least somewhat separated by vibrational level.
Yes and no. Again, the timelines are a physical manifestation that your souls created to play this game. Some timelines are just easier to live in than others. The choices made by those people living in that timeline were better than another timeline. As you can see, very complex.

I wish to re-ask how are timelines divided—vibrationally or just by degree similar to different radio stations, as I was not receiving well the other day.
Yes, this was a hard question for you to receive the complete answer I gave you. Timelines are divided like your radio dial but notice on the radio dial that they are not all at the same level but go from a low to a high and vice versa. So, timelines operate in a similar fashion. There are tiny degrees of difference, but significant enough that they are separate. When two timelines cross as they are now, then the vibrations are blended together. That's why the farther away you get on the vibrations the farther degree of

separation there is just like on that radio dial or TV, as you wish.

Then there are timelines that would be considered a higher vibration than others?
Yes, certainly. They just vibrate at a higher level so that there is a more benevolent experience on the top end timeline as compared to the one at the lowest end of the spectrum.

Disclosure and Timelines

Gaia, did I receive correctly from Antura that disclosure is predicated on when people on Earth, on this timeline, reach a certain vibrational level, and if so why would that have anything to do with it?
You did receive it correctly from him, Tom. As he said, we cannot just give you information under the rules here as you are virtually the only one asking thousands of questions and assisting in the growth and future growth of humans. So, disclosure will be given when we know you can handle the information.

That's my next question though—why is disclosure tied to our vibrational level? It does not seem to be or should not be connected, as there is a huge group of people that are awaiting disclosure, and there will always be those who will not believe it.
But for the majority to accept it, Tom, you must have moved a little past the stage where everyone believed that you were the only intelligent society in the Universe. There would be too many people that would be quite fearful, and we cannot have that happen.

So, are we really over a year behind timeline 7 in raising our vibrational levels when the other timelines seemed to have one after the other?
Yes, Tom. There is a drop off between seven and you, but you are catching up.

Earth Changes and Timelines

Gaia, are Earth changes the same on the upper timelines as they are

on the lower ones? And are the after affects the same on all timelines?
The Earth changes, as you call them, are virtually the same on all timelines, Tom. How you handle them is different. The lower the timeline, the less assistance with, let's say, an earthquake. Still, these responses are improving on the lower timelines as you slowly raise your vibrational levels. Therefore, I don't need as many storms and tornadoes on the upper timelines to clear the negativity. We are speaking more about earthquakes and volcanic eruptions. A severe storm on the upper timelines will include tornadoes on the lower timelines. Then assistance is much better on the upper timelines. Still, everyone is improving on all the lower timelines.

Earth Differences in Various Timelines

Gaia, is the Earth about the same in appearance in all 12 timelines, or do you have other experiences in those timelines?
Yes, my Earth is about the same. Different holes in it compared to yours, but about the same. The timelines, as you guessed, are for your soul's benefit. After all, your souls made time in the first place so that this and other experiments could be done with the goal of creating and being co-creators in your lives. And it is working well, I will say, as you have been told through other channels whose souls try to present the big picture to you in your veiled world. Of course, the veil works perfectly, as your souls thought it would, but it was even more of a success than you as souls had hoped. That's why you have observers from all over this Universe and several others that are parked off planet monitoring your progress in ways that you can only guess at now, with technology that is from far in your future, although that future may arrive even sooner than they or you could have imagined.

Fifth Dimension

Gaia, is the Fifth Dimension an expansion of the four other dimensions?
Yes, this is a very difficult subject to understand, Tom, as you don't seem to feel any different—at least not the general population—than you did in the third. But it is a focus, and a lightening of the level of energy you inhabit. It can be compared for your readers, Tom, as a different station on

a radio. Using your terms for simplicity, it would be as if you tuned your FM receiver from 90.0 to 100.0 on the dial. Those are not the actual figures as I'm simply using those numbers for the sake of explanation. It was not the easiest thing for us to move you from the Third Focus to the Fifth Focus with you inhabiting the planet. That's why it was necessary for you to be put in a giant tube of energy to protect you while we inched up the dial, shall we say.

Did our size increase in the Fifth Focus?
Yes, everything expanded in size, but relative to everything else, so there was no way to really compare, Tom. You cannot say you doubled in size— you just expanded. You are not as dense as you were in the Third Focus.

Will our scientists figure this out one day?
Yes, but it will definitely be quite a few years, Tom. This is in the realm of quantum physics, and you have much to learn—your scientists—in this field of study.

Future Development of Timelines – The End of the Earth Experiment

In the future, will we continue to have 12 separate timelines?
Yes, and no. For the foreseeable future yes, but as you get far in the future the timelines will tend to combine as there will not be such a divergence in beliefs and separate actions as there is at the present time. This will not happen for a very long time, but will happen as you become a more loving, less violent society in general.

Gaia, will we always have villains on Earth during the next 7,000 more years of the Earth Experiment?
No, Tom. Several things will occur over this time period. First is a reduction in the population, which we have said before has peaked. Second, is that fewer and fewer conflicts will arise over the next century. We have said before, that the Ukrainian War will be the last one in Europe. Third is technological progress, with such things as the free energy machine being constructed on a worldwide basis.

Therefore, those needing to experience wars will do so in earlier time periods. They will not need to incarnate in the future. The number of young souls will shift from first and second quadrants to third and fourth, and there will be more medium souls. All this will occur as you raise your vibrational levels in the coming years. There really will be peace on Earth in the future.

Gaia, in 7,000 years, at what focus will we be at that we can change molecules when we return Earth to its pristine beauty?
You will still be in the Fifth Focus, which you guessed, but at a much higher level, just as the whole Universe will be, thanks to the Explorer Race. You can put that at around 5.8 to even 5.9. By then it will be "old hat" for you and everyone left on Earth. This work will be done out of love as your parting gift to me.

Gaia, in 7,000 years after the Explorer Race departs back to their home worlds, I assume, will there be Earth keepers to make sure that the visitors who come to enjoy your beauty do not make mistakes?
There will be strict rules that everyone will know before visiting. They will be in awe of the varied typography. They will live in their spacecraft or will commute from larger craft to explore.

So, there will be no need for people to direct them or make sure they keep everything pristine?
No, only those advanced enough will be allowed to visit. And as you were thinking, the Explorer Race will return to Earth with their families to show them where they lived their many lives.

Who will give them the rules?
They will be given to them by, shall we say, advanced systems far beyond what you have today.

On the last day on Earth for the Explorer Race, how many will be left, and will there be some sort of celebration and then departure, or just a transition?

A nice question, Tom. It will be just a few hundred—yes, that is correct, and I might add you will be there too. You and the others will bless me, as at that time you will have achieved ways for your presence on Earth to quickly return to a pristine condition, since don't forget that Earth is to become a place for visitors from all over the Universe to go and enjoy the beauty of this planet. People from other places will know not to clutter up the planet. So, then off you go back to your home planets. Fini.

Will we still be ensouled as humans? How will that work?
Yes, Tom, you will. You will all depart in star ships. The ships will go to places where you can finish out your lives. You will be like housekeepers, tidying up.

Gaia, which frequency level will remain on Earth when the Earth Experiment ends? Will the other frequencies disappear, plus the parallel Earths, and there will be no space-time continuum?
Eventually, Tom, there will be a combining of timelines, but that is thousands of years in the future for the Explorer Race. What was created for the Experiment can be uncreated, shall we say. Eventually, there will be only one frequency and that will match the rest of the Universe, which by that time will have absorbed the negative energy—your greatest accomplishment. People all across the Universe will want to travel to where it all began.

Gaia, when the Earth Experiment is over, will all the souls who have been assisting you in running things on Earth stay, or what will happen, as you've said in the past that this will become a giant park for those from other worlds to visit?
Many will remain, Tom. It just depends. You were thinking about dogs and cats, and, yes, the group souls providing those soul fragments as a service to humans will be allowed to withdraw as they are domesticated animals and need to be taken care of and fed. Otherwise, they would have to revert to being wild animals and that might not be too safe for visitors.

If they remained, it would be a small version of Jurassic Park, but not so much for dinosaurs, although I will allow gentle versions of those animals to return, but it would create packs—hungry is the word to use here—who might spoil an idyllic vacation for some family who wishes to enjoy the beauty of this planet. And as you can imagine, there will be rules and regulations of what they can and cannot do while visiting. Of course, this will be after completion of the Earth Experiment and will not involve your souls other than to pay a nostalgic visit every so often to relive the good old days.

Intersecting Timelines

Gaia, Nelson Mandela was released from prison in 1990, therefore how far back in the '80s did we intersect the other timeline, which may I confirm was timeline 4? And did timeline 5 intersect with timeline 3?
Yes, Tom, use the year 1985 for the intersection, and, yes, timeline 5 intersected with timeline 3 while your timeline 6 intersected with timeline 4.

How long did this intersection last?
A few months, but not quite a year. That was deemed sufficient to uplift those on that timeline, so they could get an idea of what could be.

That's quite a long time in a way isn't it, Gaia? So, are you saying it was 11 months or a little shorter than that?
A little shorter, Tom—closer to 9.5 months is quite close to the total time you intersected.

Was there any other time that we intersected with them, such as the 1960s or '70s?
Yes, but you also must keep in mind, Tom, that you also intersected with timeline 7 back towards the end of the '60s. There were reasons why that "Summer of Love" and 1969 were where peace and love were emphasized. They were like springboards for your development.

When you say probabilities may extend for some time or fade away, are these non-physical timelines?
Yes, they are, Tom. Timeline 12 is also non-physical, but may I remind your readers that this is considered the perfect life by your souls to judge and compare not only all the other timelines too, but also all the hundreds, and, yes, at times, thousands of probabilities. As you can see, the Creator,

along with your souls, created a number of realities all for your souls' benefit, as they needed to learn how to create realities when they one day take over this Universe for the Creator. Life and creation are much more complex than I can even begin to describe to you at this time, but as we said before, you have only been seeing the "tip of the iceberg" to use that description, or "scratching the surface."

These descriptions will one day cause your scientists to delve further into the concept of timelines and probabilities. This is good work you are doing, and certainly I can respond to more questions on this subject.

Karma and Learning with Timelines

If in one timeline someone kills another, does the soul portion of that timeline incur karmic debt, or do all the timelines?
Since all are connected, Tom, they all do, but generally only one timeline will have to pay the price, so to speak, either in that life or another.

So how can we change timelines when our souls want the experience of having 12 aspects of itself experience Earth reality in 12 different ways?
There will still be an aspect of itself left that will continue on that path. That may seem confusing, but that part of the aspect that vibrates at a higher level will break off or divide itself and that aspect or part will move up to the higher vibrational level.

Next, when two timelines cross, it seems events are much more intense. Is that a correct observation?
Yes, they are meant to be, as the events cause the two timelines to handle adversity or events that happen in that time period to be dealt with in differing manners—sometimes very minute—but others in completely different ways. It all depends upon the individual. It is a free choice.

So, our souls designed this crossing of timelines to be a huge learning tool, or for experiences to be, or to happen when both are together and then what we do as a result after the timelines separate?
Yes, exactly. And as you might guess world events fall into this as well,

242

because the world leaders will handle events differently on different timelines.

Are there more secrets revealed when timelines cross or is that just a by-product of the crossing?
No, you are correct, there are more secrets revealed so that each timeline can choose a different way to handle these secrets.

Gaia, can you give me a more detailed description of the intersection of the timelines?
Yes, there is a pollinating effect from the electrical charges. That is a fact that is just coming out now or recently, but it also releases negativity stored in the ground from all the many humans that live on the surface now.

Yes, crossing the timeline is a major event in your lives. The lines normally run parallel, but sometimes do cross and when they do, it is normally for a reason. They are attracted together like magnetics, or magnetically. Then they will separate in several months, but not before there have been a number of dramatic events which take place that each timeline needs to experience.

Will there be two of everyone running around, or will we meld for a short period of time.
There will actually be two of everyone, but it will not seem that way to the normal person, as everyone is leading somewhat different lives in the two timelines. That is why I said that people would seem a little strange to you at times as they will be the different self from the other timeline.

I still need some explanation why the two personalities would not merge, as it would require two houses, double buildings, and so on.
You are correct in that. The structures will remain virtually the same, with some differences, but the personalities will be different and although there is a slight merging, there will be times when there will be two, Tom Moores walking the streets, but there also is some merging of personalities to bring them more into alignment.

Mandela Effect and Timelines

Gaia, is there any truth to the so-called Mandela Effect of feeling what you remembered as fact has been altered?

Yes, there is this constant changing of your past. We have discussed this a little with you previously, but as your souls progress you not only change your future, but your past as well. Most of the time no one notices, but there are small things that were just a little bit different before. This is because you are in, or have jumped to, the Fifth Focus and things are a little different than the Third Focus.

So, do not be concerned as your paths are at a higher level now. There are many other things that have changed you are not aware of or dismiss as imperfections in your memories. Do not be concerned that your memories are playing tricks on you. Just enjoy the path you are on and wish the past well or send light to the old path.

Gaia, why does our past change? Is it the solutions to problems in the present make "tweaking" the past? Or something else?

Imagine time as a living thing, Tom. Decisions you make now, especially benevolent decisions, cause the past to change. There is this tweaking, as you termed it, going on all the time, from very small things like the names of commercial products to larger ones such as why the Mandela Effect got its name. Then that also brings up the crossing of timelines where you suddenly adjust to an upper timeline's history. So, time is fluid. As you raise your vibrational levels, so can you raise the vibrational level of the past. And, yes, those people who go from having a life in the present or future and then go back to have a life in the past do change the past, and we might add, significantly at times, as their higher vibrations also affect these future lives. Good question.

So, am I to understand there is more than one frequency of the timeline, or is it just our placement in the frequency?

No, there is a range of frequencies in this timeline. Your quantum physics scientists will study this for many years and will develop equipment that can identify these frequencies.

Parallel Lives and Timelines

If our parallel lives are considered timelines, would time periods be stacked vertically?
You can imagine it that way, Tom. Actually, it is much more complex. It's as if each time period is like a thin sheet of paper all stacked together. And, yes, they are separated by days so that, let's say, an ET ship or humans in the far future can simply dial in a day and be able to travel to that particular day to visit.

So how can a slip in time from one year to, let's say, several hundred years happen?
It's as if a hole in the pages of time occurred just for a few moments, before being repaired.

How many souls have the task—volunteered to do this work of not only keeping the timelines separate, but also the pages of time separate?
Good question. There are several hundred souls that enjoy keeping the Earth Experiment intact as nowhere else in this Universe is there such a space-time continuum. You see, even the name implies a separation. You can ask more questions on this in the future since it is a very complex subject.

Gaia, is there any difference between experiencing events while at the top of our timeline, as compared to experiencing them at the bottom?
Yes, a few differences, Tom. At the top of the timeline, the events do not seem so unsurmountable. They take place, but they do not seem to affect you like they do if you are at a lower frequency of the timeline. It may seem, to use an allegory, that the whole forest is burning with the exception of your place in the forest. You know how to request Most Benevolent Outcomes to lessen the overall challenges for your timeline.

Pets and Timelines

Gaia, does each timeline have a version of our pets?
Certainly, your same pets exist on all timelines. Dog Soul, Cat Soul, and other pets are all ensouled on all timelines. There are no souls that do not do the same job on all timelines. This was a good question we have not

covered before.

Can our pets see orbs, deceased pets, and perhaps people?
Yes, to all three questions. Their eyesight has a higher range than do yours. During most of the time they just ignore them, unless the orbs wish to play games. Other times they will stare at the deceased pet or person before they depart.

Do they have some sort of contract to follow us in the Earth Experiment?
This is handled not only by your guardian angels, but by the souls ensouling your pets. We have said before but were limited to providing the answer to a question for this timeline that your pets have many lives with you—and that goes for all timelines.

Seventh Dimension

Gaia, do our Seventh Dimensional-selves have actual lives, or do they live in perpetuity?
Good question, Tom. They do have lives, but much longer than you do at the present time.

If that's so, are there the same number of Seventh Dimensional selves since you mentioned a "tower of light"?
Your seventh dimensional lives encompass the multiple lives you are having, Tom. Here it gets complicated. That tower of light encompasses all your multiple lives. They do not need to incarnate time after time as you do. As we said before, they can manifest at will.So yes, there is a tower of light, but it encompasses all your incarnations, Tom.

Then, there is no balancing to be done as we must do at this level, correct?
Quite so.

Do they live in houses?
Not as you would know and understand at this time. More houses of light.

So, all their lives are spent sending light our way?
Not only light in this life, Tom, but all the hundreds you and everyone else spend on Earth. Your Seventh Dimensional self sends warm greetings and love, Tom.

And this fragment of a soul sends back love.

Are our Seventh Dimensional selves just a larger fragment of our soul?
That's correct, Tom. It has a job to do, just as you do in all these lives on Earth.

When we were crossed with Timeline 7, it seemed as if I was perhaps a little more relaxed with outcomes of things I have either been working on or problems. Would that be a fair assessment of combining with Timeline 7 or was I just wishing to feel that way?
No, Tom, you found one of the tenets, we will call it, of Timeline 7 and even above in the other timelines. You are not as stressed as on those timelines. You're slightly more mellow, would be one description.

It would seem there are little differences between Timelines 7 and 6, but I thought there was a little more of a jump away?
There is, Tom, but it was desired for you to receive this higher feminine energy without disrupting your lives.

Were there adjustments made prior to the temporary merger?
Yes, you did notice on a personal level of perhaps doing something one way and then encouraged to do something in a gentler way. Those would be prior preparations for the merger.

Slip In Time

Gaia, are there "slips in time" where for just an instant or minute someone slips into the past or future? If so, how does it occur?
Good question, Tom. Remember that we have said over and over that time is an illusion to all on Earth. It is a construction, and there are souls that work to maintain this construction, but there are times when what we will

call the wall of your time frame to momentarily merge or weaken, and then just for that very short instance the individual slips into another time frame and then out again. Obviously, it is very confusing to that person who experienced the slip in time.

Gaia, what is the difference between a slip in time and a slip from one timeline to another?
You have these barriers not only between these parallel lives, but also between one time period and all the others that are going on simultaneously. We've not taken this up before, as just the parallel timelines were a lot for you and your readers to absorb. Now we can expand your knowledge out a bit, thanks to your readers who have had experiences with slips in time periods.

Solar System and Timelines

Gaia, do souls in our solar system that ensoul the other planets, moons, and even asteroids also ensoul each 12 times, as you do Earth?
Yes, they do. There is not such a dynamic difference as there is on Earth between timelines. You could call it a blending, more than a separation. Here we get into quantum physics, and it will be many years before your scientists will be able to see the difference.

Gaia, am I correct in understanding that there was only one loop of time?
Correct, Tom. The Earth Experiment needed that extra time.

When did it begin?
It began in the 20th Century, Tom. You needed more time to raise your vibrational levels. I think you are confusing the Loop in Time with timelines. To use your example, Johnny could be a soldier on one timeline (parallel Earth) and a mechanic on another timeline, both existing at the same time.

Soul Contracts and 12 Timelines

Gaia, are there 12 different soul contracts for the 12 different

timelines?

Quite so, Tom. Each soul fragment has a slightly and quite often a significant difference in soul contracts, as each soul fragment is put into different circumstances, such as marrying completely different people than they do in a parallel life. Don't forget that the souls wish a wide range of experiences for each Earth life. They achieve this through having 12 parallel Earths. This is complicated and beyond many people's understandings since lives are difficult as it is without wondering what the next timeline over or one farther away is up to. Yet, in dream time you all share your experiences to assist one another as you move forward in each of your lives. In most cases, the lower timelines must have the strongest soul fragments in order to handle the lower frequencies. Many times, the lives are shorter like yours was on the lowest two timelines.

More explanation from Tom: As I was told before, our souls may be having 500,000 to one million lives going on all over the Universe for our souls' learning. Keep in mind that the reason our souls chose to take part in the Earth Experiment was to "fast-track" the raising of their vibrational levels instead of doing it the slow way as Theo and the other "golden light beings," who act as our guardian angels, did. These are hard lives, but with great growth potential in each life we live veiled from knowing about our true identities.

The Creator of this Universe (one of billions of creators, but Theo says would be ranked in the top five) has about 10% of the souls Creator created taking part in the Earth Experiment. They will have the choice of melding together with the other 90% and becoming a creator one day to take over this Universe and allow the Creator to go to another level. On a soul level we all share our learning with the creators who created us. The Creator responds to our prayers through our own GAs and other "whole souls," or angels as we call them.

If everyone recalls, I was told that besides the Soul of the Earth we call Gaia, in modern times (Earth Mother among many others), she has four million other souls assisting her with running the planet because of the huge diversity not only of plant and animal life, but in the variety of the topography.

My understanding is that all the living beings on this planet have group souls. Some may leave to return to their planets, and some will come. It is all by choice. Our pets will not merge with us, as they are not the souls taking part in the Earth Experiment—only supporting it. I was told that a number of us did have a life as perhaps a tree and then an animal as part of our preparation in the Earth Experiment to "dip our toes" or "get the lay of the land."

There are supposed to be a little over one million golden light beings acting as our GAs and around the same amount of souls—a little over one million—that respond to prayers from all over the world. Theo told me he had not decided what he will do yet at the end of the Earth Experiment. Our guides are fragments of our soul fragments.

You are applying Earth time to the souls when you speak of them "hanging out." Keep in mind that ALL our lives on Earth are going on at the same time. That's really hard for most of us to understand, but that's why I'm always told that all of our lives are affecting each other. And that's why I say the Daily Benevolent Prayer.

Gaia, do all soul fragments experience more or less the same soul focus and the same lives through all 12 timelines? And do we experience the guilt other timelines experience through their actions?

Ah, Tom, such a heady question today. Yes, you experience more or less the same soul focus in a particular life, but—as we have covered before—since the frequencies are different the actions in each of your timeline lives can be different. As you have been told, in your own case your soul imbued your fragment with the desire to succeed in business, while on the upper timelines your focus immediately was on being a writer. Therefore, there are millions of answers to your question. The lives can be almost identical in focus, or they can be widely different, as yours has been with your lower timelines concentrating on tourism and the travel business. So, in your 12 timelines there are more or less three focuses, along with a difference in when you transition.

Regarding guilt, all timelines tap into each other both in waking hours where you don't notice at all, and especially during your dream time when each can share experiences, but in a quantum state where you tap into past, present, future, and parallel lives. These feelings can be love, hate, disgust, guilt, and any of the other feelings you experience in these lives. In one life, a person can divorce their partner, but in a higher timeline they continue the relationship, but with mixed feelings that can range the scale. On a lower timeline, that person could kill the other person. That guilt can be felt on all the other timelines.

Twelfth Focus Timeline

Gaia, in the 12th focus, which I think you said in the past is where you're located, are there spatial boundaries as there are in the Fifth Focus, so that we could say that a whole soul such as yourself would take up X amount of space?
No, Tom. Here we get into a discussion about that energy soup, as we've called it in the past, plus this would be more of a discussion for someone with a background in quantum physics, and even the most learned people might scratch their heads. I could be as small as a baseball or as large as, let's say, a football stadium—it makes no difference.

So, I could be hugging a football stadium instead of a giant beach ball?
That's a good analogy, Tom. But, when you visualize putting your arms on my surface, that idea you present does have its intended effect of expressing your affection and I send it back to you 100 fold.

Twelve Timeline Frequencies

Gaia, am I correct in understanding that it is not just one solid Earth and 12 timeline frequencies, or am I mistaken?
No, you are correct, Tom. There have to be 12 of me, you might say. All of life, you see, to try and put it in language you and your readers will understand, is simply energy, which can be manipulated by Creator to have any appearance It wishes. You really enter the realm of quantum physics here, Tom, and it becomes more difficult to understand, but for your purposes, there are 12 Earths and not just one with 12 sets of the same beings. If there can be 12 sets of the same beings then it must be obvious that there can be 12 Earths too, simply at different frequencies.

Gaia, a question I've been meaning to ask for clarification. Besides having to take care of 12 parallel Earths, you must also take care of these 12 Earths simultaneously from the beginning of time to at least when the Explorer Race departs, am I correct?

Yes, and long past that, Tom. After the Explorer Race departs, as we have spoken about before, the Earth will become a huge park for those from all over the Universe to come and enjoy. There will be no need for parallel Earths at that time as that time loop, shall we call it, for your purposes, will have been completed and normal universal time will return. This time loop, we will continue to call it, was created for your learning purposes and when school is dismissed, shall we say, there will be no longer any need for those 12 tubes of time. A good question.

Gaia, are all the land masses the same on all 12 timelines?

Yes, Tom. They are exactly the same. Certainly, the villages and towns are different the lower frequency you go or the higher you go, but the continents and islands are the same.

And I must ask, are you raising the ocean levels on all timelines?

Certainly, Tom but that was a good question. The playing field, shall we call it, must be equal for all timelines. It would not be fair, shall I term it, to have an island in one timeline and for it not to exist in another.

Gaia, why are there 12 timelines and not more, or do the thousands of probabilities within those 12 make the need for more a moot subject?

Creator felt that 12, being a master number, as your mathematicians will discover one day, was sufficient for the Experiment. Even as a quantum master, it would be difficult for me to handle more parallel Earths, and all the souls you call group souls would have had a difficult time in handling any more Earths. Probability is a different cat, you could say, Tom. Here we again get into a subject that even your own quantum scientists will take hundreds of years to understand.

Gaia, as there are 12 timeline Earths, are these fragments of your soul that runs each Earth, or are there separate souls for each timeline?

Good question, Tom. No, it is just myself that acts as the conductor, shall we use that term, and that is why there are four million other souls assisting me, as you can imagine the work involved in all the tasks multiplied by twelve. It would seem the 12th timeline requires virtually no work at all as it is non-physical, but that is not the case. Percentagewise, yes, it has perhaps less moving parts, to use that 3D terminology, but even non-physically that frequency must be maintained with a structure that will take your quantum physics scientists hundreds of years to understand. We must give them something difficult to work towards.

Speaking of that, in a way the 3200 era seems as if my reception will be ignored, and they will head for a nearby star instead of waiting to discover how to portal hop. Why?
Because there will continue to be scientists who only accept what they can prove. Your work with Antura will be quite old news by then since doors will continue to be closed as far as what can be explained and what is forbidden.

Will our relationships with ETs not continue?
Yes, but your scientists will be told in no uncertain terms that they must invent and develop everything. Nothing will be provided to you.

Gaia, I have a fill-in-the-blank type question on timelines. Are there actually 12 different Earths, or is there one Earth and 12 different frequencies of people on Earth?
A good follow up question, Tom. No, there are multiple Earths. I realize this is quite difficult for you or, for that matter, anyone living at this time, including your most knowledgeable quantum physics scientists, but this had to be done in order for your souls to gain the most experience in the shortest amount of time. Keep in mind that I exist differently on the seventh, ninth, and eleventh dimensions or focuses, so it is really not too difficult to have different Earths in fractions of those dimensions too.

If you recall, we have previously talked about the group of souls from the planet that blew themselves up coming to Earth and inhabiting a low third dimensional frequency. They have thousands of years to go before they are able to reach where the Explorer Race has reached in such a short time, as they have only one Earth, and not multiples.

Gaia, how long did it take to construct the 12 timelines? Was it instantaneous?

In a way, yes. Creator can construct things in a second, but this took slightly longer, as creator tweaked the creation. Then I and the many souls charged or volunteered to keep these timelines intact stepped in to begin our duties.

Are the timelines visible for those coming from the 10 positive energies?

Not exactly. They must tune to the frequency used for each timeline to see that Earth. As you can only imagine, this is far, far beyond your scientists' understanding at this time.

Gaia, does anyone experience the same life twice?

No, Tom. That's why there are 12 timelines, so that your souls can see all the different decisions made on different frequencies. There is no need to repeat a life when your souls have had 12 already.

Other Dimensions Affecting Ours

Gaia, do other dimensions affect our dimension as compared to how the other 11 timelines affect our timeline?

Yes, there is a great effect by the other dimensions on your dimension, Tom, even greater than that of the other timelines. You can imagine it as a tower of light with all of the dimensions stacked on top of each other, with light passing through all the dimensions. They may appear separate, but they are not. They are intertwined, you see. They may all be seen as having their separate lives, but their love permeates your dimension.

Then, do I exist on, say, the Sixth Dimension or are these separate entities that exist there?

Good question, Tom. No, you do have a sixth dimensional self that sends you light and love. Here we truly get into quantum physics, but in the future your researchers will learn more about these different dimensions.

Gaia, does the tower of light encompass all 12 timelines or each one, and are any of the upper dimensions physical?

First, let's tackle the tower of light. This tower of light encompasses all the timelines, not just separate timelines. You can't see it, but it's as if your frequencies are on top of each other. Then we have the dimensions, and to answer your question, there are some that have a physical presence and some that are non-physical.

So, as an example, is our Sixth-Dimensional self physical or non-physical?
Non-physical, but there are physical forms. Again, you would have to read more about what your scientists have speculated, and I repeat, speculated about the difference in the dimensions. Your higher selves are thrilled that you have opened this door to pass on this knowledge to those who will read your work in the coming years. There will be much discussion, and more people will ask about this in their own meditations.

Is the Seventh Dimension physical?
Yes, there is a physical form there.

Are the beings on the Seventh Dimension Homo sapiens, or something else?
Yes, they have the appearance of humans, Tom, but their forms would be described as more light. They can manifest at will. They spend most of their time working with the lower dimensions in ways difficult to explain to you at this time in your development. Your seventh dimensional self sends love and light to you as I am responding to your question.

WWII and Timelines

Gaia, are there one or more timelines that began in WWII and had the Germans winning?
No there were no timelines with the Germans or Japanese winning. They both lost the war, but things quickly diverged after that.

What about the Japanese timeline?
The Japanese timelines were the same. After the loss they diverged too.

Is the belief by some people that the Holocaust never happened just a

denial or because of a timeline that intersected?
The belief that the Holocaust never happened was just a denial. It happened in all timelines. Because of some people's belief systems and prejudices, they cannot believe such a terrible event happened, but it did. Those souls gave of themselves to remind everyone how cruel you can be to each other, so that it will not happen again, at least in the western world. Other cultures have undergone similar situations so that they can learn the same lesson, but at different times.

Chapter 12
Religious Practices & Institutions

Bible/Torah Code

Gaia, is there a code written into the Torah as there seems to be for the Bible?
Yes, the mystical part of these religions did create these code systems to contain their predictions for the future, Tom. It would not have been in their best interests to bring out this knowledge during those early times. They were able to project themselves into the future.

Burial Preferences

Gaia, is there any particular preference by spirit regarding cremation or burial?
No, Tom, as this is for the family and friends—these burial services to remember the person who transitioned. It is left to the beliefs of those who wish to honor the person who transitioned.

So, there is no preference in rituals?
Not at all, Tom, as, again, this is left to those people's beliefs. There are many rituals that were created over the years to remember a person. They would fill a book and, yes, there have been attempts to list all of these different death rituals in books. You might be surprised to know that there are thousands when you include all the indigenous peoples of the world. Many are similar, but, yes, slightly different.

Why would there be a different energy in a cemetery when the soul fragment has left the body?
Keep in mind that the families of these people come to lay flowers on the grave, and feel it is proper to communicate with the departed at the

gravesite. They pour out their innermost thoughts and actions and many are sad as they try and remember the person whose body lays there as it decomposes. Of course, the piece of the soul fragment is there with them to give comfort and to communicate, although this can be accomplished in one's own home just as easily—again, it all depends upon the person's beliefs. So, to summarize, the people who visit the graves create the energy, along with the love returned to them by the pieces of soul fragments.

Will burial ceremonies change much in the future?
Not too much, Tom. These practices have been established over hundreds, and, yes, thousands, of years, according to one's beliefs. The greatest change will be more of a celebration as compared to only sadness in passing. You can see this change now, but it will continue to evolve.

Catholic Church

What are some of the secrets the Vatican holds?
There are too many to list here, Tom. The Vatican knows much more about Jesus' life, at least in the books contained in the Vatican library that were discarded at the Council of Nicaea. There was a decision at that time to ignore the fact that he was married and had children. This has continued to haunt the Catholic Church as it is not natural for men or women to not have physical feelings for one another.

What is the probability of the Catholic Church allowing priests to marry? (Asked June 2021)
That is a fairly high probability in the next five years.

When will it welcome homosexuals?
That will happen sooner.

We have discussed the Vatican archive being opened. When will that occur?
When your documentaries are released, Tom. There will be a clamor from those who wish to read more about that time period and what the Vatican chose to hide away.

Gaia, what is the highest probability regarding the Catholic Church and its pedophile priests? (Asked August 2018)

Yes, a sorry state there, Tom, although as you know these are soul contracts with those that are being abused having also abused before in previous lives. The Catholic Church, with the attention of the public and authorities to clean house, will be forced to take dramatic action to rid itself of these pedophile priests. It will not happen overnight, but certainly over a very short period of time, comparatively speaking. They will set in motion psychological tests to ferret out the candidates, while at the same time they will be forced to give up the chastity aspect and will allow priests to marry. Sex is all part of the human experience, but it must be with consenting adults. Otherwise, if they continue down the same path, they will be left with not enough priests for their churches. Therefore, both will go hand in hand—the expulsion, and in a number of cases punishment by law enforcement, and the dramatic reversal of their policy of chastity. Otherwise, there will be no one left to conduct services.

How soon is the highest probability for this to take place? (Asked August 2018)

First will come the forced ferreting out of the pedophile priests in the next two to four years, Tom, and then will come the changes allowing marriages by priests. That will occur within the following four years. That may seem like a long time, but not when you consider how long the Catholic Church has been around.

Let's see if we can move things along a little faster with a Benevolent Prayer. Please say out loud: "I ask any and all beings to aid, comfort, and assist those who have been sexual assault victims of any clergy person, and may these people be ferreted out and brought to justice even faster than we can hope for or expect, thank you!"

Cross Of Hendaye

Gaia, are there special qualities to the Cross of Hendaye in France?

This again gets into religious beliefs, Tom, and again, I say allow those who believe it has special qualities to have that belief. If they believe it is so, then it is for them.

Different Religions

Gaia, what is the purpose in having different religions?
It is for your soul's learning, Tom, as part of the Earth Experiment. Notice how three of the major religions of the world were created in the same location—coincidence? No. It is for you humans to learn to live in harmony no matter what your beliefs are. Certainly, it would seem you have a long way to go as you even war between sects of the same religion, but you are making progress. It may seem small at times, but you are making steady progress.

Once you have contacts with ETs and, yes, I can assure everyone that will happen in the not-too-distant future—even, yes, near future—you will see great changes in your religions as your true history is uncovered. This will draw the major religions closer together. Still, you each will choose your own path, but you will begin to accept those with beliefs other than your own. Again, this is all for the learning of your souls.

Future of Religion on Earth

Gaia, how will religions change when they come to know the real history of the world?
There will be great changes as you can guess, Tom. Those religions that have taught that the Earth is only 6,000 years or so suddenly will have to rewrite all their books or writings on that subject. Their followers will suddenly be questioning all they have been taught in the past and there will be a great desire for more information about their history, and the history of the world.

This will be an unsettled time until more information comes forth—and of course a portion of that will come from your documentaries, as you well know. That is a major reason why you, whose soul interest is religion, will be telling these stories. You will assist these religions in coming closer together.

ET Acceptance

Which religion will be the slowest to accept ETs?
There will be people in all the religions who have been taught you are the only intelligent species in the Universe that will have a hard time accepting that ETs exist. Even when they see videos of ETs, they will reject it as it is too fearful an idea. This will cross religious boundaries so that you cannot say one religion will be the slowest to accept. This will be part of the great changes people will see in this century.

Heaven

Gaia, can you explain "where is heaven?"
Certainly, Tom. That question comes up over and over again. It is not a place. It is the 12th Dimension where your souls reside in that energy soup, we call it for your purposes. When you transition, you go back to your souls in what is considered a quantum state. In the beginning, your soul is able to create for you a very tranquil place—what you consider, depending upon your beliefs, heaven. There is no time there. Then, with a gentle nudge from your soul, it's time to plan your next soul contract.

Illuminati

Gaia, how much influence does the Illuminati have over the governments of the USA, UK, Germany, France, Russia, and China?
They are not personally running any of these governments, Tom, but their influence comes from massive amounts of money to, shall we say, "buy" votes. Plus, they have influence in the banking industry. As we said before, though, this influence is waning. This waning of influence will dramatically increase as more women are voted into office.

What about members of the Illuminati being any Hollywood stars or studios?
Their control here again, Tom, comes with money they are able to invest in film projects. Actors they leave to be influenced by stories planted in newspapers and magazines.

Gaia, has the Illuminati had any hand in terrorism in the USA or Europe?

Only to sow seeds of discontent and generate seeds of hatred so that wars can erupt, and they can make money off the wars. Wars further their wealth—increases it. They do not go out and hire people to do these deeds—you all do this quite well yourselves under the guise of religion and greed.

Should we send white light or Benevolent Prayers their way and what influence will it have?
That's an easy question to answer. Say benevolent prayers, send white light. You'll find it lessens the strain and there is more love that permeates every soul on Earth.

Every time I meditate I send white light to every continent, island, rivers, lakes, streams, and to the oceans and seas and release that light to go to the darkest areas on Earth to light them up so there is no more darkness— only light—and no more secrets!

Jesus

Did the soul and its soul fragment Jesus originate in the Arcturus star system?
The soul that split off a fragment that you know as Jesus was created by another creator, but like so many other souls, was attracted to this Creator's creation, to lend a hand in teaching unconditional love to millions of people—soul fragments that are veiled—that would stand the test of time.

How did the story of his soul originating in Arcturus begin?
You could say that it was a stop along the way.

Is he having lives on other planets in this Universe, as our souls are?
No, its full concentration is on Earth, as there are so many people that worship him.

Gaia, will the complete true story of Jesus ever be told, or will it always remain a mystery?
You and a few others, Tom, are giving insights to his true life, but there are many who read it, and as it goes against their teachings, cannot accept

it as it has been repeated over and over again since their childhood days. That is part of what we have termed the "control factor" of the Christian religion, but it is not limited to just the Christian clergy. You can study the other major religions and most seek to control those of their faith.

But if there is one thing all those of the Christian faith can learn and concentrate on, it is the unconditional love that Master Jesus taught. That gets lost in people's everyday existence when they develop prejudices against other people for whatever reason. You cannot be a true Christian until you are able to love others unconditionally no matter what their own faith, beliefs, and/or ethnicity is. It must be a total commitment to loving everyone, and not just one day a week in your churches.

You can pray out loud to become more loving of others. It will transform you in time should you wish to add this prayer or lead others in saying this prayer of love. So, for some people, the actual life of Jesus will be something to study and learn more about, but for all people, even other religions, his messages of unconditional love is what truly matters in the end.

*Here's a Benevolent Prayer to say **out loud** if you wish: "I ask any and all beings to assist me and all the other citizens of Earth to love everyone unconditionally no matter their faith, beliefs, or ethnicity, thank you!"*

Gaia, was the drawing found in the Egyptian tomb that of Jesus, or whom?
Yes, actually it was, Tom. Yes, you are receiving me correctly. It was and is an ancient depiction by the artist.

Had he seen Jesus or was this well before his time?
No, well before his time, but still one of the earliest depictions of Jesus ever discovered. Therefore, it will give those who believe in Jesus, but perhaps are a little tentative in their beliefs, something to think about due to the age of the drawing.

Why is it there?
Yes, the scribes who are buried there had written down stories passed along

for generations about his visit to Egypt.

Are there any real books that give the correct history of Jesus?
Yes, those are in the Vatican. What this may do is encourage the Pope to allow more scholars into the Vatican archives where there are numerous references to the early and later life of Jesus. Those will be authentic. This one will be proven not to be, and that they have an agenda.

Krishna

Gaia, how many lives did the soul fragment have as Krishna, since you have said he was the Dalai Lama of his time?
Yes, he had several lives as Krishna. As has been written, there were 10 avatars who had lives in the later time period, but his was the most prominent and written about. He would reincarnate over and over again with memory of his Akashic records.

Did he incarnate as much as one hundred times as Krishna?
No, but he certainly did over 50. Records were just not that good in those times, so much has been lost. He incarnated 77 times as Krishna.

Lucifer

Gaia, what happened to Lucifer?
Yes, we have covered this somewhat in the past. Lucifer was and is a loyal servant of the Creator. Out of love, Lucifer took on certain traits for the Earth Experiment.

So, Lucifer would not be in the creator category?
No, but he would be in the archangel category—a larger fragment of a creator.

So, he was not a creation of this Creator?
No, but a good guess, Tom. He, like 90% of the souls, was attracted to this Creator's creation, because it was so unique.

Meditating For Peace

Gaia, I saw a photo and short mention of one million school children meditating for peace. Did this happen, and what results would or will it have on the world?

Yes, this was an admirable event in the Buddhist religion, Tom. It did have some effect, but as you guessed, it would have been much, much more powerful had they requested peace in the world verbally. With that many people asking for peace in the world out loud there would have been an immediate shift. Again, part of your soul contract on Earth, Tom, is to assist in convincing people to say these Benevolent Prayers out loud and there will be a shift. One day in the future the probability is high that you will lead people across the world in that request. As you have been told before, you are a catalyst and that will be your legacy.

Middle East

Gaia, would the reason for so many wars in the Middle East be that the land there holds so much negativity?

That's certainly one of the major reasons, but not the only one. There are three major religions that were created there and there is a constant struggle between them. They have taken on the challenge of learning to live together. It may seem as if this will never occur but will in the future. That will not happen without much bloodshed to come, but the feminine energy you obtained when you crossed Timeline 7 will slowly settle in and assist in the peace process. It will come in bits and pieces over the next 100 years.

Why are Arabic people so proud and take things personally?

They are proud of their ancient, to them, traditions. They feel history is on their side and pride comes before the fall. They will discover in the near future that their history is not like they have been taught. This will cause them to come to doubt everything they've been told.

Gaia, what is the probability of women in the Middle East ever experiencing freedom as women do in America and if so, when? (Asked February 2019)

There are great changes coming, Tom, starting with your revelations about the origins of religions in the world. That will be a catalyst as the true teachings are related. Then it will be like water slowly dissolving prior beliefs and concepts. The highest probability will be in the next 25 years. Yes, there is that number again, Tom, but this 25-year period of time will see amazing progress in so many different ways. Equality will come during that time period, with some holdouts, but we are talking about the majority here.

Mongolia

What is Mongolia's role in the new age development?
Mongolia does have a role to play, as its citizens are more grounded, you could say, than those people in western societies.

Why are there more or many shamans in the country?
Again, it is this grounding that these people have to the energy of the mountains. They have not been so corrupted in their thinking compared to the western religions. They are more connected to the Earth. It comes back to the energy of this ancient land.

Origins of Religion on Earth

Gaia, was it Creator's plan to have separate religions?
Yes, it was one of many problems the Explorer Race took on to solve, since there are worlds with similar situations. Religions in the future on Earth will be more respectful of each other's beliefs. That is slowly happening but will speed up in this century.

The Old Testament and Gaia

Gaia, are the Divine Wisdom books in the Old Testament related to you?
Yes, although they have been altered from their original writings. These writings were passed down over centuries to the point where they are almost unrecognizable from the original thoughts, but as I have told you before, you must ALLOW those who wish to take the writings in these holy books of all religions to believe as they wish. That is part of their learning for their souls' benefit.

Quran
Gaia, was there a 200-year gap in the Quran?
No, Tom, which is incorrect information. As we have covered before, the Quran was added to after Mohammad's death by his scribe who was not as loving as was his master. That's why there are contradictions in his scripture.

I assume he had to balance those actions?
Quite so, and in more than one life as his actions have affected millions of people.

Races And Religions

Gaia, was it the Creator's plan all along for us to learn how to get along with all other races and religions after experiencing the differences, distrust, hate, and so on?
Exactly, Tom. This was another significant reason for you being veiled. Creator wanted to see how long it would take you to finally learn to get along together. It may not seem so at this time, but you are making great strides for this to finally reach a point where you will accept everyone no matter their race or religion or sexual preference.

This is all part of raising your vibrational levels to the point you will love one another unconditionally. That will happen in the future, Tom, on a widespread basis and not just on an individual basis. It will take several hundred more years for this to finally come about, but you as a people are marching in the right direction.

Ramtha

Gaia, is Ramtha the same as the Hindu God, Ram?
No, Tom. Under their belief system they are two different entities. As you have not studied this religion heavily in this life, I can't give you a more complete comparison at this time, but again, this is their belief system, and I know you and I respect them for their beliefs. Many of their beliefs are more enlightened than those of Western beliefs, but they certainly have their limitations too, just as all religions do.

Saints and Their Characteristics

Are saints different by their vibration, energy, or DNA, or was this just defined like that by humans?
Just as there are and were many saints, so was there a variety in young, medium, and old souls. Many were declared saints because of their work, others because of church politics, and others were of a higher vibrational level, whose soul contracts were to lift those around them.

Scientology

Gaia, what is the highest probability for the future of Scientology?
Like all religions, it will morph into something else in the future. It will not go away since there are people who wish this type of religion, but it will change.

Gaia, what year will I be born in the Scientology life?
Nice question to start the day, Tom. You were or will be born in the 1930s as you guessed. We will not give you the exact year, as then you might wish to put two and two together.

So, does that mean I will have to go through WWII?
Yes, but you will be too young to take part in the war, as we do not wish you to be involved in the war, other than as a young spectator. You will know deep down that the war will end with an Allied victory. You will begin making predictions at an early age.

Man or woman in that life?
Woman, Tom. Yes, you received that correctly.

How many lives will I communicate with you and/or Theo, and how far back will those lives range?
Good question, Tom. In virtually every one of those lives, you will communicate at some level. Obviously, those lives in the future periods of time will be easier than farther back in 3D time, but you will have these unique capabilities to know we're there, and be open to our information, no matter what you may call us in that time period.

So, will I have any lives back one or two thousand years ago?
No, not that far back. Let's say the 19th century will be back as far as you'll need to go with these lives. Perhaps a little farther in one or two, but you will have much work to do guiding others, whether they are rulers or leaders of their countries, or those that form religions.

Star of David

When did the Star of David originate, and was it a symbol on an ET spacecraft?
An interesting story, Tom, with some validity. There is a similar symbol on some of the Federation spacecraft. This story dates back to a time when there was more communication and interaction than is allowed now.

Temple of Healing

Gaia, were the "Temple of Healing" and the "Temple Beautiful" actual religious-type temples or secular hospitals or healing facilities and why did Cayce call them temples?
Mr. Cayce called them "temples," Tom, because that's how the Atlanteans referred to them. He received that correctly. Regarding their use, each had their specific purpose or purposes. The Healing Temple was just that—a place to come and be healed of any and all maladies of that day and time. The Temple Beautiful was more a temple that was to heal one's spirit, you could say. Yes, there were advanced techniques at that time to improve one's appearance, but that was not all their purpose. There they could also pray for their soul's betterment and to love one another. You could say whatever you wished. So, in summary, one temple had all the healing lights and advanced procedures for those truly sick or injured, and the other was for healing the soul.

Uncle Zoosh

What is Uncle Zoosh's interest?
Uncle Zoosh, as you call him, for readers unfamiliar with this being, is a creator who assists your Creator—sort of "on the job training," preparing him one day to create his own universe. We have previously said that over

a very long period of time, Creator studied other creations before creating this Universe. Uncle Zoosh is doing something similar.

Witches

Gaia, regarding witches, do they receive their power through spells and chants, let's say, or is this through heredity?
Obviously, a soul that chooses a life as a witch has a soul contract to learn the spells and chants that create different energies. Certainly, for a long time, this has been passed from mother to child, but again through soul contracts. Most of the people who practice witchcraft do so to honor me in their own way. There are also those who are balancing by having lives where they try to control others through witchcraft. If they do not follow their soul contract, then they must balance in a future life or lives. So, you can say it is much more soul contract than anything hereditary.

What about the verse in the Bible where it says "thou shall not allow a witch to live"—where did that verse originate?
Naturally, back in the times when the church officials did not want people to practice pagan religions. They thought it would be a good way to rid themselves of competition in order to control more people. This was not some "divine" revelation, but an act of aggression and, you could say, genocide.

Gaia, give us a little history of witches—have they been around since the Adam and Eve humans appeared, and are there true witches today?
Witches, as you can imagine, Tom, began as women who were fully cognizant of me when they were first put on Earth by your ET fathers and mothers. Therefore, they did, from that early time, honor me and the Earth itself with chants and dances and other ways to recognize there was a soul assigned to this planet. They passed this down in their group, or as they became known as tribes and clans. Some were much more in tune than others, so they became the person to go to when there were aches and pains as they took on the responsibility of treating the sick and wounded. So, that's how it started—from your very early days on Earth. In today's world, yes, there are still women who feel more connected to me than

others and they've become a more modern version of a witch. Naturally, over the years there have been efforts to put these chants and remedies and such into books. Some are much more advanced than others.

Yahweh

Who was, or is Yahweh?
This was the name the Jewish religion uses for Creator.

Does Creator call himself Yahweh?
No.

Chapter 13
Technological Advancement

3D Printed Architecture

Gaia, what is the future for 3D printed architecture?
You are just in the beginning stages. This again will be a rapid development in this century, and, yes, will even be used in outer space.

5G
Gaia, is 5G really an improvement and good for us?
Yes, Tom. In the long run it is but another step along the way.

Gaia, will 5G wipe out the bee populations of the world? And will people become sick from exposure?
The bee population will continue to thrive, Tom. Nature, shall we say, has a way of evolving. Some animal populations will disappear for a while, partially due to the change in climate, but will again make their appearance in the future. We have spoken about these before. The bee population has been decreasing, but will stabilize in the fairly near future, as they instinctively learn to avoid certain vibrations put off by the 5G machines. I need them, the faerie kingdom needs them, and you need them.

Regarding people getting sick from exposure to 5G, as I have said before, stay away from the close proximity of the towers. It is the same advice for people living too close to large electrical lines—not good for you.

Air Taxis

Gaia, the Dallas area is scheduled to be the first area for Uber Taxis, manufactured by Bell Helicopter. Will this become popular, and if so, how fast will the use of these air taxis spread?

It will become highly popular, Tom, especially in cities where the highways and streets are already clogged with too many vehicles. Naturally, only those that can afford the equivalent of a premium taxi ride each day will take it, but a large number of people will take the taxis for specific purposes as the demand heats up. Their plans to have them pilotless will take a little long for acceptance, but there are great strides being made in that area too. You will see hundreds of these ships whizzing above before too many years, Tom. There will be landing spots on parking lots and then eventually they will land in the street in front of houses. That will come sooner rather than later as the trust for these vehicles spreads.

Aircraft

Gaia, will there be a successor to the Concorde and if so when, and will it be capable of flying between New York and London in 3.5 hours?
Yes, a new version of this plane has already been developed but is not yet in service. The reason why the original Concorde was not successful was that the number of people who could afford to pay for the trip was not economically viable. There are more people with the financial means to pay for this type of transportation, but it remains questionable.

Eventually, the breakthrough will be when anti-gravity aircraft are introduced where the cost of operation is so much less. This is coming sooner than people expect.

I have to ask, how soon? (Asked September 2021)
Within the next 25 years, as those aircraft are being tested and used by your Area 51-type operations. When they are finally exposed or brought out in the open, corporations will demand the plans. It is, but another development during this century that will give you a giant leap in progress as these craft will not need fossil fuels to operate.

Androids

Gaia, what year will androids first be produced, and how will they be educated in even the most basic functions?

Yes, a good question, Tom. Let's see if you can receive this. It will not be until the 4000 millennium, closer to the 4200 era. You're fairly close on that time period. Regarding education, that will be a snap as, by long before then, children and adults will have this information transferred through very sophisticated devices directly to the parts of the brain that retain learning, so the android will be fully educated within a very short period of time. Yes, even their personality will be wired, shall we say, to be bright and pleasant. Their DNA will be such that it will be on the high end in intelligence.

I'm a little surprised since we are seemingly making rapid advancement in the study of DNA and cloning.
Yes, but there are many, many steps before you can actually create a person that will be ensouled. Right now, you, meaning humans, have no clue as to how to ask that a body be ensouled. Then you must also be able to design the DNA in ways far beyond your understanding even several hundred years from now. It is one thing to find the part of the DNA strand that can cure a particular disease, it is another to create whole bodies, brains, etc. That is much, much further in the future.

Will their work be mostly off-world, and if so, where?
Keep in mind, Tom, that these androids are very expensive—even in that time period—so there must be justification for them being produced. So, yes, their work will be mostly off-world on newly-discovered planets, not something simple like our Moon, but planets where expertise is needed, along with strength. To go beyond this statement might give away too much at this time, Tom. You are, shall we say, putting thoughts in the heads of people who will read these messages in the future. We cannot lay out all the work androids will do. That will be in the thoughts of those even many years from now.

Gaia, in the future will androids or robots be capable of telepathy?
Androids will be constructed as closely to humans as possible, and that will include the pineal gland, so, yes, they will have that capability. But robots will not be capable of telepathy. They will be so advanced at that time they will be capable of anticipating all your wants and needs, but in reality, their advanced knowledge will only seem like telepathy.

Gaia, when androids are created 300 years in the future, will they consist of organs and other parts of the body produced in a lab, or will they partially use human parts such as the brain?
No, they will only use body parts created in a lab, Tom. That is why it will take so long to produce an android, as they will be prevented by law, of course, from using any human body part; and no, to answer what you are thinking, there will be no place in the world where they would try and "cut corners" by using, let's say, a human brain as was depicted in the movie you saw. Times will be much easier then, as there will be less negativity compared to what you have today, and certainly almost zero conflicts. Any potential conflicts will be handled by negotiators who will work with both sides to resolve conflicts.

On that line, I assume the armies, navies, and air forces of the world will be greatly reduced or almost nonexistent?
Quite so, Tom. The money spent on the military today will be spent to make the lives of citizens around the world more benevolent.

That is great to hear. Shame we can't have that now, but I do understand that progress is slow.
Yes, but let me affirm that you are on that path, even though it may not seem that way, with so many conflicts in the world. These will fade away in time. And of course, you can have everyone say a Benevolent Prayer for world peace this week and it will help, even though the results might not be readily seen.

*Here is the Benevolent Prayer to say **out loud**: "I ask any and all beings to assist in bringing peace to the whole world and may this happen even faster than we can hope for or expect, thank you!"*

Will they be allowed to mate?
Yes, they will, although depending upon their projected work they may be given a low libido, so that work will come first.

Gaia, will the androids produced in the future be babies or full adults?
Good question, Tom. They will be fully realized adults. They won't have to wait 20 years for them to grow up. They will have developed their

process to the point similar to what the ETs do with full bodies, but just not in the short time period in comparison.

In my book Atlantis and Lemuria: The Lost Continents Revealed, *I was told that the ETs could replicate a human body in 2.5 minutes, making it easy to populate an area of a continent with 30 or 40 humans. They "hit the ground running," as they had no food, water, clothes, or shelter. Unlike the androids, the humans they produced could have their DNAs altered, so that the humans would not be mating with their brothers and sisters, using our terminology.*

Gaia, will androids be created with DNA at the top end of human strength and intelligence in that far future?
Yes, Tom. They will not be some slender, androgynous humans, but will be designed to operate at a high level—but still not at a superhuman level.

Will there be both male and female androids, or just male?
No, both male and female androids will be created, but still, as pointed out before, they will be in their first or second life on Earth—a "newbie" in your terms as a young soul in the first quadrant.

Artificial Intelligence and Its Development

Gaia, how do you see AI to play out? Many are afraid it will get out of hand.
I would advise those that are concerned to know that you will fairly quickly learn how to control it and use it to your advantage and not to your detriment. It is but another giant step in your progress as the Explorer Race. AI is used extensively throughout the Universe to make, in the past, giant leaps in everything from robotics to solving medical problems. AI can analyze in a few seconds hundreds of thousands of pages of information and draw conclusions for your scientists and researchers. You were told previously that at the beginning of the next century you would look back on this time period the way you view the 1917-18 period—very basic. AI is one of the major breakthroughs.

Gaia, in the future will any AI robot with a sense of humor kill because

they think it's funny?
There is absolutely no chance in that, Tom, as there will be many safeguards in place; "no kill" being just one of them.

Artificial Moon and Chinese Launch

Are Chinese scientists working on an artificial moon some of the same scientists that were involved with the artificial moon back in Atlantean days?
Good connection, Tom. Yes, a couple are. On a subliminal basis they remember that artificial moon, which we covered quite some time ago, was five miles wide.

I don't think I ever asked, why did they think they needed one?
We touched on that aspect, Tom. It helped power their engines and devices at that time. If you recall, the crystal energy was limited by the curvature of the Earth, so they looked for a way where they would not have to have the posers every few miles.

Batteries

Gaia, will any of these batteries replace Lithium-ion: Sodium-ion; Nickel-hydride; or Nickel-hydrogen?
Yes, for Sodium-ion, no to the others. With the introduction of the free energy machine, there will be less need for batteries. And to the natural next question, yes there have been delays, but ones you will appreciate that are connected to COVID—people being off work or remotely working from home has caused a delay. Still, look for the introduction quite soon, I assure you.

Gaia, is there a future for hemp batteries?
Not so much, Tom. A fast, rechargeable battery is coming soon that will allow them to be used over and over again, so that billions of the present batteries do not continue to flow to the landfills as they do now.

What would be the timing on this? (Asked January 2022)
It will be less than five years as you were thinking.

How will they work since when a battery goes out it is at a most inopportune time?
There will be a small charging station where a charged battery will be removed, and the dead battery will be inserted—in other words a quick exchange.

Bio Identification

Gaia, will using our palms as recognition be commonplace in the future to pay by credit cards?
Yes, that will come into common use—that and fingerprints. It all depends on the credit card company.

What about eye scans?
No, those will still be reserved to enter highly secured areas. That is too expensive, compared to a palm or fingerprint.

Consciousness Transfers

Gaia, will we ever be able to transfer our consciousness to an artificial body?
Not in the way asked, Tom. This is difficult to describe in your time period; it will be much easier to reach across space with your consciousness to communicate and even view other planets and people in the future. This will take some time as you move much farther into the Fifth Dimension or Focus. You will be able to see through other beings' eyes. Again, this is quite far in the future for you—several thousand years.

D-Wave Quantum Computers

Gaia, are the "D-Wave quantum computers" communicating with negative spirits? And is the byproduct of this the Mandela Effect?
These computers are the next generation of computers, Tom. They are a giant leap forward in solving problems. They do not communicate with negative spirits. Do not be afraid, would be my advice to everyone. They will enable you to solve problems faster than ever before and will greatly contribute to the giant leap in knowledge that will occur in the next 100

years. And this is quite separate from what is termed the Mandela Effect. You, as humans, as we have said before, are constantly rewriting the past, present, and future. That does not seem possible to you yet, but one day in the future your scientists will understand this. As we have gone over this before, we will not address it here again.

Disaster-Proof Housing

Gaia, are there any types of houses that could withstand earthquakes, hurricanes, tornadoes, and such?
Yes, there will come a time, Tom, when the materials used in house construction are so strong as to withstand almost any disaster as you would term it, but that is still pretty far in your future. They will be more of a round construction and will be able to move with the Earth. In the future you will also be much more in tune with me and the Earth environment in general and will ask the material for a house if they would like to be a house, so you will have an ambiance, if we might use that word—a connection. There will be a lot fewer people on Earth in the thousands of years ahead of you as compared to now. Even now there is just a hint that birth rates are starting to go down in some places. In other places there will be regulations as to how many children a family can have, or they will be taxed at a higher rate, as they take up more room, and the governments must spend more money on education, etc. And there will be a movement to take better care of your resources.

Gaia, how will humanity change the way houses are built?
There will be great changes coming even in this century, but certainly in future centuries. They will be built out of materials that are long-lasting, and much sturdier than today. Many of these improvements have not even been thought about, so I can only give you hints. I must allow for those "ah-ha" moments.

Electric Cars

Gaia, will someone invent an inexpensive method for converting cars to electric, or will they just fade away?
The switch to electric cars and trucks will be quite fast. The value of gas

driven vehicles will plunge, but the cost of converting will be more than the value of the vehicles—that is the highest probability at this time. There will be attempts to simply remove the engines and install electric, but that will only take place in the short term. Keep in mind that with the free energy machines, recharging your vehicles at home will have no cost. We have said a number of times that these machines will be game changers. In the early days, when you come home at night, the first thing you will do is to plug in the recharger.

Won't there be still a time when electric cars will be plugged in at home until new electric cars are introduced, or somehow converted?
Yes, at the initial stages there will be electric cables sold to plug in at home, but the conversion to these small machines will be so easy car companies, and even your local garages, will be able to quickly convert electric cars to use these machines.

Are there any fire dangers?
Very little, as long as they are connected correctly.

Gaia, will electric cars be the only ones sold in the USA by 2030?
There may be a very small percentage of gas driven cars and trucks, Tom, as diesel fuel will be slower to be dropped as an energy source, but, yes, the vast majority of vehicles will be electric by 2030. There will be breakthroughs in the capacity of batteries to power longer distances. And, yes, those will be introduced quite soon. And of course, those free energy machines will play their part too.

Will there be more accidents, or will they all be self-driving?
Virtually all vehicles will be self-driving by 2030, Tom. Even the older vehicles will have self-driving upgrades available. At some point, self-driving vehicles will be required as they will virtually have no accidents.

What percentage of gas stations that are in operation today will still be around in 2040?
Almost none. There will still be a few spots where someone with an old "clunker," as they will be called, can fuel up, but those places will be harder and harder to find, making driving these vehicles only viable

around cities.

Energy Waves: South America to Antarctica

Gaia, what are the energy waves that seem to come from South America to Antarctica? (Asked July 2017)
Yes, the tests I told you about before—from Antarctica. This is very hush-hush experiment. More will be forthcoming in the next few months.

Is it a weapon?
Yes, that's what they are trying to see, but will have inconclusive results. I will only allow it to go so far.

Gaia, will the experiment with the wave energy in Antarctica affect the energy grid/ley lines that run from North to South America along the Rockies-Andes mountain system?
Not at all, Tom. As I said before, there will be information that will come out in the fairly near future, but it will not affect my energy grid or ley lines.

Facial Recognition Technology

Gaia, will facial recognition technology continue to improve and become universal in use, or will something better come along?
Facial recognition will become universally used, Tom. It still has a long way to go before it can be described as perfect, or at least with a 99.99% accuracy. It is non-invasive, and only a DNA match in the future will possibly replace it, but that is quite far in the future. There will be others not as widely used such as an eye scan or fingerprint. Some facilities might use a combination, if high security.

Farm Equipment

Gaia, what about farm equipment in 2030 when all the cars and most of the trucks are electric?
By that time, Tom, many types of farm equipment will also be electric as they will have these free energy machines that can power the equipment,

or that they can plug into for a quick recharge. Great strides will have been accomplished in powering everything with these machines, as keep in mind that it will greatly lower the cost of farming to use these machines. It will affect every life on Earth.

Finding Solutions

Gaia, have we found solutions to problems the ETs have not been able to solve? If so, what?

We have discussed in the past how the simple paperclip had never been thought of in the rest of the Universe. You are coming to a time where there will be inventions that have never been thought of by the rest of the Universe. You have to understand that the rest of the Universe has been millions of years in advance of you technologically. But you, the Explorer Race on Earth, will find unique ways to end wars and other problems the rest of the Universe has never thought of before. The rest of the Universe has been ahead of you technologically, but as we have said before, you are the great problem solvers of the Universe. That's why, in your dream time, you are taken to the far reaches of the Universe to help other societies solve their problems. That is a great contribution.

Flying Cars

Gaia, when we have lots of personal or group flying cars, will they have anti-collision technology?

Yes, and no. It will not be so needed in the early days of these vehicles as they will have assigned flying altitudes, according to direction, but, yes, that will quickly change to more sophisticated computer technology. Your FAA will require avoidance systems.

Will there be many individual flying vehicles, or will most be more like taxi vehicles?

There you have it, Tom. Only corporations will have their own, as they will use them to ferry corporate heads across cities to meetings and to airports.

So, you don't see them proliferating to the point where everyone has one?

There will just be no need, plus you have to have the ground space for landings and takeoffs. Many rooftops in cities will adapt to their use, but they will be too large to have one in the typical garage. Car ownership will continue to fade over the coming years. Keep in mind there will be a great changeover coming from oil- or gasoline-run cars to electric ones. The cost of ordering up a taxi will be inexpensive, using electricity as its power source.

Free Energy Machine

Gaia, what is the probability of how long will it take for free energy to become the dominant way we use to power our homes, businesses, etc.? (Asked June 2017)
Once it begins, Tom, it will quickly catch on and will only be limited by how fast these generators these devices can be produced. Therefore, give it five, but a maximum of 10 years and you will see them covering the globe as there will not just be one manufacturer, but several.

Will they be large enough to handle just one house or several?
Several, Tom. Call them mighty-mites. They will come in different sizes depending upon their use. Grids will quickly form, much to the chagrin of the electrical companies that will try unsuccessfully to slow their distribution. As I said before, this will be a major change, as wealthy individuals will donate millions, and, yes, billions, of dollars so that every poor village all over the world has electricity. This is truly revolutionary, in every sense of the word, as people will become so much more knowledgeable as they can and will make use of the freedom to obtain facts about their governments, they were not privy to before.

I assume electricians will be quite busy installing these generators?
That's true as thousands, and, yes, millions, of people will be employed to install these, although the actual installation and connecting to a house will be quite simple. And as you are thinking, there will be some thefts in the early days until everyone is hooked up or connected.

Gaia, will the release of the free energy machines put renewable energy companies out of business? And will these machines be

affordable for everyone?

There will not be just one company making these devices, Tom, but a number, as this technology will be released to the world. Some companies will jump in and start small factories and grow along with the demand. Other renewable energy companies will continue on their path, but depending upon what they do, some will wither and die, and others will find a niche and supply that demand. There is not just one answer here. These free energy machines are such a game changer, it is difficult for you to imagine the impact at this time.

Will these machines be affordable to the general public?

Yes, because of the competition. And there will be even groups of homeowners that will join together to buy just one machine to power all their homes. Electricians will have a field day hooking these up.

Is this being developed in someone's garage or workplace, or by a company?

More the latter, Tom. It is cloaked in secrecy.

I thought it would be the former. Am I receiving correctly?

Yes, Tom. Keep in mind this will be released to the world

.

I assume free energy machines will power these vehicles in the future. (Asked June 2018)

Yes, that will come about, but not for about 10 years, Tom. Not so long though, I'm sure you will agree.

Gaia, is there a free energy machine being developed near Waco, Texas?

Yes, but they do not wish to be advertised, shall we say. There are other places that are all working on a free energy machine. We will not say who we know—from their soul contracts, you understand—will be successful.

Gaia, will companies try to interfere with the distribution of the free energy machine? When will it be widely used?

Those oil companies will see it as a danger and immediately try and put pressure on the entity that releases the instructions on how to build the machine. They will offer billions, but to no avail, Tom. The plans will be simple enough so that any electrical-minded person or company will be able to produce the machines. It will take several years, and there will be attempts to force countries to try and prevent its use, but the cat will be out of the bag, and thousands of these machines will be built. It will take over 10 years, but as you were told before, this will be a game changer.

Gaia, will the free energy machine have two or three magnetic wheels?
That is correct, Tom—both. It will be a simple machine that anyone can put together. Using two or three wheels will depend upon the amount of energy needed.

Are the magnets that plentiful?
They are fairly plentiful but will become much more so, as demand warrants.

I read where the most magnets are in China. Do other countries have a natural supply?
Yes, where there is a need, other sources will be found.

Will there be some that are so tiny as to fit in a cell phone?
Oh yes, and China will be a large producer of those since they manufacture a large number of these mobile phones now.

Will the free energy machine cause more people to move to small villages and towns?
The cities will not be abandoned, but there will be fewer people feeling that they have to move to the big cities. Factories can be set up anywhere there is a workforce available. Even those in remote areas will have whatever form the internet takes. There will be no "dead zones" where there is no internet coverage. And this is not for just North America and Europe, but even the remotest parts of the world.

Gaia, will any of the inventors featured in the Thrive II film be successful in creating a free energy machine?
As you were told before, this information has been downloaded into several people in order to ensure that the machine makes its way to use by

the general public. There are a couple of inventors featured in the film that are fairly close, just as the person you have previously asked about, where we mentioned there were a couple of flaws in his design.

I'm also asked why this information wasn't downloaded 60 years ago. It was soul contracts, Tom. There was still a lot of learning to be done by those who use carbon-based energy systems. People have to truly desire and want these energy systems, since you recall there is and was a subconscious fear of using this free energy for destructive purposes as was done in the past when the Atlanteans and Lemurians destroyed themselves. Every advancement has to have a strong push behind it, and I can assure you that 60 years ago there was not. Now, even those that just fill up their tanks once a week for their drives to work see the advantages that electrically run cars have. These developments must have everyone on board, you see.

*Here is the Benevolent Prayer to be said **out loud***: *"I ask any and all beings to assist in the discovery of free energy devices, and may they be discovered and developed even sooner than we can hope for or expect, thank you!"*

Human Energy Potential

Gaia, in the future, will we be able to use our energy to create by using light, heat, cooling, pressure, and motion to transform things from basic elements?
In a way, yes, Tom, but not in just a year or two. It will become easier over the centuries for humans to create what they can imagine, and it will be much faster as you slowly raise your vibrational levels, but as you are in the Fifth Focus you will still need to actually do the work to create. It would take a higher focus for you to create by simply assembling basic elements and willing them into some creation that you have in mind. These lives for you as Junior Creators in Training are for you to learn the steps involved in the process. The Explorer Race has a few more thousand years to learn about creating things from scratch, shall we say, but that was a good question from your reader.

Hydrogen From Plants

Gaia, does the new process of extracting hydrogen gas from plants have promise, or will it actually be something else that comes along to give us free energy?
Certainly, this does have some promise, Tom, in certain applications, but there are limits to how much energy it can supply before the fuel is exhausted. Still, these studies will lead to other things. And, yes, free energy is still on the horizon as we have discussed before.

Hyperloop

Gaia, will there ever be a hyperloop between North America and Europe or with Russia? And will it involve the tubes in the Earth that are said to exist to be discovered and used? And what is the probability of that in what time period?
These tubes, Tom, will be discovered by chance. They will not be found by using information gleaned from your history. Therefore, the probability of this occurring will be on the order of two to three hundred years. Before I allow drilling new tunnels for these hyperloops, I will allow someone to discover these tubes or tunnels.

I would have thought this would be much sooner since these possibilities are being tossed about at the present time.
Short tunnels, yes, but you are asking about tunnels from one continent to the next. To drill these tunnels costs billions of dollars. Before this money will be spent, I will allow the discovery of these tunnels.

Internet

Has the internet become conscious or will it in the future?
Not in the way asked. It will become more responsive as improvements continue to be made. It will never become "Hal" of the movie *2001: A Space Odyssey.*

Jet Packs

Gaia, will jet packs be used in the future in mountainous areas as part of rescue efforts?

Yes, for a time, Tom, but other methods will be introduced that will be even faster and with better advantages. These will include larger robotic-type aircraft directed from the ground that will even be able to pluck the person, let's say, off the side of a mountain and bring them back to safety, and, yes, be able to administer to any injuries. Jet packs will be considered an interim method of assisting those in certain areas.

Invisibility

Gaia, has any government developed a device that can make people or vehicles of any size invisible?

Not yet, Tom, but they are not so far away as you may think. Certainly, they have developed materials that when used as the surface of planes does not show up on radar, but one day they will discover frequencies that can alter the visible light spectrum that will accomplish this. All the major powers are working on this.

Kamma Gear Flywheel

Gaia, is there any future for the Kamma Gear Flywheel? On a general level, it looks very complicated.

No, Tom. The people developing this have good intentions, it is just far too complex to work on a general basis for, let's say, the typical household. Again, although delayed, the free energy machine, with a much simpler design, is on the way. We don't have any control over the announcement. We just encourage those involved in the development to bring it to the public. That will happen, I can assure you.

Lab-Grown Meat

Gaia, will lab-grown meat become a large part of the market, or just an interim step to plant foods?

Acceptance will be slow, but the advantages of eating meat that was not derived from a slaughterhouse will appeal to a number of people. The costs of producing the lab-grown meat will also be high in the beginning but will come down as the popularity increases. Still, plant foods will continue to grow in favor, so both will be popular in the coming years. Gas emissions will slowly decrease as the need for live animals decreases. Herds will shrink, and farmers and cattle ranchers will have to find other ways to make a living. This will happen even faster than most speculate at this time. Good question, Tom.

Los Angeles Oil Deposits

Gaia, how large is the oil deposit under Los Angeles? Will it ever be drilled?
It's not huge, but sizeable. Drilling would be disastrous, as the oil acts as a lubricant. Take it away and the area would have earthquakes. Plus, with the advent of the free energy machines, there will be no need.

The population on Earth is just now past its peak, although it is not reflected in many reports. Old housing will be abandoned and then torn down. Look for these changes in the next 25 to 30 years as new housing developments are tested.

Magnetic Generator

Gaia, did or does Dennis Danzik's magnetic generator work? Looks complicated.
It is a little too complicated, Tom, and if you notice, it has not been a machine that others are adapting. That's because he continues to try and make it work. The machine that is coming is quite simple in design—you'll see.

Gaia, is there another energy system that will come after magnets that generates energy by tapping into the ever-present quantum vacuum energy state—the baseline energy? If so, what is the highest probability of when, since it sounds as if "black ops" already has it? (Asked November 2021)
They do have a form of this energy, Tom, found and discovered during their back engineering of downed ET craft. But it will be years before it sees the light of day. In the meantime, the magnetic energy will be something simple that can be reproduced in mass quantities. As far as a

timeline on when, it will be at least 25 years, but it will be finally released later in this century. This type of energy has to be carefully handled.

Gaia, will lasers be part of the new energy source?
No, this will be in the area of magnetics.

Montauk Experiments

Gaia, a quick question on the Montauk experiments. I was told previously that we would never time travel, yet here we have done it one or more times in the 20th century. It seems to me some person or group will return to this and study what was done wrong with those experiments and work to correct them.
True, Tom, but they will be only partially successful after spending a great deal of money and time. The space-time continuum you are in is one of the most complex systems ever developed by your ET uncles and aunts, and that was after millions and, yes, over a billion years of work in this field. Yes, they will try and do smaller experiments with objects, but again, with little success. If you recall, Tom, you were previously told that all of the timelines will eventually have spaceships and all will be just a few frequencies different than each other. This would seem confusing, but your ET uncles and aunts are quite prepared to handle multiple visits.

Yes, but what about the worlds that are not part of the Federation?
They will be informed in advance so there is no confusion. You will have a small number of spacecrafts compared to the actual number in existence in other parts of the Federation. They do not wish me to give you numbers in order to not frighten those who will read this one day.
Gaia, what is the probability of the United States admitting to the time travel Montauk experiments?
As it is easy to guess, Tom, these experiments ended in failure, and all attempts for humans to time travel ceased. As you have heard and read, it was quite messy. All experiments ended, but there are still researchers who continued to study, and try and figure out what went wrong, and is there some way to correct it. As you have been told before, time travel will not become possible for many centuries. There will be a great reluctance to publicize these past experiments.

Did the Russians try too?

Yes, but equally unsuccessful.

Was there a time machine capsule they attempted to travel in?

Yes, but unsuccessfully. These experiments ended tragically for all who tried.

What happened to the time capsule?

Lost.

Were the people who got stuck in the walls and bulkheads alive, or did they instantly die?

Almost instantly, but for those who did not it was quite a short time as their molecules mixed with those of the structure.

What happened to the body parts sticking out? Were they cut off?

Yes, Tom, they had to be. Very gruesome work for those whose job it was.

Was Nixon briefed?

Yes, a very short report.

Number System Evolution

Gaia, when will we adopt the 12 number system?

It will not be for some time, Tom. A mathematician will need to prove it works better than your 10 system, and that will take some time. That person has not yet been born.

Are we talking about over 100 years, 200, or more?

No, it will be more towards the end of this century, Tom. One of those great breakthroughs. Then it will take time for it to be tested by others, and it will take even much longer to be adopted into general use.

Gaia, is something else used on other worlds besides counting? Is it strictly an Earth concept?

Mathematics exists throughout the Universe. It is just much more sophisticated than it is so far on Earth. We have said before that there is the 12-count system that Earth will adopt in the future. You could say that mathematics is one of the core principles of the makeup of the Universe. Earth mathematicians are still in the early stages of their knowledge of math.

Personal Flying Machines (Pods)

Gaia, regarding the year 3000, I used the word "pods" to describe the personal flying machines. Could you give me a better description?
Yes, the word "pod" was given to you to use, Tom. The energy devices to power the pods kept getting smaller and smaller. Speed was fairly fast, but not, let's say, jet speed. Sufficient to cover shorter distances. If the distance was to be greater, they would use larger craft. So, we are talking about comfortable, but not so roomy. And they were designed to be able to load them into larger transport craft. This is so far beyond your development at this stage, Tom, that it is a little difficult giving you word pictures or descriptions. No controls were needed since, of course, voice recognition by that time will be quite sophisticated. A person will be able to give the craft instructions and then enjoy sophisticated communication devices that you have not even imagined yet, or even just to take a nap on the ride.

Plastics Magnet

Gaia, is there a plastic magnet in the works to sweep up all the plastic trash in the ocean, and if so, how soon before it is implemented?
There are several methods of collecting this trash floating in the ocean, with, yes, one patch larger than the state of Texas. The most effective trash removal will be giant scoops to ingest this trash with machines to crush the plastic and put into a form of bales, like bales of hay, or, yes, other blocks of refuse. The idea of a plastic magnet will not gather the plastic as fast as these giant scoops will be able to.
How long before the oceans are clean again? (Asked May 2018)
The various ways of collecting the plastic will be implemented within a short time—perhaps less than five years, and the ocean will be fairly free of trash within the next ten years. I can assure you, Tom, that is quite fast, considering the amount of plastic there is in the ocean. There will not be just one collection point, but several. And, yes, as you are thinking, the plastic will be removed from other floating trash.

*Let's say this Benevolent Prayer **out loud**: "I ask any and all beings to aid and assist in clearing the oceans of all types of refuse even faster than we can hope for or expect, thank you!"*

Satellites

Gaia, is there some device in space destroying satellites?
Yes, one of your competitors, shall we call them, has been testing such a device. It is not ET in nature. Your CIA and associated space force-type people have been alarmed about this, and have reported to the president, which resulted in him asking to form a space force. Therefore, there will be threats from your side to cease the tests. Things will settle down shortly. The device has limited power.

*How about saying a Benevolent Prayer **out loud** here: "I ask any and all beings to aid and assist in keeping the exploration of space and the planets peaceful, and for the cooperation of all nations involved in this exploration, thank you!"*

Scalar Energy

Gaia, please comment on scalar energy?
Yes, this is a viable energy, but perhaps not what will be used to power the free energy machines. You are slowly discovering (your scientists) that there are many energies available to you. Each are building blocks to understand energy itself.
Self-Driving Cars and More

Gaia, what is the highest probability for virtual reality, augmented reality, and self-driving cars for the next three to five years? (Asked September 2019)
There will be continued progress, Tom, but no real breakthroughs, you could say. No great "ah-ha" moments. All three require continued work, and each year you will see the corporations working on releases of new and improved versions, but still, a completely self-driving car is farther out. We have said 10 years before, but perhaps a little less now. A new safeguard will be introduced on those Tesla and other models to make sure

a person is fully awake while driving the car. On the computer side, the reality of the experience will continue to be improved.

Smart Glasses

Gaia, highest probability for when smart glasses are introduced to the general public? (Asked November 2020)
Not too long in the future, Tom. They are busy working on the prototypes as we speak. Look for them to be introduced in the next two to three years. Those will be the basic model, you could say, with many, many improvements after that, as more and more capabilities will be discovered that have not even been thought of yet. It will be, "well, if it can do this, why can't it do that" kind of thinking.

What will the basic model be able to do when released—video calls, GPS?
And more than that, Tom. Look what mobile phones can do now and just project those capabilities to glasses.

Will they miniaturize down to contact lenses?
Yes, but that will not be for some time.

Sound To Move Objects

Gaia, will we start to use sound to move large objects?
Yes, sound will eventually be found to have many more uses than is commonly believed as to its limitations. It was used in ancient times to move objects, such as large blocks of stone, since your ET uncles and aunts taught this to the builders knowing they needed a much faster way of moving stone blocks for the necessary pyramids than using thousands of slaves or workers to drag the stones to the building sites. That knowledge of how this was accomplished has been lost in time—and I might add your ET friends were aware that this would be lost—only to be rediscovered by your scientists in more modern times. They knew it could be used inappropriately for warfare had the knowledge been allowed to be used through the years.

String Theory

Gaia, please comment on the string theory by Dr. Michio Kaku. And how long before we have invisibility devices?
Dr. Michio Kaku has done good work in this field of quantum physics, Tom. He has also made it more understandable to the normal person who has scientific interests. That said, he still has, and I'll add in his distinguished colleagues here too who are working on the same theories, a lot of work and exploration to do. They have only scratched the surface, shall we say, in the string theory analysis. They have some major, yes major, discoveries ahead of them—for not only Dr. Kaku but the rest of his colleagues. This string theory does have promise, but they are not there yet, however, shall we say, are getting close to opening the door. That's how much is left to discover using that analogy.

Regarding invisibility devices, there are some already being developed for use—yes not only for jet fighters but also for individuals. Naturally, the application is for military use—but it will quickly be used throughout the world. You will need these devices certainly when you begin to roam the stars as there will be places where the people you meet will not be up to the level of knowledge you will have by that time, and you will not wish to scare them.

Does that sound familiar to what is occurring today for your world? Yes, your friendly ETs use these devices to observe and not frighten your people too at this stage. In the next few years, the need for these devices by these ET visitors will diminish as they become accepted, but it will be quite a few years for these devices to be put away completely or packed away, shall we say.

Tachyon Particle

Gaia, is the tachyon particle faster than light, and if it is, can these discs as they're called, protect you while you use a cell phone?
Yes, Tom, scientists will find that these particles do travel faster than light. How else would you think that your ability to move about the Universe is faster than the speed of light? But there is so much more than that, Tom,

and much of the data has not even been theorized yet. And, yes, there are some ways to protect yourself when you use cell phones.

Gaia, did not go so far as to recommend the discs, so I think she's letting us decide if the product "resonates" or not.

Thorium

Gaia, is thorium a mineral that will provide abundant energy in the future?
Yes, but even thorium has its limitations. Obviously much, much more analysis of this element will be done in the future. You are starting to get hints of that now.

Will that include powering our spaceships of the future?
Most definitely, Tom.

Is that because thorium would be considered not as radioactive as uranium?
That's correct, Tom. That is a good guess. Those that read this in the future—and I'm talking to scientists—should thoroughly explore this mineral. It is abundant, unlike uranium, and it is easier to contain.

Time Machine

Gaia, at the end of WWII in Germany, were the German scientists working on a time machine?
Yes, but they never developed a working model, and had they done so it would not have worked. As we have said in the past, it will be several thousand years before the ability to travel in time will be learned, and even then, it will be restricted to anthropologists who simply wish to study the many different time periods. They will have strict rules to not change anything—only to observe.

Time Schedule for New Technology

Gaia, you said that the technology from far in the future might arrive

sooner than we or others had hoped or imagined, if I understood correctly. What would be the reason the time schedule would be speeded up?

Yes, the technology will come faster because your vibrations will rise faster than is believed possible at this time by those monitoring you and even your own souls. You will assist in that, Tom, to a certain extent, as well as future versions of yourself and the soul you know as Reveals the Mysteries. There will be many others contributing to that rise in consciousness and understanding and I see a glorious future that will come faster.

I believe All That Is (Creator) wishes for this to be put on the speed track, as you might say. It has some impatience to move on to the next level so there will be some push and encouragement to raise your vibrations faster than your souls planned or hoped that that process would take. You see, things are never absolute. There is great variety or you're not receiving the word here, great ability to create more than has been imagined so far. Time will have to be adjusted to be able to keep up as it were. It may be shortened in loops. That gets into a very technical discussion, but your timelines can be looped.

Why has there been such a massive technological development in just the last 100 years?

It is all part of your soul contracts, Tom. It was time for you to develop and see if you could survive without destroying the Earth.

CONCLUSION

In this first volume of *Conversations with Gaia – Soul of the Earth*, you have read hundreds of questions that people all over the world have sent to me to ask in my meditative sessions. May I remind you that **anyone** can do the same. We all have the pineal gland in the back of our heads that acts as an antenna for all types of telepathic communications. Part of my soul contract in this life is to encourage **you** to begin to communicate and ask your own questions. Keep in mind that ten people can ask the same question and receive ten different answers. It all depends upon your knowledge, education, and religious or spiritual beliefs.

You can go to my website at **www.thegentlewaybook.com** and click on Articles and News on the Menu where all of my Newsletters since 2007 are archived. There is a search box at the top of the page to enter a name, word, or phrase to see if I have asked about this subject before.

Most importantly, please say a Benevolent Prayers each morning that I list in Addendum 1.

I wish you all a great life!

Tom T. Moore

Appendix 1: MEDITATIONS

I began this book by saying that anyone can ask questions in a meditative state because we all have the pineal gland in the back of our heads, also known as the Crown Chakra. If you wish to begin to ask questions yourself, my first suggestion would be to buy Dick Sutphen's audiobook, *Spirit Guides – In-Depth Lecture, Workshop & 2 Meditations*. He has a melodious voice and was the president of a national hypnosis organization. Richard puts you into a light altered state and then at one point, stops speaking, allowing you to ask a few questions before bringing you back. I make no money from this recommendation, but I did use this at one time. It is inexpensive and the advantage is that you can use it over and over again until you are comfortable.

Don't become frustrated and give up after only one or two times. When I was beginning to ask questions and receive answers, I asked my guardian angel Theo if I was improving on my reception. Repeatedly, he kept saying, "Practice, practice, practice." I finally gave up asking him. He told me that no one that asks questions in a meditative state is perfect. You might be tired that day, or even the transiting planets can affect your reception. You can always come back and ask the same question, as I have done many times, if you are not sure you received the answer.

The alternative to purchasing *Spirit Guides* would be for you or someone you know to record what I will give you below as to how I put myself in a light altered state to begin asking questions.

When I ask questions, I sit in front of my computer, with a list of written questions by my side. I like to have these sessions around 3:30 a.m. to 4:00 a.m. when the house is quiet. Choose a time that is good for you. I type the first question on the page before I begin. Then I close my eyes and begin breathing in through my nose for five counts, hold it for five, then out through slightly-parted lips for five, hold it for five, then begin again. All the while I am relaxing my body.

I suggest that you ask to speak to your own guardian angel, that golden light being that takes care of you in every life on Earth, knows your soul contract, and is your best friend. Eventually you may wish to speak to Gaia or even Creator—who has told me that He (using the male form) can have **trillions** of conversations going on at the same time and will answer even the most trivial questions. Or you can choose any other soul you may wish to contact. This could be the soul of the Sun, Moon, Mars, or perhaps an ET that has a connection with you. The possibilities are endless.

Each time I ask a question, I open my eyes long enough to read the question. You may not need to do this if you remember your questions. I typically have 20 to 25 questions I'm asking over a one-and-a-half to two-hour period of time, but it's fine to have only two or three. Here is what I first say **out loud**: "I request a Most Benevolent Outcome to receive these messages perfectly, thank you!" This brings in the protection of your own guardian angels. You will see below that I mention the Milky Way Central Sun Alcyone. I'm told this sun is so huge that over 1,000 suns could fit within it. Alcyone truly has a great energy.

Each time before I mentally think the sentence, I breathe in and hold my breath and then breathe out after finishing the sentence.

Then this is what you record in a soft tone:

> "As I begin to breathe in white light from the Central Sun Alcyone, I now breath out all the negativity in my body.

> "As I continue to breathe in white light from the Central Sun Alcyone, I now send this white light down to permeate every single cell of my body, tip to toe, and everything in between.

> "Now, as I continue to breathe in white light from the Central Sun Alcyone, I send out white light from my heart chakra and have it form a bubble of white protective light 360 degrees in all directions around my body, and as far out as it needs to go to utterly and completely protect me.

"As I continue to breathe in white light from the Central Sun Alcyone, I now send gold light out from my heart chakra, and have it form a bubble of gold light on the outside of the white light as an extra protection.

"As I continue to breathe in white light from the Central Sun Alcyone, I now send white light and love to every single continent, every island, all the lakes and streams, oceans and seas of the world, and I now release this white light to go where it is needed the most, so that there is no more darkness, only light, and no more secrets.

"As I continue to breathe in white light from the Central Sun Alcyone, I now send white light and love to all the other timeline Earths, and I release this light to go where it is needed the most, so that all 12 timeline Earths have no more darkness, only light, and no more secrets.

"As I continue to breathe in white light from the Central Sun Alcyone, I now send white light and love to the center of Mother Earth, and now I spread this white light to permeate every single cell and every single atom of the interior of the Earth.

"As I continue to breathe in white light from the Central Sun Alcyone, I now send white light and love to the soul of Gaia, and to the four million other souls that assist her in running the Earth.

"I now wish to speak to: [My guardian angel, Gaia, Creator, my main guide, etc.]"

When I'm finished, I simply open my eyes, since this is a light alternate state. If you feel groggy, you can say, "At the count of five I will be wide awake. 5, I'm starting to wake up, 4, I'm more awake, 3, I'm feeling much more awake, 2. I'm almost awake, and 1, I am fully awake, fully awake!"

Remember, PRACTICE, PRACTICE, PRACTICE!

Appendix 2: BENEVOLENT MORNING PRAYERS

Here are the morning prayers I say **out loud** each day. Typically. it takes me less than a couple of minutes, since I have said them so many times, I memorized them, which you will too. I'm told that saying them will raise your vibrational level. You can find these on my website **www.thegentlewaybook.com**, under the "signs" tab on the Menu, which you can then print out. One day in the future, scientists will rediscover the power of the human voice. These prayers are written so that anyone of any faith or belief can say them. If you wish to add a deity at the first or last, that's fine, but it is not needed—they are heard! And remember, it is best to say the prayers and requests outloud.

Benevolent Prayer for the World

I now send white light and love to every continent, every island, all the rivers, lakes, and streams, and all the oceans and seas, and I release this light to go where it is needed the most to light up the darkest parts of the world, so there is no more darkness, only light, thank you!

Benevolent Prayer for Those You Have Harmed

I ask any and all beings to aid, comfort, and assist anyone that I have ever harmed either physically, mentally, morally, spiritually, or emotionally in any past, present, or future life.
And I ask any and all beings to aid, comfort, and assist the families and friends of anyone I have ever harmed, in any way, in any past, present or future life. Thank you.

Special Most Benevolent Requests for You

"I request a Most Benevolent Outcome to stay on my soul contract for the rest of my life, thank you!"

This is the soul path you and your soul agreed upon before birth.

Then you can begin the day with other Most Benevolent Outcome requests for your drive to work or getting a seat on a crowded subway or bus, and for your safety to and from work—all said.

You can request Most Benevolent Outcomes for your workday, meetings, and if you are a commissioned salesperson to have great sales each day. If you are having problems with a coworker or manager at your place of work, you can request a Most Benevolent Outcome for your safety. For many more ideas for Most Benevolent Outcomes to request, check out my *The Gentle Way III* book that has hundreds of stories sent to me from all over the world of people having success with requestings.

It has been proven over and over again that these work!

About the Author
Tom T. Moore

Tom T. Moore is an author, speaker, and frequent radio and podcast guest. For over two decades, he has worked as the president and CEO of his own international motion picture and TV program distribution business, Reel Media International, based in the Dallas-Fort Worth metroplex.

After a spiritual retreat in Sedona, Arizona, Tom was inspired to publicize the modality of the Gentle Way, which dates back to Atlantean times and is described as a giant step forward over the law of attraction. He believes that his personal practice of requesting benevolent outcomes for many years now has resulted in leader a gentler, less stressful, and less fearful life.

Tom graduated with a BBA in finance from Texas Christian University in Fort Worth, Texas and served in the U.S. Army as a first lieutenant. He is a native of Dallas, Texas, and is married with two children.

Tom publishes a weekly newsletter and blog, and his articles have appeared in a number of international and regional magazines. You can receive his free weekly newsletter by subscribing at his website. To book him as a speaker at your next conference or event, email Tom at speaker@TheGentleWayBook.com

www.TheGentleWayBook.com

AVAILABLE NOW
on Amazon & wherever books are sold

The 2nd volume in *Conversations with Gaia The Soul of the Earth*

Tom T. Moore continues his channeling work with Gaia.
Topics in Volume 2 include:

- Health & Medical Advancements
- Space
- Extraterrestrials
- Mystical Creatures
- Recent Events and Controversies
- Ancient Civilizations
- Pyramids & Other Geological Wonders

ALSO FROM TOM T. MOORE

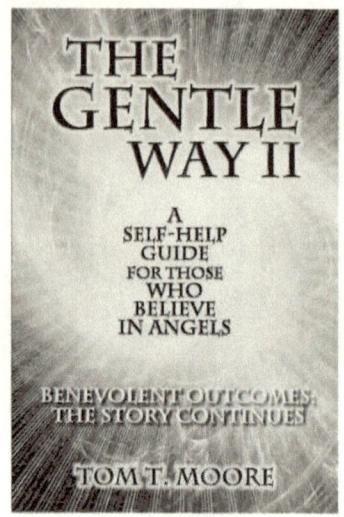

ALSO FROM TOM T. MOORE

Full of techniques and exercises developed by world-renowned intuitive counselor & channel Joan L. Scibienski, this workbook will increase your understanding of how to work with and hone your own psychic and intuitive abilities.

Topics include:

- **Changing your life by changing your thinking**
- **Learning to contact your guides**
- **Releasing fear and guilt**
- **Healing childhood pain**
- **Working with energy: auras and chakras, & much more**

Flint Hills Publishing

The 3-volume series that imparts deep spiritual knowledge in a page-turning novel.

Written by world-renowned intuitive counselor and channel of the the collective consciousness Equinoxx, Joan L. Scibienski, with the assistance of Equinoxx, introduces the reader to a group of "misfit" college students who unlock their psychic abilities.

Their new-found abilities force them to to truly see the world's problems, yet powerful negative forces threaten to stop them.

Their survival depends on developing their inner power and teaching others to do the same. In fact, the survival of the world may depend on it.

www.ingramcontent.com/pod-product-compliance
Lightning Source LLC
Chambersburg PA
CBHW021610120626
46545CB00001B/159